By the Seat of My Pants

BY THE SEAT OF MY PANTS

HUMOROUS TALES OF TRAVEL AND MISADVENTURE

EDITED BY
DON GEORGE

LONELY PLANET PUBLICATIONS
Melbourne • Oakland • London

By the Seat of My Pants: Humorous Tales of Travel and Misadventure

Published by Lonely Planet Publications

Head Office:
90 Maribyrnong Street, Footscray, Vic 3011, Australia
Locked Bag 1, Footscray, Vic 3011, Australia

Branches:
150 Linden Street, Oakland CA 94607, USA
2nd floor, 186 City Rd, London, EC1V 2NT, UK

First published 2005
This edition published 2011
Printed in China

10 9 8 7 6 5 4 3 2 1

Copy edited by Janet Austin
Designed by Daniel New
Cover design by Roberto de Vicq de Cumptich

National Library of Australia Cataloguing-in-Publication entry

By the seat of my pants : humorous tales of travel and misadventure / edited by Don George.

2nd ed.

ISBN 978 1 74179 524 0 (pbk.)

1. Voyages and travels - Anecdotes. 2. Travelers' writings.

808.8032

CONTENTS

INTRODUCTION

Travel is funny. Not always, of course, and often it's funnier in retrospect, but you can be pretty sure that just about any journey is going to offer some moments of unadulterated hilarity or at least unanticipated irony. And usually at your own expense. That's just the way of the road.

In thirty years of wandering the globe, I've learned that the one thing I can reliably expect when I travel is that something unexpected will happen. And when it does, I'll be forced to call on all my grace, sensitivity, courage and wisdom. And when they don't respond, I'll be forced to call on my sense of humour.

That's why my #1 rule of the road is this: if you don't pack your sense of humour with your sunscreen, sooner or later you'll get burned.

By the Seat of My Pants springs from this notion. These thirty-one tales of on-the-road adventures and encounters encompass the full comic spectrum, from the wryly ironic to the laugh-out-loudably absurd. While the stories vary widely in setting, subject and tone, they all remind us that some of travel's greatest treasures are those unexpected, unimaginable situations that make us laugh – at the world and at ourselves.

That's one reason for this book. Here's the second. Thirty years ago, on a soaring spring day on the Princeton University campus, I made a momentous decision. I decided to forego the familiar paths most of my graduating friends were taking – grad school, med school, law school, jobs in long-established firms –

and follow a different track: I would live in Paris for the summer on a work-abroad internship, move to Athens for the academic year on a teaching fellowship, and then... I had no idea.

I had absolutely no idea what I would do next. I just knew that something deep and irresistible was impelling me to go to Paris and Athens, and that if I ignored this urge, I would regret it for ever. The rest, I trusted, would take care of itself. So the week after graduation I packed up my life and set off for Europe, without any friends to meet me, with no place to stay and no coherent overall plan. I was making a grand leap into the unknown – flying by the seat of my pants.

That was the beginning of my life as a traveller, and the beginning of my resolution to trust the pants-seat and make the leap – a resolution that has conferred innumerable and life-changing gifts over the ensuing thirty years.

———————————

Flying by the seat of your pants is a quintessential part of the traveller's act and art. You'll be cruising along with everything seeming to be working out just fine, when suddenly reality tilts and teeters and you're confronted with something entirely unexpected – a flat tyre, a missed train, a mystifying meal, a kindly but incomprehensible villager, an unmapped fork in the path. Time to put on the pants.

The tales in this book illustrate this principle and the wide variety of forms it can take. Sometimes the need arises in the middle of an otherwise uneventful trip, as Jan Morris discovers on her first trip aboard a *vaporetto* voyage in Venice, and Michelle Richmond learns in a hotel room at the end of the world in Ushuaia, Argentina. Sometimes entire trips can go horribly wrong, as on Pico Iyer's wide-eyed, white-knuckle, four-wheel whirl through Ethiopia, Chris Cox's decidedly not-as-advertised boat to Angkor Wat, and Danny Wallace's assignment in Prague with an Uzi-toting kidnapper-cum-tour guide.

Sometimes travel thrusts us into unexpected encounters with locals. Jeff Greenwald peers into dusty Indian depths in a confrontation with a luggage *wallah* in Calcutta's airport, Edwin Tucker gets much more than he bargained for when he unwittingly trades his last pen for a shepherd's lamb in Tibet, Laura Resau befriends a Mexican village boy and receives an unforgettable lesson in traditional bathing rites from his mother, and Deborah Steg is treated to an award-worthy dinner performance by an unctuous new *ami* in Cannes, in southern France.

At other times our travelling companions are the challenge, whether it's Tim Cahill's exasperatingly annoyance-proof caving partner in Thailand, Judy Tierney's wrangler-wannabe boyfriend on a boot-shopping spree in Texas, Sean Condon's exhaustingly enthusiastic uncle in Vermont or the family from hell that Karl Taro Greenfeld lands among when his girlfriend introduces him to idyllic Ibiza. At other times we put on the pants of the fool ourselves, as Bill Fink discovers on a spontaneous expedition to climb Mount Fuji in Japan, Doug Lansky understands inside an exit-less Dutch toilet and Jeff Vize realises as a crowd-pleasing pedestrian in Bangladesh.

Finally, on some journeys it's the destination itself that dissembles, as the alluring marble marvels of Italy's Apuan Alps do for David Downie and a reputed Buddhist Shangri-La near the India–Tibet border does for Rolf Potts. Amanda Jones's youthful escape to the United States becomes a nightmare when she discovers that her promised apartment isn't available and she is suddenly homeless in San Francisco. Holly Erickson's dream job as a live-in cook in a London apartment takes a tilt when she breezes in to find that the garden kitchen is literally so.

Ah, the rewards of the road!

When I first set out to compile this anthology, I knew from my own experiences and thirty years of conversations with friends and fellow travellers that the theme was resonant – but I had no idea we would end up with this rich repository of tales. I owe a deep debt of gratitude to the numerous writers with whom I have worked in the past, who agreed to share their favourite on-the-road bungles, bumps and bounces. And I owe a second debt to all the writers who responded to the competition we sponsored on www.lonelyplanet.com, which elicited – much to our amazement and delight – more than six hundred submissions. Wonderfully, and fittingly, the compilation that resulted brings together stories from some of the world's best-known travellers and storytellers side-by-side with works by writers who have never been published before.

Compiling this collection has been its own glorious seat-of-the-pants journey, but now that it is nearly over, I can look back and discern four fundamental and interwoven lessons revealed along the way.

The first is that the world offers an inexhaustible supply of surprises. We may think we know what's around the next corner, but we never do. And this is precisely why travel continues to excite and delight.

The second lesson is that whatever surprises the world throws our way, we can cope with them gracefully and generously, as long as we maintain our sense of humour, which is compass and counsellor all in one.

The third lesson hearkens back to Plato, who famously wrote that necessity is the mother of invention. The tales in this collection amply illuminate the traveller's corollary: adversity is the mother of invention. Travel thrusts us into all manner of unexpected situations, with all kinds of unimagined people, and in so doing, it challenges and stretches – and teaches – us in unexpected and unimagined ways. Adversity offers us irreplaceable lessons in humility, flexibility, open-mindedness, open-heartedness, resilience and resourcefulness. In this sense, our seat-of-the-pants adventures ultimately teach us not just about the people and places of the world that we didn't know existed – but about the unknown, unexplored corners of ourselves.

And the fourth lesson springboards from this truth back to the principle I have followed countless times since that soaring spring day on the Princeton campus thirty years ago: trust your instinct. If you're faced with a sticky situation or a daunting divide, listen to the small, still voice deep inside you– it will tell you what to do, which way to go.

Don't be afraid to fly by the seat of your pants. Just enjoy the ride.

Don George
San Francisco, May 2005

THE SIGHTS OF PRAGUE

DANNY WALLACE

Danny Wallace is a comedy writer and producer. He has written two books, *Join Me* and *Yes Man*, both of which are currently being adapted for film. He recently wrote and starred in his own BBC2 TV series, and lives in London with a girl and no cats.

You can call it whatever you like.

You can call it a hunch. You can call it instinct. Some might call it a well-honed eye for detail, carved by experience and years on the road – while others might go so far as to call it some kind of secret sixth sense.

But let me tell you, I *knew* something wasn't right about my trip to Prague when the stranger who picked me up at the airport reached under the front seat of the car and pulled out a semi-automatic machine gun.

'It is Uzi 9mm!' he said, grinning at me in that special way that only men holding Uzi 9mms so often do. 'It is good, solid. But... *dangerous.*'

I nodded, and tried a vague smile. To be honest, I'd already *guessed* that an Uzi 9mm was probably a bit dangerous, despite the fact that I'd never seen one before, let alone been shown one by a bald Eastern European in a car. Maybe I *do* have a sixth sense, after all.

I had flown to Prague at the last minute to write a piece for a music magazine. An up-and-coming British band happened to be playing in town, and I'd been asked to cover the gig. I'd said yes straightaway – this would be my first chance to see Prague, and the trip would include several hours where I'd have nothing to do. I could see the sights, get a feel for the place, go to the gig and come home. I'd be meeting the photographer in a couple of hours, in the centre of Prague. But that was only if I made it that far.

I'd been told I'd be picked up by a local driver called Honza, a friend-of-a-friend of the man who usually picked people up – and here he was, holding his Uzi 9mm with a grin. I grinned back. Now we were just two men in a small white car, grinning at each other – one of them armed.

'You want Uzi 9mm?' he asked.

'I'm fine for Uzi 9mms', I said, quite honestly. I could only hope that by offering me an Uzi 9mm, Honza wasn't also challenging me to a duel.

'I mean, to hold?' he said. 'You want hold gun?'

He was looking at me with what seemed to be real hope in his eyes. I didn't quite know what to say. I didn't really want to hold the gun, but being British, I didn't want to *not* hold it either, in case by not holding this man's gun I made him feel uncomfortable or offended him in any way. As a well-raised Briton, I find it difficult to refuse anybody anything they might want whatsoever. This is also, incidentally, why I tend to avoid the gay nightclub scene.

'Okay then,' I said, slowly, 'I will hold the gun.'

He passed the weapon to me, his face aglow, and I held it for a moment. It was heavy and metal. That's all I can tell you. I was, it seems, never destined to be a reviewer for *Guns 'n' Ammo*.

'You like?' asked Honza, eagerly.

'It is brilliant', I replied, handing it back almost immediately.

'Okay!' said Honza. 'Now we go!'

Honza tucked the Uzi under his seat, and reached into his pocket for something. I figured so long as it wasn't a hand grenade, I'd be happy.

It was a knife.

A knife that he then jammed, with some considerable speed and force, into the ignition of the car. He twisted it once, and the car roared into life. We sped out of the airport car park so quickly that for a moment I wished for the safe old days, when we were just two strangers, in a foreign country, playing with guns.

'So, um, why exactly do you have a gun under your seat?' I asked, after a silent ten minutes or so.

'Ah', said Honza, sadly. 'To protect. Local gangs, mafia people. Some bad gypsy people, too. They look for tourist, or foreigner. They steal list of people flying into Czech, and then they make a small sign with name on, and stand at airport and wait for you. They bribe real driver away. And then they take you out of city, to country, and rob you with gun.'

'Oh', I said, slightly relieved.

Until I realised that Honza had met me at the airport with a small sign with 'Mr Wallace' written on it, and that Honza had a gun, and that outside the window of the car, the grey of the city was instead becoming the green of the countryside...

———————·———————

It turned out, of course, that Honza was not about to rob me. He just had a few errands to run before he could drop me off in town. I mean, of *course* he did. When else would you run errands but when you've been asked to pick up a British journalist from the airport? You certainly don't do them before you've picked him up, as that would be a waste of valuable time, and you don't do them afterwards, do you, because then you'd get home late. No, no. You wait until you've picked him up, and then you spend nearly an hour and a half driving around the Czech Republic picking up bags of plant pots from women in floral dresses and getting your windscreen washed by a dusty minor. Then, and *only* then, do you take the journalist to his destination, which, in this case, was a pub. Still, I didn't mind too much. So I wasn't going to see Prague straightaway. I could see it later – after I'd met the photographer or after the gig.

The photographer who was supposed to be waiting for me in the pub was not, of course, waiting for me in the pub.

At first, I didn't mind too much. Surely he'd be along in a minute or two. Perhaps he was off buying film. Maybe one of his flashbulbs had broken. There was still time. The gig didn't start for a few hours, and he was only a little bit late.

Honza had decided to park the car and come inside with me. He even said he was going to come along with me to the gig. So together we sat, awaiting the arrival of the photographer, and nursing two inordinately cheap pints of beer. I'd hoped that at least our rendezvous point would be an example of proper, old-fashioned Czechoslovakia. It wasn't. The main clue was its name: Mulligans. There were other clues, too – the bicycle bolted to the wall and the giant plastic bearded leprechaun being just two of them. It appeared that we were sitting in an Irish theme pub designed by someone who had never actually been to Ireland. This was back in the late nineties, when Prague seemed on the cusp of huge commercial change – that is, it was gracelessly changing from a priceless fairy-tale village to a city entirely sponsored by McDonald's.

It was this aspect of Prague that I was rather pompously contemplating (I do, after all, live in London – a city that proudly claims as one of its main tourist attractions a big neon sign with the word 'Fuji' written on it), when a stranger sat down next to us.

He was scruffy, unkempt and reeked strongly of whisky. In other words, he looked like he was probably the photographer.

'This is Jiri', said Honza. 'He is butcher.'

It wasn't the photographer.

I raised my hand in greeting, and would have said hello had I not then immediately remembered my encounter with the Uzi. I found myself hoping that 'Butcher' was this man's occupation, as opposed to his nickname.

Jiri looked at me and smiled, then uttered a sentence which impressed me as much for its speed and confidence as it did for its total and utter lack of any discernible vowels. Not able to speak Czech, I blinked at the man a couple of times, and said, 'Um...'

'American?' he said. 'British?'

'British', said Honza.

'What you are doing here? Holidays?'

'No', I said. 'I'm just waiting for someone.'

'Who you are waiting for?' said Jiri. 'Tony Blair?'

And then he laughed and laughed and laughed, smacking the table with the palm of his hand, and turned to Honza, who was also laughing. Then they both stopped laughing and looked at me.

'No', I said, quite calmly. 'I am not waiting for Tony Blair. That would be ludicrous. I am waiting for a photographer.'

Jiri brought his hand to his chest.

'I am photographer', he said.

I blinked again.

'Are you?' I queried.

'No', he said. 'I am not photographer. I am butcher.'

'Oh.'

I couldn't help but wonder what had prompted Jiri to play such an elaborate hoax on me.

'But!' he said. 'I have camera!'

At this, Honza and Jiri started to talk very excitedly in Czech. And then Honza got out of his seat and said, 'I come back soon.'

I looked at my watch. There was still no sign of the photographer. Perhaps he wanted me to meet him at the gig. I reached into my pocket and tried to find the piece of paper on which I'd written the name of the venue. Jiri watched me do this, then leaned forward, conspiratorially.

'What do you want, my friend?' he whispered, his eyes darting nervously around the room.

'How do you mean?' I asked, confused.

'Anything you want, I can get you. You are friend of Honza, you are friend of my. What do you want?'

I thought about it, and shrugged. Perhaps he thought I wanted a tour guide, which, come to think of it, wasn't such a bad idea.

'You want to smoke something? I can get you something. Anything I can get you, in Praha it is all possible. You want class A, I get you class A.'

Oh good God. The Butcher was trying to sell me illegal substances, when all I wanted was an hour to myself and someone to tell me where all the pretty buildings were. First I'm picked up by an armed stranger, and now I'm sitting underneath a bright-green leprechaun with a criminal butcher who wants to find something he can sell me.

'A girl? You want a girl? I get you girls. Anything you want, my friend, it is possible.'

'To be honest, I'm okay at the moment...'

'A gun?'

'No!' I said. 'No, I don't want a gun. Or a girl. Or any Class A's...'

Jiri leaned back in his chair, cast his eyes round the room, and then leaned forward again. 'Anti-tank missile?'

Anti-tank missile?!

'Whatever it is,' he said, 'it all can happen. It can take time, yes, but...'

'Um, look...'

'Ah!' he said, suddenly, pointing a finger in the air. 'You want Chicago Bull? I can get you Chicago Bull!'

'*Chicago Bull?* What's a Chicago Bull?'

But the truth was, I didn't *want* to know. I had a hunch he was referring to something illicit and dodgy, but to be honest, even if he was referring to the basketball team itself, I wouldn't have been interested. There is a time and a place for illegally purchasing massive, millionaire basketball players, and the corner table of an Irish pub in Prague isn't it.

'Really', I said. 'I am absolutely fine for all the things you have mentioned. Even the anti-tank missile and the Chicago Bull, whatever that is. I am simply waiting for the photographer to arrive and then we are going to go and see some music.'

Honza walked back into the pub just then, and Jiri put his finger to his lips, willing me not to let on about his minor indiscretions, such as drug dealing, pimping and the potential kidnap of some nine-foot sportsmen.

'I have camera', said Honza, placing a small and battered disposable Kodak camera on the table. 'Now we go.'

———————————

'*You're* the photographer?' I asked, as we drove over the Charles Bridge, heading for the gig. '*You*?'

'No. I am not photographer. But photographer did not come tonight. So I help you. We have camera, what is problem?'

We were alone again now. Jiri had stayed on at the pub and given me a knowing wink as I walked out the door, mouthing what I *think* were the words 'grenade launcher'.

'We go Dlouhá', said Honza, and I nodded, even though I didn't know what he was saying. I was growing a little nervous now. I'd been told the venue was only moments away from the pub, but already we seemed to have been driving for a lot longer and in what I irrationally believed to be the wrong direction. Plus, the photographer was missing. Oh my God, the photographer was *missing*. He was probably *dead*! He'd clearly got to the pub early and run into the Butcher. Or maybe Honza had got to him earlier today with his Uzi...

'How much you paying photographer?' said Honza.

'I don't know. The magazine was paying him.'

Honza made an odd grumbling sound. We were thundering over a cobbled street now and into a square, where trams were stopping and people dashed through slanting rain.

Honza slowed to a halt. 'There it is. You go in, I follow.'

And I did as he said.

———— - ————

The band came on half an hour late to mild and scattered applause from a bored-looking audience. But they played well and won the crowd over, and soon the place was rocking. I looked around, trying to catch a glimpse of anyone with a camera, anyone who might be the guy I was supposed to meet. But there was only Honza – clutching his disposable camera in one hand and a beer in the other and clicking away from the back of the room. I made a few notes and drank a bottle of water. And then the gig was over.

'I only make seven photograph', said Honza, back by my side. 'Already this camera was full.'

'I'm sure that'll be fine', I said, eager to get away, to finally be free. 'Thank you very much for that.'

There was an awkward silence.

'Well', I said, offering Honza my hand, hoping that this would be the moment I could make a break and flee into the night to see all that Prague had to offer.

'And now we eat!' said Honza.

An hour later we were sitting in a fine little restaurant, chewing bread and meat and drinking beer. A few of Honza's friends had turned up, and although I couldn't understand them, the atmosphere was warm as we sat there and laughed and drank and laughed some more.

I suddenly felt quite guilty. I mean, this wasn't so bad, was it? So I wasn't exactly seeing Prague – but maybe, by hanging out with the locals, I was experiencing a more important Prague, the Prague of the people.

I looked over to Honza. 'You like the food?' he asked. 'Good food, huh?' I nodded, and realised something shocking. I had clearly jumped to some very wrong conclusions about this man. He hadn't *needed* to invite me out. He hadn't *needed* to fetch his camera and take pictures of the band. He was a genuinely nice, hospitable and friendly man. Someone who was only supposed to pick me up from the airport, but who was now spending all evening looking after me. Just because he had a gun in his car and his friend had tried to sell me black-market weaponry didn't necessarily make him a bad person.

As I accepted another beer from this table of strangers, I resolved to be less judgemental in the future. I'd learned an important lesson, and if someone tries to sell you black-market weaponry one day, I hope you'll remember my experience in Prague and not think too badly of them.

'Here, Danny', said Honza, holding a small shot glass filled to the brim with something green. 'Drink!'

I downed the shot to the cheers of the table, and we ordered another.

'Tonight, Danny, you stay with me', said Honza.

'No, no', I said. 'It's okay. I've got a hotel booked.'

'Which hotel?'

'It's called Hotel Pyramid, or something.'

'No, no – that is terrible! You stay with me. Please!'

'But it's booked!'

'We unbook it. You stay with me!'

And I looked around the table at the smiling faces and said humbly, 'Thank you, Honza.'

When the bill finally came I suddenly realised that I hadn't had time to change any money yet. Honza just smiled and waved my objections away, and the bill was paid. I smiled. What genuinely lovely people.

A few of us went back to Honza's that night, and as the clock edged towards 3am, I fell asleep, drunk and happy, on the sofa in the living room.

———— ——— ————

Four hours later I was being shaken awake.

'Danny! Come! We must leave!'

It was Honza.

'Eh?'

'We must leave now! We go!'

'Where?'

'To the airport!'

He was smiling the broadest smile I think I have ever seen.

'But it's only seven in the morning! My flight isn't until two.'

'I have things I must do.'

'I'll get a taxi to the airport later on. I want to see some of Prague anyway. I still haven't managed to see it.'

'I show you sights in car', said Honza. 'Please, we leave now.'

Confused and tired, I quietly got my things together.

I'm not sure what sights normal tourists get to see when they visit Prague. I'm told they're entranced by the majesty of the old town. I'm told they stand and stare for hours before the gates of the mighty castle. I'm told some fall in love with St Nicholas Cathedral, while others never want to leave the Old Gardens. Evidently, Honza didn't think any of these were the slightest bit important. Which is why most of what I saw of Prague was a motorway, a brewery and the back of Jiri's block of flats. Honza had more errands to run – the very last of which, it turned out, was dropping me off at the airport.

I began to thank him for looking after me in such a – well – *unusual* way, but he had one last thing to say.

'This is for you', he said, and handed me an envelope. I was touched. Honza had obviously written me a letter, thanking me for my friendship and wishing me the best. Or perhaps it was the photos, which he'd secretly had developed as a parting gift. Or maybe it was an invitation to come back sometime, to enjoy more of his generous hospitality.

I opened it. It was a bill.

Car. Drinks. Photos.

I couldn't quite believe it.

Meal.

I was being charged for the meal? And not just for *my* meal, either. It seemed I was being asked to pay for *everyone's!*

Hotel.

He was calling his sofa a hotel?

Prague Tour.

Prague Tour?! A brewery and the back of his mate's house!

I was dumbstruck, and not a little vexed.

I looked at Honza, who looked at me and smiled. I remembered the Uzi under his seat. And the knife in the ignition. It was all I could do not to scour the horizon for Jiri and an anti-tank missile.

And so I bravely said, 'I only have British money on me.'

'Okay', said Honza.

Twenty minutes later I stood in the check-in queue and considered the fact that my trip to Prague had actually cost me more than I had earned. And then I looked up and caught a glimpse of bald, beefy Honza walking towards the arrivals area, carrying a small sign that read 'Mr Thomas'.

Mr Thomas, if you are reading this, please get in touch. It would be nice to reminisce about all the things we saw in wonderful, unforgettable Prague.

BLACKOUT IN USHUAIA

MICHELLE RICHMOND

Michelle Richmond's books include the story collection *The Girl in the Fall-Away Dress* and the novel *Dream of the Blue Room*, which is set in China. Her stories and essays have appeared in *Glimmer Train*, *Playboy*, the *San Francisco Chronicle* and elsewhere. She lives in San Francisco and edits the online literary journal *Fiction Attic*.

At first glance it may seem that Ushuaia is sleeping, but in truth the city is fully awake, groping in the dark. It is seven-thirty on a Friday evening, rather early by the standards of this South American ski resort, the capital of Tierra del Fuego and the southernmost town in the world. Perched on the southern tip of Argentina, Ushuaia borders the frigid Beagle Channel and is backed by the awesome Andes. In the depths of winter it is a haven for serious ski bunnies from around the globe. By day, the steep mountains behind the town are dotted with veteran skiers; by night, the discos along San Martin serve overpriced alcoholic drinks to a young, disorderly crowd and pump out dance music so loudly one can feel the thunder in the floor, and one fears an avalanche. Winter in Ushuaia is also host to a number of grand events I've read about in my guidebook: the Longest Night National Party, the Snow Sculptors' National Meeting and the much-anticipated End of the World Rally – the Stanley Cup of sledge dog racing.

Or so I am told. But it is not the depths of winter, not quite. It is August, and ski season is apparently over. The best snows have gone, and the slopes are dotted with old snow and slush. One can still take the ski lift to the top of Martial Glacier, but the café is closed and the few people milling about at the top are pretty unfriendly. In the lull between ski seasons – a lull made even quieter by the wretched state of the Argentine economy – the town reverts, for the most part, to the dominion of the locals.

I say for the most part because a few tourists have managed to find their way here despite the blandness of the season. My husband and I are among them. It has become an accidental routine of our travel modus operandi to visit a foreign city or country only at the most inopportune time – thus the Scottish Highlands in January, when the castles and B&Bs were closed; Baja in August, when the heat and humidity put everyone on permanent siesta; Costa Rica's Caribbean coast during a particularly precipitous July, when it poured 200 millimetres in three hours. It is in our nature to arrive anywhere and everywhere just after the parade has passed or weeks before the party starts. While our taste in destinations may be superb, our timing is atrocious.

So, upon our arrival in Ushuaia the slopes are no longer skiable, the town's best chefs have gone on vacation, and the gift shop proprietors are desperately hawking wool sweaters and wooden ashtrays as if we're the last tourists they'll see this year. None of this is surprising, given our history, but we aren't prepared for the possibility that even the electricity might take a hiatus.

It happens on our second night in town. To save money, we have checked out of the pricey Del Glacier Hotel and into the Tolkeyen, a small, one-storey, lodge-like affair perched on the edge of the continent. To get here, we took a ten-minute cab ride from the city centre through winding suburbs filled with large, unattractive houses. The blank-faced homes with their small windows and smoking chimneys seemed adrift in a sea of black ice and snow. Hardly anyone was about.

Our room at the Tolkeyen features dark-panelled walls, a single queen-sized bed with a seventies-era quilt, some cheaply framed pictures of mountain scenes, a three-drawer dresser with missing knobs, two lamps and an ancient TV with no remote control. The room is simultaneously ugly, cosy and warm, and we are both happy to be here.

Our new room reminds me of the night my husband and I spent together eight years ago at the Bucksnort Inn in Bucksnort, Tennessee. We were at the fragile beginning of our relationship, driving from Fayetteville, Arkansas, to New York City through blizzards and sleet storms in a tiny Mitsubishi pick-up with no power steering. We arrived at the Bucksnort Inn the night before the opening of deer season, and the clientele consisted almost entirely of hunters. All night long we could hear men in the adjoining rooms cleaning and oiling and racking their guns. We woke at six in the morning to find the place deserted; the hunt had already begun.

The Tolkeyen has the same abandoned feeling, as if it is only by accident that someone left the door unlocked and the vacancy sign in the window. When we checked in, the concierge seemed surprised to see us. He was wearing a funny hat, the kind favoured by the children of Finland. 'Where are you from?' he asked, sliding a skeleton key across the wooden counter.

'California.'

'Oh.' The fuzzy balls on his Finnish hat jiggled. 'Hollywood. Your movies are very big but not very interesting. You are in room number one.'

My husband empties the contents of his backpack into the top drawer of the dresser and takes a moment to brush his extraordinarily unruly hair. The effect of the static, combined with an orange-and-green striped scarf he purchased from a street vendor in Buenos Aires, makes him look something like a misguided English gnome.

'Want to go for a walk?' he asks.

'Sure, a short one.'

I pull the gingham curtains aside and take in the view. Just a few hundred yards from our window, the sea whips against the flat brown beach. In truth I'd rather stay right here and catch up on sleep and Argentine TV, but compromise is in order. Earlier today, my husband consented under duress to ride the toy-like Tren del Fin del Mondo through a flat, dull landscape made remarkable only by the stories piped out of the train's loudspeakers. From the moment we arrived in Ushuaia, we had been bombarded with literature and coupons for the Train at the End of the World, apparently the only tourist attraction currently in operation. Long before it was a tourist destination, Ushuaia was a prison town, where criminals were sent to labour and die under unbearably harsh conditions. The electronically delivered Disneyesque narrative made it sound as if the prisoners had enjoyed a pleasantly reformative exile, complete with arts and crafts and organised football. We met a friendly family from Buenos Aires on the train, whose eldest son pulled out his harmonica and serenaded us with 'Candle in the Wind'. By the time we got back to the little station my husband's cranky knees were suffering the ill effects of an hour crammed into a Small World-sized seat. I owe him a walk on the beach.

The evening is windy and grey, beautiful in its bleakness. As we walk along the dirt path from the motel down to the beach we are followed by a scraggly yellow dog. My husband has been picking up dogs all over Argentina and Uruguay. Not at all a pet person at home, in this part of the world he has become a natural magnet for unkempt, affection-seeking canines. Just a few days ago in Colonia, a scabby brown mutt who decided he belonged to us got us chased out of a laundromat, and as a result we have had to put our unlaundered socks and underwear on a second rotation.

From the beach we can see the twinkling lights of the town centre in the near distance. The Beagle Channel is shrouded in darkness. I am beginning to suspect that, like Tolstoy's unhappy families, all bleak coastal towns are bleak in exactly the same way. The place reminds me of other coastal towns we've visited in winter: Akranes, Iceland; John O' Groats, Scotland; Crescent City, California. There is the same saltwater smell, its vague fishiness somewhat mitigated by the cold, mingling with the scent of coal fires; the same grey sky meeting grey sea; the same sense of loneliness, of having arrived at the last place on earth. These places trigger a similar feeling of sadness, despite the fact that, when on vacation, one generally does not have much to be sad about. A by-product of the drenching melancholy is a desire to connect in an intimate way with another human being, to shrug off the cold and the vastness of windblown spaces by warming up to another body. To put it simply, bleak coastal towns always make me want to get laid.

I turn to my husband, who is having a rather dignified conversation with the mutt on the subject of *submarinos*, a delicious kind of hot chocolate served in Argentina and favoured mostly by schoolboys. 'The secret is in the little foil-wrapped chocolates', my husband is saying to the dog, who sits eagerly on his haunches, panting and taking in the lecture. 'You have to swirl them into the hot milk at precisely the right speed.'

'Do you want to go back to our room and do it?' I ask.

Both my husband and the dog tip their heads towards me as if they'd forgotten my presence. The dog makes an uninterested whimper.

'Excellent idea', my husband says. One thing I have always admired about him is that he is always up for that sort of thing, no matter the time or the weather.

Just then the lights go out.

'What was that?' I ask.

We both look towards the town, which only moments ago twinkled like a Christmas tree in the distance. Now it is entirely dark. We have been plunged into that kind of darkness one finds only in the most rural places. The only illumination comes from the glow of the moon seeping through the fog. I reach for my husband's hand. The mutt is panting between us, his damp dog smell penetrating the air.

'A blackout', my husband says, pulling me close. 'I could have my way with you right here and no one would know.'

'*He* would', I say, feeling the pressure of the dog's small, muscular body against my legs.

The headlights of a single car wind slowly towards the shadow of the town. I think of the prisoners in their wooden shacks down by the water a hundred years ago, feel the sweet thrill of being on a grey beach beside a grey sea in a black night on the edge of the world, hand in hand with my husband.

We pick our way along the dirt path back to the motel, and leave the dog whimpering by the door. The lobby, deserted only a short while ago, is now crowded with about a dozen guests who seem to have emerged from the woodwork. There's a sense of jovial camaraderie about the place. The concierge in the funny hat is distributing free candles and flashlights for a fee. We wait in line for a couple of candles wrapped in foil. There are no candlesticks. 'Use the drinking glasses in your room', the concierge instructs us. As we walk away, I can hear him mumbling something in Spanish to one of the other guests about Hollywood.

Minutes later my husband and I are unclothed and in bed, the candles glowing softly on the dresser. Making love during a blackout in a foreign country is something like making love on a speeding train or in the office after hours. It's so new and different that one irrationally assumes, in the blissful midst of the act, that nothing could possibly go wrong. The walls are very thin and our room is just off the lobby; we can hear the happy commotion of the other guests just outside our door, a pleasant background noise. It's so noisy, in fact, that it takes me a couple of moments to realise that someone has opened the door.

The father enters the room first. He's holding a candle in one hand and a large piece of luggage in the other, and he doesn't appear to notice us as he heads for the dresser to set down the candle. By the time he sees us, his entire family has followed him into the room: two small children, a teenaged son, and a skinny wife bringing up the rear. I can't help but let out a shriek. My husband is on his back, eyes closed, concentrating on the business at hand, so he naturally assumes that my cry has something to do with his technique.

'Was that good or bad?' he asks, opening his eyes. At which point he too sees the family, who are now standing in a line at the end of our bed. Not one of them is moving, as if by their stillness they might disguise the disconcerting fact of their presence.

There is the feeling of a train wreck about the whole thing, the family standing in paralysed horror while I sit astride my husband, my entire torso exposed. I tug at the sheet, trying to cover myself, but it's too short and I can only get it to come up to my waist. My back is to the family, but the teenaged son begins to slowly inch around the end of the bed, as if to get a better look. My husband pulls me down towards him in an attempt to hide my nakedness, and the wife's face takes on a horrified expression. It occurs to me that she must think my husband is trying to get on with the lovemaking.

In the candlelight I can see that the two younger children are dressed identically, except that one is wearing a white cap and the other is wearing a red one. The child in the red cap finally breaks the silence, pointing and blurting out something in Spanish that I can't decipher. The child's voice seems to jolt the mother from her paralysis. She grabs the children's heads and pulls them to her, then backs out the door. The teenager and the father are in no hurry to go anywhere.

'You must be the Californians', the father says in slightly accented English. I get the uncomfortable feeling that he's waiting for us to invite him to sit down for a friendly chat and a cup of *mate*.

'Yes', my husband says.

'Sorry for the intrusion. We must have the wrong room. Have a nice vacation.' He picks up his candle and suitcase and says something in a scolding voice to the teenaged son, who shrugs, gives me a polite nod, and walks out as if nothing has happened. The father follows his son into the hallway and softly shuts the door.

The blackout lasts for another hour. It's too dark to read, we can't watch TV, and both of us have given up on romance for the night. The following afternoon, having exhausted all the possibilities of the town, including the kitsch prison museum, we find ourselves on a catamaran taking an excursion into the Beagle Channel. The main attractions of the cruise are supposed to be Isla de los Pajaros and Isla de los Lobos – two small, rocky outcrops whose only distinction is that they are home to cormorants and sea lions. We have just settled into our seats and are loading film into the camera when the family of five appears. The teenager spots us first and smiles awkwardly. The mother is momentarily caught off guard and holds my gaze too long, as if trying to recall exactly where she's seen me before. The child in the red hat points again, and I wave. Now that my embarrassment has faded, I feel a vague satisfaction. Like us, the family missed the skiing, the snow sculptures, the Longest Night National Party, and the rest. But at least they saw *something* on their trip to the end of the world.

THE SNOWS OF CARRARA

DAVID DOWNIE

Paris-based David Downie writes for leading publications worldwide, from the *Australian Financial Review* to the *San Francisco Sunday Chronicle*, *Gourmet*, *Bon Appétit* and the London *Sunday Times*. His latest travel-cookbook is *Cooking the Roman Way: Authentic Recipes from the Home Cooks and Trattorias of Rome* (www.cookingtheromanway.com). David is currently working on *Paris, Paris*, a collection of travel essays.

'The snows of Carrara never melt', said my wife, Alison, as she read aloud from the guidebook we'd bought a week earlier in the Cinque Terre. She paused to regard me with a gimlet eye. 'If it snows, how am I supposed to take photos to go with your article?'

'Snow?' I repeated, chuckling. 'No, dear, that's not snow. It's marble dust. All the books say so. Besides, it doesn't snow on the Italian Riviera in May.'

The idea of snow seemed completely out of place in this Mediterranean paradise, where Tuscany meets Liguria. The rocky beaches were already colonised by large pale bodies and just yesterday we'd been hiking and building up a sweat in the spring sunshine.

Our guidebook had informed me that marble discards and dust have been accumulating on the Apuan Alps' craggy slopes since antiquity, which was why I knew that what Alison was looking at wasn't real snow. The Apuans lie eight kilometres or so from the coast, forming an amphitheatre around Carrara, Pietrasanta and Massa. The trio of towns have been synonymous with stone since Roman slaves wrenched Trajan's Column from the Fantiscritti quarry high above the Colonnata Valley (so named because its marble is ideal for columns). The mountains' deposits are estimated at twenty-five kilometres long, almost ten wide and two deep. In them lie forty kinds of marble, an alphabet of colour and texture nuances, from swirled grey Arabescato via snowy Statuario to zebra-striped Zebrino.

Our assignment for an English magazine was to explore Carrara as an unusual destination for intrepid travellers. We looked forward to seeing and photographing what friends had told us was overwhelming, spectacular scenery. Squiring us around would be a local marble expert from International Marble Machines. I'll call him Giovanni. When I'd phoned Giovanni several weeks earlier to go over the details of our private tour, he'd immediately boasted – rather gleefully, I thought – that the area's 'snow' is visible from outer space.

'You've had Martian visitors?'

'Ha, ha, ha... You are the spirited type of American', he'd laughed. 'Come, you'll see the eternal snows. Seeing is believing.'

As arranged, Giovanni was waiting for us at the headquarters of International Marble Machines, on the outskirts of Carrara. A wiry, moustachioed, dark-haired man in his fifties, he shook hands vigorously then opened an umbrella, holding it out for Alison and her photo equipment. 'I'm sure the rain won't last', he said apologetically, 'and you will be able to take stupendous photographs. Shall we take my car?'

It was a rhetorical question. The company Fiat Panda was compact but unstoppable, he said; the ideal vehicle for visiting quarries. 'Since precipitation appears to have begun unseasonably,' Giovanni added, 'perhaps we should start by visiting an artist's workshop? The rain will stop soon, and then we can head up into the quarries.'

Again, the question was rhetorical. We sped along wide modern avenues into Carrara's historic heartland, a heart reportedly carved from purest marble. The white Fiat darted through spring showers among trucks and Formula One wannabes driving SUVs.

'The entire area is a vertically integrated factory', said Giovanni amiably, swabbing at the windshield. 'The history and livelihoods of countless people like me revolve around marble and always have.' As he spoke, the rain drummed on the car's tin roof. He raised his voice, a sonorous baritone. 'Marble follows us from the baptismal font to the tombstone.'

'Is that fog up ahead', Alison asked nervously, 'or snow?'

'Mmmm', acknowledged Giovanni vaguely. 'Fog, definitely fog. Be gone in a minute, I'm absolutely sure.' He motioned beyond the steamy windows. 'Look up at the hills', he directed. 'To us, the mountains are beautiful titanic sculptures, the greatest work of art of all. Did you know that Michelangelo in the early 1500s decided to transform the top of Monte Sagro, up there, into the statue of a giant?' I began to roll down my window for a look but the rain was coming down too hard. 'Never mind, you'll see it later', Giovanni said confidently. 'Michelangelo would have succeeded except that the Marquis Alberigo Cybo Malaspina, who was Lord of Carrara, did not have the funds and workmen. Mount Rushmore would have seemed nothing in comparison – a bagatelle, a molehill!'

We were creeping through what seemed to be the old part of town; the streets were narrow, the traffic thick and slow. '*Bello, bello!*' Giovanni bellowed suddenly, a rapturous smile lifting his moustache. 'You'll see, once the fog lifts...'

Alison nodded, trying not to shiver. We were underdressed. To stop her teeth from chattering, she asked Giovanni whether it was true that Carrara's medieval centre was chock-a-block with marble churches, theatres and aristocratic *palazzi* constructed from choice white stones.

'Yes, yes', Giovanni agreed, his hands leaving the wheel to flutter, bird-like. 'And the humble dwelling houses were built from marble leavings – you know, bits and pieces – covered with plaster.'

Beyond the windows I caught sight of a handful of vintage buildings in what appeared to be hazy pastel tones, though it was hard to be sure because of the rain.

'Piazza Alberica,' Giovanni declared, his hands alive, 'paved with marble blocks. See the sculptures of lions, of giants, of statesmen, of heroes and quarry workers? All are marble.'

Glimpsed through the precipitation they looked like chess pieces on a glistening marble chessboard, I said. Giovanni liked that. Alison was itching to stop and take a picture but the weather was too awful.

We parked under what I assumed were trees on a square and stepped into the downpour. The barn doors ahead turned out to belong to the famous eighteenth-century sculpture workshops of Carlo Nicoli. Giovanni danced over the puddles, holding up his umbrella. 'They have been in the Nicoli family for six generations and are Carrara's most illustrious', he explained.

The studio was an Aladdin's cave of busts and statues, shrouded in a heavy layer of dust. It merged with the mist coming in from outside, making photography impossible. We could barely see the heads of flesh and stone that surrounded us. 'Giuseppe Garibaldi', Giovanni shouted over the din of drills and hammers. 'There, there', he pointed, coughing and waving. 'That's Disraeli, there's Christ and Queen Victoria.'

Moments later Signor Nicoli, a distinguished man with a scarf wrapped stylishly around his neck, emerged from the dust cloud and beckoned us into his office. After a brief introduction he seemed eager to show us records proving that around three hundred marble busts of Queen Victoria had been sculpted here. It was unclear whether they were originals made by Nicoli's great-grandfather, grandfather and father, or copies of sculptures owned by the Royal Family. 'You are writing for an English publication, are you not?' Nicoli enquired. 'Bad luck with the weather...' He glanced at Alison's cameras.

The rain had eased by the time we found our way through the fog to the invisible white Fiat. 'Above, it will be sunny and beautiful for photography', said Giovanni, undaunted. 'We'll drive up through marble villages, shall we?'

As the two-lane road chased its tail uphill the fog turned into low cloud. Water rushed down the road carrying chunks of rock and clots of white mud. I'd read that the systematic devastation caused by quarrying had inadvertently wrought man-made majesty in a stunning natural setting, and the little I could see of the landscape seemed brutally beautiful. We passed through hamlets and villages perched over gaping ravines that seemed set to swallow them.

'Isolated houses occasionally do disappear', Giovanni said mildly. 'They are engulfed by the vortex of quarries.'

'Sounds poetic', Alison remarked.

'Very. Have you read Dante?'

We pulled over onto a shoulder and got out of the car. I could hear a river thundering below but all I could see was wet whiteness, as if we'd become stuck in a milking machine.

'The Garrione runs white', Giovanni murmured, sounding like a soothsayer.

'What does that mean?'

'The name of the river is Garrione. It means, perhaps there will be a little more precipitation', he admitted. 'That's good, the rain will wash away the fog and then you'll be able to see for yourself the beauty of the setting.'

As we continued to motor upward the jagged hills seemed to have been softened by cotton balls. Mist dampened the staccato percussion of pneumatic tools. We slowed as Giovanni looked around him, and suddenly an outsized bulldozer appeared a few feet away from us and began piling up shattered stone. Giovanni fiddled with the emergency blinkers and headlights as he pulled off the road again.

'Do you think maybe you should honk the horn?' I suggested.

Giovanni laughed operatically. 'Oh no, no, no. They see us, believe me. They very rarely have accidents – well, rarely, occasionally, let us say.'

'But the car is white...' Alison added meekly.

Transported by hilarity, Giovanni opened the door and stepped into a puddle the size of a fishpond. We followed suit and sank to our ankles in white mud.

'Look!' Giovanni commanded. 'At the base of sheer rock faces such as this the bulldozers make mounds of chips to cushion the fall of massive blocks. Do you hear the whir of the high-speed diamond wires overhead? No? The blocks weigh up to twenty tonnes each. See?' Directing our attention to rows of truck headlights penetrating the fog in perilous proximity, he lifted me by the arm and led me forward. 'Below us is the Ferrovia Marmifera', he explained, conducting an unseen orchestra. 'It's a railway through tunnels and over bridges. Very spectacular. You see?'

'Oh yes', I lied, wondering how I would be able to describe the scene without having seen it.

'Wonderful', Alison added as she wiped the rain off her cameras.

We'd admired photos of the Ferrovia Marmifera's elegantly arched bridges in the guidebook. The bridges had been built at the turn of the twentieth century, specifically engineered for trains, but now monster earthmovers used them.

'Many of the quarry roads leading to the old train line down there are too steep and narrow to turn on', Giovanni said. I could no longer see his arms but sensed he was waving them. 'Even specially designed vehicles like these cannot turn,' he added, 'so the trucks go up or down one section of road in first gear, then they do the next section in reverse.'

Alison and I held hands and stared into the abyss like actors in some Absurdist drama. As the wind picked up, snatching at the fog and low clouds, we caught sight of a truck doing a mesmerising, heavyweight ballet towards the valley floor.

'I don't usually eat lunch,' Giovanni remarked, rainwater streaming across his wrinkled brow, 'but perhaps, given the meteorological conditions, we could retire to a local restaurant?'

'Good idea', I blurted. 'Alison? Where are you?'

We bumped into each other on the way back to the car, our lips bloodless, our faces beginning to turn blue.

'You will have heard of our famous *lardo di Colonnata*?' Giovanni enquired hopefully, putting the Fiat into gear.

We had. New York restaurateur Mario Batali calls it 'white prosciutto' so that diners won't be turned off by the prospect of eating pickled lard. Giovanni laughed when I mentioned that. 'Very good, white prosciutto', he said, repeating the words several times.

The rain was coming down harder than before, mixed with sleet. The wipers couldn't cope. 'Now we're definitely coming to the end of this storm', he said brightly. 'White prosciutto! Ha, ha, ha...'

As we drove skyward in first gear, Giovanni kept up a running commentary. In the year 1570, he said, the Marquis Alberigo's son, also conveniently named Alberigo, inaugurated the use of gunpowder in quarrying. It was thanks to him that some of the most spectacular avalanches of Carrara marble 'snow' had been created. 'Honestly, I am glad it's raining and foggy now, because when it clears and we're up top it will be even more breathtaking for your article and photographs. White prosciutto – I love it!'

We darted across the village square to a restaurant whose simple exterior hid a luxurious and – thankfully – well-heated interior. It was hung with vintage photos of marble quarries and workers from the bad old days.

Giovanni and the proprietor embraced and confabulated about the menu, and within minutes a procession of blubbery delicacies began to arrive. Smiling from lobe to lobe, the owner leaned over and sang a snatch from an aria, his index finger counting the beat. 'I see you've brought the rain with you', he joked. 'No matter, it will stop soon. In the meantime, enjoy your lunch, then we will visit the lard works.'

'Ah, the lard works', Giovanni repeated. 'Amazing...'

Ten thousand calories and several bottles of local Vermentino Nero later, we waddled on webbed feet to a stone building 500 metres away. The temperature had dropped close to freezing and the continuing downpour had caused a power outage in the factory. Inside the dark building it was even colder than outside. Half a dozen giant sarcophaguses lurked against the walls. Bumping into one, I put out my hand instinctively and felt it subside into something clammy.

'Colonnata lard is salt-cured in these vats of Carrara marble', the proprietor's voice explained in the darkness. 'Usually the vats are made of a greyish or slightly swirled variety – never the white statuary marble prized for making sculptures, which is not porous enough.'

'The marble, it is said, maintains the perfect temperature for curing and also imparts a peculiar, inimitable marble-powder taste', added Giovanni.

Alison tried to get a photo or two using her flash, but we knew they wouldn't come out – the interior was black. Back outside I plunged my right hand into the rushing rainwater to get rid of the cold salty brine. My hand was numb as we said farewell to the lard-maker.

By now the river flowing down Colonnata's main road was up to mid-calf level, but the Fiat started at the flick of a key. Giovanni beamed. As we descended into another soggy valley, he delved further into the past. 'Here, all around us, are dozens of sleigh paths first used by the Romans to slide marble down from the mountains...'

'So it does snow here', Alison observed. 'I thought so...'

'No, not that kind of sleigh', Giovanni laughed. 'No, no, no.'

The Romans did not, as might seem logical, quarry the most accessible stones, Giovanni insisted. They followed the best veins of marble, even if that meant making their slaves climb a 1500-metre mountain. 'In ancient times,' he said, pointing at the mist beyond the window, 'marble was the stone of the emperors.' As the ultimate status symbol, no price – in money or human lives – was too high to pay for it. 'Once the marble was loaded onto the sleighs,' he continued, 'they were dragged by men with teams of oxen. The sleigh routes were very, very steep.' Slippery logs, coated with soap, were laid in front of the advancing sleigh, a juggernaut whose progress could never be fully halted. 'Like the big trucks now – sometimes they cannot stop', Giovanni remarked, his right hand doing somersaults.

Before arriving at the celebrated Carbonera quarry, he explained that the primitive and dangerous sleigh technique was still in use in 1926. Benito Mussolini's marble monolith at the Foro Italico stadium in Rome came from Carbonera.

We parked and, no longer bothering to use an umbrella, squelched across the quarry. 'The monolith was dragged by sixty oxen from here to a ship at Marina di Carrara. Look – you can still see the spot from which it was detached, there, there!'

Somehow, despite our best efforts, Alison and I could not make out the gash in the sodden hillside Giovanni indicated. 'I'll take your word for it', I said.

'Lovely, really', Alison added, convulsed by the cold.

'The 300-tonne block is still the largest ever quarried', Giovanni continued once we were back in the car. He turned the heat up to full blast and swept at the windshield. 'The sleighs and oxen only disappeared from here in the 1960s – I remember them. Now we have trucks.'

'I see', I said, blanching. A very large specimen of truck was hurtling at us, its lights blazing. Giovanni popped the clutch and the car bucked through the mud out of harm's way.

'*Fantastico!*' he enthused, turning to admire the quarry vehicle. Its wheels were taller than the Fiat. 'That's efficiency!' Giovanni exclaimed as we surged toward another quarry road. 'Gone are the days when hillsides were dynamited', he explained, denouncing the destructive extraction process used until World

War II. 'Nowadays, with diamond-wire cutting machines and high-tech equipment like that earth-mover, there is no waste. None! Marble discards are crushed to make gravel or composite paving stones', he sang. 'Marble dust goes into glossy magazine paper and cosmetics, and is used as a filtering agent in anti-pollution scrubbers for smokestacks.'

'You must be very proud that the great sculptures of the world are carved from Carrara marble', I said, holding onto the armrest as we swerved up another curlicue road that had been transformed into a river. I rolled down my window to look out. The water was above the seams of the car's doors. I could feel the tyres spinning to get a grip.

'Sculpture?' Giovanni asked. 'Oh yes, very prestigious. But artwork represents only a tiny fraction of marble's uses', he added, gunning the engine and swerving. 'Sculpture is to marble what Ferrari is to cars. The construction industry is the Fiat of marble – the real thing.' He pounded the dashboard.

'What would happen if a truck like that big one we saw were to come down this road right now?' Alison asked.

'A truck? Here? Now? Oh no, I doubt it, highly unlikely. Well, it might happen but... Ah, here we are at the summit at last and you see it's no longer raining.' We paused by a large road sign that read 'panoramic piazza'. 'I know it's here somewhere...'

Dizzy and only partly thawed, we got out of the car. 'Giovanni, where are you?' I called.

'Here, don't you see me?' he asked, then began to point and explain.

'This is snow', Alison said, interrupting. 'This is definitely snow.'

'We call it a white-out', I added.

Giovanni frowned. His moustache twitched. 'Mmmm, it does appear to be snow of the non-marble kind', he conceded. 'But that's excellent. At my office, I have many photographs and brochures. And now you have a reason to return!'

THE BOAT FROM BATTAMBANG

CHRISTOPHER R COX

Christopher R Cox is a feature reporter on the staff of the *Boston Herald*. He has survived Cambodia's transport system on six trips for his newspaper and such magazines as M*en's Journal*, *Travel & Leisure* and *Reader's Digest*. He is the author of the adventure travel book *Chasing the Dragon: Into the Heart of the Golden Triangle*, about Burma's narco-warlords, and can order cold beer in more than half a dozen languages. When not experiencing Third World gastro-intestinal distress, Christopher lives in Acton, Massachusetts.

The route from Battambang to Siem Reap makes a long sweep around the western shoreline of the Tonlé Sap, Southeast Asia's largest lake, via kidney-rattling roads crowded with death-wish buses, overloaded lorries and plodding ox carts. In Cambodia, it's an immutable fact that travel is 90 per cent perspiration and 10 per cent sheer terror. So it seemed a miracle when the Angkor Express Boat Company promised to whisk me from Battambang down the Sangke River and across the Tonlé Sap to Angkor's doorstep in just five hours – half the time I'd spend on a swelter-ing, crowded bus fretting about an impending head-on collision.

Even the firm's ticket had the look of pure '20,000 Leagues' porn: a colour picture of a sleek, modern vessel knifing through placid waters in front of Angkor Wat. Never mind that the moated temple is miles from the lake. I plunked down my fifteen dollars for passage at seven the next morning. This was the way to travel, I thought, as I confirmed my boutique-hotel reservation and several appointments in Siem Reap. Safe, smooth, scenic.

It was March, the hottest time of the year in Cambodia, and the dawn brought enervating heat and humidity to Battambang. It had rained briefly but intensely overnight and puddles filled the potholed streets of the sleepy provincial capital. The dry-season downpour, however, had not been enough to raise the Sangke to navigable depth for our boat. 'River' seemed a bit of a misnomer for the waterway I now regarded ten metres down a sandy, rubbish-strewn bank. There trickled a latte-brown stream that would barely float a bathtub toy.

Where was the speeding boat that was pictured on my ticket?

'Don't worry', Bounhet, an Angkor Express employee, said brightly. He pointed to a battered, fifteen-passenger Ford van. 'We drive to Bak Prea. Maybe one hour. The river is still deep in Bak Prea. There we meet the boat from Siem Reap.'

I consulted my maps. There was no sign of Bak Prea on anything a tourist might buy, but on a detailed, 1:100,000-scale Cambodian map of greater Battambang I found a thin black line (a fair-weather 'cart track', according to the key) meandering through open country until it fizzled out at a small cluster of riverside huts thirty kilometres northeast of the city. This was Bak Prea; literally the end of the road, the dry-season relay point for other travellers equally petrified by bus travel or locals who lived in the villages along the great lake and its tributaries.

A half-hour beyond our scheduled departure, but still well within Cambodian parameters for on-time performance, we set off. I shared the van with an elderly Khmer woman and a trio of Euros: Ales, a forty-eight-year-old Czech train engineer, and two twenty-something backpackers called Ben and Remy, who hailed from England and Holland, respectively. Ben wore a Red Bull T-shirt and a dazed expression; Remy sported a nasty purplish laceration running halfway around his neck.

'Did it surfing the train up from Phnom Penh', he shrugged. 'I was standing on top of one of the coaches. Someone had tapped the power and run a line over the tracks to their village. Almost lost my head.'

Luckily for Remy the condition of the nation's railways was so appalling that trains barely moved above a trot. This time, he'd decided to ride inside.

For a while we rolled along a decent sealed road shadowing the left bank of the Sangke, passing fruit orchards and sturdy wooden homes. From somewhere in the back of the van rose the distinctive, urinal-cake bouquet of a durian fruit. Bounhet ignored the stench, cranking the van's radio and fielding incessant calls on a mobile phone that had a jaunty 'Jingle Bells' ring tone.

Beyond Wat Ek, the site of tenth-century Angkor ruins and a Khmer Rouge killing field holding at least five thousand victims, the villages receded and the tarmac faded, leaving only a stark floodplain. This was Cambodia's rice bowl, which owed its productivity to a remarkable annual phenomenon. During the monsoon season, the rain-swollen Mekong River overflowed into the Tonlé Sap River, actually reversing the current of the hundred-kilometre waterway that connected the lake to the Mekong. By September, floodwaters would extend almost fifty kilometres inland from the great lake's dry-season shoreline, quadrupling the size of the Tonlé Sap.

This inundation deposited fertile silt and nurtured one of the world's richest freshwater fisheries. It also made for terrible roads. Less than an hour from Battambang, Bounhet gingerly entered a small wash without the momentum necessary to send the hulking van up the opposite slope. Too late, he desperately gunned the engine; the tyres only sank further into the slick muck. We were stuck.

Luckily, a nearby farmer had a tractor and cheerfully extricated the road rubes. While we thanked him, a convoy of mud-covered Chinese trucks rolled up from Bak Prea. Forget a one-hour drive: the lead driver said they'd left yesterday and spent the night in their vehicles when the rains struck and the track became a metre-deep quagmire. The route was impassable in our vehicle.

Bounhet ruminated on this, then announced, 'We go to Bak Prea another way.'

His optimism proved short-lived. Less than a kilometre down a faint trail through squash fields, he once again had us mired in a small gully. Eventually a passing four-wheel drive pulled us out. Bounhet pushed on – for all of two hundred metres. Then another muddy patch; another bog-down. After half an hour of fruitlessly spinning our wheels, another Good Samaritan with a Toyota Hi-Lux gave us a tow.

Bounhet decided a break was in order. By now it was almost eleven o'clock. At this pace, Bak Prea was days, if not months, away. A half-dozen Cambodian travellers in another underpowered car joined us in the meagre shade of a solitary, desiccated tree.

'You will make it to Siem Reap today', Bounhet said.

'Tonight', I corrected him.

Ben butchered the durian, then recoiled. He thought he had bought a jackfruit in the Battambang market. The undaunted locals fell on the reeking delicacy with gusto. After another hour of putrid, ninety-five-in-the-shade limbo and a few 'Jingle Bells' ring tones, Bounhet made an executive decision: we would bash on to Bak Prea.

By trial and repeated error, Bounhet had finally grasped the concept of off-road driving. While we shouted and goaded, he powered the van through the dips and puddles and ruts. But after another half-hour scramble, our exhausted driver suddenly stopped and pointed at the thorny underbrush enveloping our path.

'*Steng*', he uttered. River.

The Sangke was nearby. Our speedboat? No one knew.

We bushwhacked through fifty metres of thickets to the river, which hadn't changed much since Battambang: still brown, still slow, and perhaps six metres across. A wide-beamed cargo boat wallowed against the left bank. For a dollar apiece the captain was only too happy to take on passengers.

'One hour to Bak Prea', he said brightly. I'd heard that one before.

For the next two and a half hours the skipper spent more time in the river than at the tiller, dragging his boat through the shallows and over mudflats. In the stupefying midday heat, even the birds – swallows, a black trogon, a piebald kingfisher – seemed to fly at half-speed. Whenever the Sangke deepened, the boatman was content to punt like a Venetian gondolier rather than run his engine.

It was after three o'clock when we poled serenely into Bak Prea, a collection of slapdash bamboo-and-thatch huts and a few tired concrete-block homes at the confluence of the Sangke and Mongkol Borei Rivers. The entire place reeked of raw sewage, dried fish and hard labour. A durian would have smelt like sweet relief.

Incredibly, the Angkor Express boat for Siem Reap was there, tied up at a ramshackle dock that ran from a hut listing above the shallows. The boat, of course, looked nothing like the ticket illustration. Rather, it resembled a large, covered dugout filled with wooden benches fit for galley slaves.

We gathered our packs and leaped from the cargo boat into a scrum of backpackers at the abject marina.

'Is this the boat for Battambang?' one sunburned man asked desperately. 'We've been waiting since ten this morning.'

'I don't think there will be a boat', I replied.

He took the news as well as a terminal-cancer prognosis. I approached a teenaged boy who looked like he could be a deckhand on the Siem Reap vessel.

'Where is the captain?'

Not here, to judge from his reaction. I gestured at my watch and the sun. We needed to get under way soon if we hoped to make it across the Tonlé Sap before nightfall. The boy smiled at the sweaty, addled *barang*, hopped from the boat and disappeared up the gangway to Bak Prea. I would not see him again for hours.

A policeman in plainclothes appeared. 'The driver has gone to Battambang', he said in soft English. 'He will return tonight. Then we will go to Siem Reap.'

How the captain had got himself to Battambang was a mystery. There was nothing to do now but wait. Remy and Ben pitched their bags onto the dock and wandered into Bak Prea. I bought a litre of bottled water at the marina's shack, then gagged on its diesel-fuel taste. It took two shots of travel-stash rum to cleanse my palate.

When the policeman, Mr Kousou, eventually reappeared he didn't look too happy. 'You must stay tonight in Bak Prea', he said. 'There is no guesthouse or hotel here.'

Mr Kousou gestured towards an abandoned-looking structure on the far shore. 'You can sleep across the river, in the schoolhouse', he added. 'The boat will leave tomorrow morning at seven.'

'Is there a phone? I need to make some calls.'

'There is no phone in Bak Prea.'

'Do you have a mobile?'

'There is no coverage in Bak Prea.'

So much for the on-time performance of the Wanker Express Boat Company. My drinking water was gone, I'd run out of food, and the mosquitoes had begun their evening strafing. Well, duty-free Captain Morgan rum and cheap paperback novels were made for magic times like these.

Just after 7pm, I had to rub my groggy eyes when another boat rumbled through the gloom and tied up alongside us. A dozen Khmer passengers flung themselves, their suitcases and fifty-kilogram sacks of rice onto the dock.

'From Battambang', Mr Kousou said. 'Now it goes back.'

The waiting backpackers boarded with the urgency of refugees; they wanted to escape Bak Prea come hell or low water. Overcome with pity, I thrust my fifth of Captain Morgan into the hands of the nearest passenger.

'Drink it wherever you end up tonight', I said.

In a moment the travellers had vanished, and only the fading throb of the engine broke the silence of the night.

During this flurry of activity Ales, our captain and the deckhand miraculously materialised and prepared to get under way.

'Now we go to Siem Reap', Mr Kousou said.

As our boat's engine sputtered to life, Ales seemed disappointed. 'I don't want to leave tonight', the Czech told me. 'I want to leave tomorrow morning, so I can photograph the river. Now it is impossible.'

'Look around', I replied. 'There *is* no other boat to Siem Reap. The next boat is *this* boat, and it has to make it to Siem Reap first. It might come back here tomorrow, or it might not. If you wait, there's a good chance you'll spend tomorrow night here, too.'

I intended to be on the next, and only, thing smoking from Bak Prea. Any forward progress was a small victory. Ales considered his grim options: flee now or possibly spend an eternity photographing this dismal hamlet. He dropped his pack into the boat.

Remy and Ben were still nowhere to be found. While I stalled for time, Mr Kousou sent a boy off in a pirogue to search for two *barang* in a karaoke bar across the river. It was eight o'clock before the pair strolled back to the dock with an Angkor Beer glow.

'You been waiting for us?' Remy asked.

As they boarded, a sense of dumbfounded panic overtook Ben.

'Where's my pack?' he asked.

We shifted around the rice sacks, to no avail. In the backpacker chaos of loading the earlier boat for Battambang, someone had tossed Ben's luggage aboard. He sank glumly onto a hard seat. At best, Angkor Express might find his bag and hold it in Battambang. I thought of a line from *Apocalypse Now*, an even worse river voyage through Cambodia: never get off the fucking boat.

I kept the moral to myself. We set off downriver with no life jackets, a single, naked hundred-watt light bulb for a running light, and the young deckhand on the prow with a flashlight. Our boat blundered along the Sangke for hours, ploughing over fish traps and through islands of water hyacinth, occasionally backing off sandbars or swerving to avoid tiny, unlit sampans. There were other maritime hazards as well: floating pigsties, gardens, homes – even billiard halls and saloons.

Every few kilometres the captain nosed the bow ashore and deposited a Cambodian passenger and an enormous sack of rice. Around midnight we arrived in Prek Toal, a large floating village where the Sangke emptied into the Tonlé Sap. Thankfully, our captain now had no appetite for crossing the pitch-black lake.

'You stay with me', Mr Kousou announced. 'Here.'

The boat tied up to a barge along the left bank of the river. Above the doorway of the bobbing building, I could make out a Cambodian flag hanging limply in the heat. We would spend the night in Prek Toal's floating police post. Mr Kousou intended to make damn sure nothing untoward happened to four foreigners on his beat.

Reed mats were quickly unrolled on the hardwood planks, mosquito nets were strung up from the rafters, and in a few minutes I had succumbed to flat-line sleep. I'd never imagined a Third World jail would feel so good.

The next morning passed as if in a fever-ridden dream: up at five-thirty; a dash through fishing weirs and across the placid Tonlé Sap at sunrise to Chong Khneas, the port of Siem Reap; then a five-dollar taxi ride (an outrageous price) to my hotel. I stumbled into the chic, art-filled lobby of the Shinta Mani a day overdue and immediately dispatched my filthy clothes to the laundry. The five-hour trip had taken more than a full day.

My travelling companions were still back at Chong Khneas, haggling over the cost of motorcycle taxis to Siem Reap. The Angkor Express Boat Company had promised free transfers into town, and they refused to pay the dollar fare the *moto* drivers demanded. It was their principles versus local poverty – a long, unwinnable argument.

As I soaked in a warm bath the size and – thanks to my dirt-encrusted condition – colour of a buffalo wallow, I thought of Mr Kousou. Earlier that morning, I'd given the dutiful policeman a few thousand *riel* for his hospitality, as well as a small bottle I'd been given from a drink cart on my flight to Bangkok. He had cradled the screw-top container in his hands with a wonder beyond that of any economy-class passenger, then summoned an English word rarely heard along the brown, greasy banks of the Sangke River.

'Wine!' Mr Kousou said delightedly.

I didn't have a durian. The Burgundy had to do.

ON SAFARI, ONLY THE ANIMALS SLEEP THROUGH THE NIGHT

KELLY WATTON

Kelly Watton has been chased by wild horses on Georgia's Cumberland Island, stalked by a hyena in Botswana and jumped on by a monkey in the Peruvian Amazon. She has travelled near and far to see animals in the wild, but she's starting to get the impression they're not so happy to see her. When she's not daydreaming about Africa, Kelly writes travel stories for newspapers in the US. She lives in Atlanta.

When I woke up it was cold and black inside the tent. It felt like I'd been asleep for hours. The sweet, charred smell of citronella incense hung in the crisp air. At first, I didn't know whether I had heard a noise or caught the tail end of a dream. I lay still, holding my breath and listening for anything.

Before long, the sharp crack of breaking wood punctured the silence. Only this time, it didn't stop. Limbs snapped repeatedly, as if something was walking over the fallen branches outside. I had every reason to believe that something was a lion.

Yesterday after arriving in Botswana, my husband, West, and I had flown into the Okavango Delta, where southern Africa's

Okavango River empties into the flat sands of the Kalahari Desert. Supplying much-needed nourishment, the Delta draws Africa's magnificent wildlife into this untamed and unfenced region. We were visiting during the dry season, when the streams that spill out from the river would be dried up, and those animals would stay close to the few remaining waterholes.

When our plane touched down on the parched, dirt airstrip, a game ranger named Phinley greeted us and took us by Land Rover to our safari camp. As we approached it, I noticed charred wood lying all around. Phinley explained that last year lightning had struck a tree and started a fire. In the blaze, the entire camp had burned to the ground.

The rebuilt Chitabe Trails was now a fairly primitive place with just five tents sitting directly on the uneven earth. Phinley showed us to the common area, a couple of wooden decks and another tent with the sides rolled up, where Kenny, the camp manager, waited for us.

Kenny explained that for now West and I were the only guests. As we sat on wooden stools under the canvas roof, he went over our schedule for the next few days. While Kenny was talking, Phinley walked out onto a platform ahead of us. Peering across a sea of golden grass, he turned back and waved an arm wildly. 'Lions', he called in a tempered shout.

We rushed along the deck to where Phinley stood. About fifty metres away, three female lions were walking on the other side of a small waterhole. A cub wandered along behind them, barely visible in the knee-high grass.

After two weeks in Africa, West and I had seen lions regularly, but we had always been sitting in a Land Rover, a game ranger ready at the wheel to drive away in the event of a problem. Standing in the warm sun, I looked around for a place to retreat to, and that's when I realised – here, canvas tents were our only option.

'Wow, they're right there', I said, feeling more than a little exposed. 'But it's safe to be out here on the deck, right?'

'Sure', Phinley replied.

As we watched, the lions plopped down for a nap. I kept one eye trained in their direction as Kenny walked with us down the sand path to our tent. A quiet man with a habit of whistling under his breath, Kenny explained that, since we were spending our anniversary in the camp, the staff had given us the tent with the best view. Admittedly, I should have been grateful, but I had noticed that it was also the tent closest to the waterhole. I told him it wasn't a special anniversary, so there really was no need to give us such a tent, but Kenny insisted.

Our army-green home for the next few days sat to the left of the common area and away from the other tents. A large sausage tree shaded one corner of it. Beneath the tree, the grey mud of a termite mound rose two metres into the air.

Once inside the tent, Kenny turned to us and said, 'The animals really like this camp. It's probably because we don't have the raised walkways that other camps have, so it's easier for them to walk around. They come into camp all the time.' Then he picked up a red metal canister that sat on a rattan shelf between the bed and the toilet. Kenny explained that if we had an emergency in the middle of the night, we should sound the air horn, adding, 'An emergency is not a lion rubbing up against your tent. An emergency is a lion trying to get into your tent.'

That night, as I lay in the dark listening to the snapping of branches outside, it occurred to me that I should have asked Kenny what a lion trying to get into a tent would sound like. And what did he mean by 'trying'? What would it take for the king of beasts to get through canvas? Wouldn't one swipe of a clawed paw be enough?

'Do you think it's a lion?' I whispered.

'Probably', West replied.

With that, I tried to remember what our time in Africa had taught me about lions, and this is what I came up with. Lions hunt at night. They need only one-seventh the light that humans need to see. If you come across a lion on foot, stop and don't move. Like all cats, they will chase you if you move. There wasn't one encouraging fact among them.

And then, having awakened in the middle of the night, I realised that I had to go to the toilet. I looked towards the flaps on the front of the tent. They were nothing more than mesh screens. In the silver moonlight, I could see the faint shadows of tree limbs outside blowing in the breeze. I knew that whatever was out there could surely see us inside the tent.

'West', I whispered, 'I have to pee.'

'Then go', he said.

'I'm not getting out of this bed. What if it sees me moving?'

'Can you wait?' he asked.

'Maybe.'

As we whispered, the cracking of wood outside grew louder and louder, until finally it sounded as if the animal was right behind our bed. West and I were silent, and then suddenly there was a dry *whoosh* as the animal brushed against the canvas. I began to shake uncontrollably.

'Are you cold?' West whispered.

'Terrified', I squeaked.

I reached through the tangled mosquito net and slowly moved my hand through the dark until I felt the cold metal of the air horn. I grabbed it, pulled it through the netting and hugged it to my chest.

'What are you doing?' West asked.

'I want to blow the horn', I whispered.

'Don't you dare.'

'It rubbed against the tent', I pleaded.

'What do you think it's going to do if you blow that horn? Put it down.'

'No.'

While we bickered, we began to hear crunching. It sounded as if the animal outside was eating.

'Great. There's no way I'm going to the toilet now.'

'It's probably fine', West insisted.

'Probably?' I asked. 'Will you go with me?'

'No, it's right there', he argued. 'Just go.'

'I'm not getting out of this bed', I said.

'Well, you're certainly not going in the bed.'

I tried to summon the courage to get up, but each time I imagined I could see a lion lying in the pale moonlight, gnawing on a bloody bone. If it saw my shadowy figure moving inside the tent, it would surely burst through the canvas. My pyjama pants would dangle around my ankles as it dragged me off the toilet and my husband finally decided it was time to sound the horn.

As I imagined all the painful ways a lion could kill us, the animal began to make a deep, guttural noise that sounded vaguely like a purr. Or maybe it was a growl, I couldn't be certain. All I knew was at that moment the only thing that separated West and me from a 225-kilo, man-eating cat was a sheet of canvas. I began to pray. I knew we'd tempted fate on this trip: first a cage dive with great white sharks, then a microlight flight over Victoria Falls and now a remote camp in the Okavango Delta with a hungry animal outside. I vowed to reform my daredevil ways, if only we were spared from the jaws of a lion.

I don't know how long the purring lasted, but it felt like hours. All the while, West and I lay still, listening for the sound of ripping canvas, and I prayed that the pain that was spreading into my ribcage wouldn't cause my bladder to burst. When the guttural noise finally stopped, it wasn't long before we again heard the rhythmic snapping of branches.

'It's leaving', West whispered.

I waited until I could no longer hear a sound before racing to the toilet. When I returned to bed, there was, of course, no point in trying to sleep. I knew the company that owned this camp had thirteen other camps in the Delta, and I resolved that first thing in the morning I would beg Kenny to move us to a place with raised walkways. For good measure, I rehearsed my request until it had just the right mix of reason and unabashed hysteria.

I was still practising my plea when the blue light of dawn crawled across the Delta and a member of the camp staff came to wake us for breakfast. As West and I sat in the cool morning air having coffee and muffins with the staff, West explained our rough night. At first, Kenny looked amused. But when he heard that I was ready to sound the horn, the look on his face changed to something resembling dread.

From the far end of the wooden table, Moss, one of the guides, had been listening to the conversation. 'Did it sound like this?' she asked, making a rasping sound in the back of her throat.

'That was it. Was it a lion?' West asked.

'You heard an elephant', Moss laughed.

'An elephant?' I said.

'Yeah. They like to sleep propped up against the termite mounds. I used to have one outside my tent every night. It would snore something terrible.'

Maybe I should have been relieved to learn that West and I had not spent the night about to be devoured by a lion. But I was too busy imagining what a sleeping elephant might do if it were suddenly awakened by an air horn.

SOMETHING APPROACHING ENLIGHTENMENT

ROLF POTTS

Rolf Potts is the author of *Vagabonding: An Uncommon Guide to the Art of Long-Term World Travel*. His travel writing has appeared in *Condé Nast Traveler*, *National Geographic Adventure*, Salon.com, *The Best American Travel Writing 2000* and numerous Lonely Planet anthologies. Though he keeps no permanent address, he tends to linger in Thailand, Argentina, rural Kansas and France, where he is the summertime writer-in-residence at the Paris American Academy. His online home is www.rolfpotts.com.

For weeks after returning from my ill-fated journey to the Indian Himalayan village of Kaza, I had difficulty explaining to people why I'd wanted to go there in the first place. Sometimes I'd claim it had something to do with the Dalai Lama – though someone would always point out, correctly, that the Dalai Lama lived in the Tibetan exile capital at Dharamsala, not in some obscure mountain outpost several days in the other direction.

I had no easy answer to this seeming discrepancy. Granted, the Dalai Lama was reputed to travel to Kaza once each summer – but I'd gone there in the winter. And while rumour had it that the Dalai Lama planned to spend his twilight years in a monastery just up the valley from Kaza, the famous Tibetan holy man was nowhere near retirement at the time of my visit. In the end, I suppose my decision to gain an understanding of the Dalai Lama by going where he didn't live was grounded in a vague fear of disappointment – a fear that (as with other religious destinations I'd visited in India, such as Varanasi and Rishikesh) Dharamsala had become so popular with other Western travellers that any spiritual epiphanies I found there would feel forced and generic.

By contrast, the Indo-Tibetan village of Kaza was the most remote Himalayan destination I could reach by road in late winter. There, in the cobbled alleyways of an ancient and windswept Buddhist village, I imagined I might find a more authentic vision of what the Dalai Lama represented. Far from the well-worn lanes of Dharamsala, I hoped I might better be able to discover something approaching enlightenment.

Thus, from the northern Indian hub city of Shimla, I'd walked to the far end of the bus terminal – past the backpack-toting crowds of Westerners headed to Dharamsala – and boarded the first in a series of buses that would take me to my far-flung Himalayan Shangri-La.

While still within the fog of my initial inspiration, it was fairly easy to rationalise a three-day bus ride through the remote Himalayas. Once I was actually en route to Kaza, however, I immediately realised that my whimsical pilgrimage could very well get me killed. The copy of the *Hindustan Times* that I'd bought in Shimla, for instance, devoted an entire front-page story to grisly mountain bus crashes. 'At least forty people were killed when a bus plunged into a tributary of the Ravi River yesterday evening', the article read. 'Earlier in the day, eight people died and thirteen were injured when a truck carrying them fell into a gorge thirty-five kilometres from Manali.'

The Indian highway signs were not much more encouraging. In lieu of shoulders or guardrails, dangerous curves on the mountain featured boulders with white-painted slogans that read 'O God help us!' or 'Be safe: use your horn'. I kept staring out at the river valley 300 metres below and imagining our driver cheerily honking the horn as we all plummeted to certain death.

The most alarming part of the Himalayan bus ride, however, was the road itself, which seemed to be buried under massive mudslides at eighty-kilometre intervals. Indeed, every couple of hours, our bus driver would screech to a halt and I'd peer out the window to see what had formerly been the road lying in a crumpled crust twenty metres down the mountain. Invariably, several dozen Indian highway workers would be making a frenzied effort to carve a makeshift dirt track into the flank of the mud wall in front of us. My fellow passengers would disembark and smoke cigarettes at the edge of the cliff, watching disinterestedly until the labourers gave a shout and our bus driver would rumble across the improvised mud road. Along with the other passengers, I'd then follow on foot at a safe distance, climbing back into the bus once the normal highway resumed. My main solace amidst all this was the promise of Kaza and the serene Buddhist environs that hopefully awaited me there.

After two days of nonstop travel, I'd made it deep into the Tibetan border region before the transmission dropped out of the bottom of my bus near a town called Pooh. Folks in Pooh informed me that there were no more onward buses that day, but I might be able to find transportation out of Kob, ten kilometres further up the road. Feeling optimistic in the early-afternoon sunshine, I set off for Kob on foot.

In retrospect, the early hours of my hike to Kob were the happiest of my entire Himalayan sojourn. Outside of Pooh, the altitude snaked up to above 3500 metres, and the hand-planted cherry trees along the roadside had just begun to sprout pink blossoms. Before long, though, I was trudging into a massive canyon of grey rock and the highway was reduced to a narrow slot dynamited out of the side of the cliff. The Spiti River was barely visible below, but I knew it was the same river that roared down from Kaza – a place where I envisioned cool air, welcoming locals and the soft tinkling of monastery bells.

Unfortunately, the transit town of Kob never materialised, even after four hours of hiking. I trudged an additional hour in the dark before I spied an abandoned blockhouse at the side of the road. Figuring it was as good a place as any to bivouac, I pulled on several layers of warm clothing, curled up on the dirt floor, and – exhausted – fell asleep. When I woke up, my watch told me it was just past seven o'clock. Encouraged to have had a full night's sleep, I walked outside to catch the sunrise.

I must have stared at the darkened eastern horizon for half an hour before I re-checked my watch and noticed the small 'PM' over the time-code.

Nervous about the gathering mountain cold, I began a search for firewood – but all I could find was the old wooden block-house door, which had long since fallen off its hinges. When repeated attempts to smash the door with rocks resulted in nary a dent, I tried tossing it into the air and breaking it over the large roadside boulders.

I had been tossing the door onto the boulders without success for about fifteen minutes before I realised I was being watched by half a dozen bewildered-looking Indian soldiers. Not knowing what else to do, I put my hands above my head. One of the soldiers grabbed my backpack and the others marched me half a mile up the road to their transport truck, where I met a no-nonsense lieutenant who (apart from the beard, turban and Punjabi accent) looked somewhat like the movie star Vin Diesel.

'My soldiers tell me you were taking photographs', he said. 'Is this true?'

'No', I told him. 'I was trying to smash up a door.'

Lieutenant Diesel shot me a suspicious look. 'This is a dangerous border, and it's not for tourists. Why did you bring a door?'

After a witheringly absurd ten-minute interrogation about my motives for trying to destroy a door in total darkness along the Indian–Chinese border, Lieutenant Diesel consented to drive me back to his army base near Pooh. There, I was allowed to sleep on a bench in a small administrative office. 'If anybody asks,' the lieutenant told me gravely, 'tell them you were taking photographs.'

——————— ———————————

The following day, I hitched a ride on a troop transport to the village of Yangthang, where I was finally able to catch a bus that took me over a final stretch of highway switchbacks and road washouts to my mountain-top destination. As I stumbled out of the bus at the Kaza depot, I marvelled at the stark simplicity of the town, which consisted of whitewashed houses and small storefronts spread along a scree-strewn basin. Two monasteries were perched on the surrounding hillsides, and I noticed with delight that the stones along the walkway had been carved with Buddhist prayers. The place looked like a picture postcard of Tibetan authenticity.

When I walked into the centre of town, however, I was disappointed to find that – save for wandering packs of stray dogs – Kaza was largely deserted. All the guesthouses were shuttered for the winter, and the few ethnic Tibetan residents I passed on the street couldn't understand my English queries. The only person who took an interest in me was a chubby, balding man at the government-housing complex, who introduced himself as Mr Singh.

'Come and drink with us!' he hollered happily. 'Today we celebrate the Holi festival. It is very important to Hindus.' I politely declined Mr Singh's offer, explaining that I had come to Kaza to experience Buddhist culture.

Since the local monasteries were as empty and gated as the hotels, however, I was quickly running out of options. Stopping to check my guidebook, I noticed that Ki Gompa, a historically isolated thousand-year-old monastery, was just fourteen kilometres from Kaza via a mountain trail. With the realisation that all my travails up to that point might really just be hints of fate leading me to the halls of Ki Gompa, I shouldered my pack and headed to the footpath on the edge of town.

As I walked, I felt a slight twinge of pity for all the travellers who made their way to Dharamsala seeking the Dalai Lama, only to wind up in guesthouses and Internet cafés full of travellers from Berkeley and Birmingham and Tel Aviv. By contrast, I reckoned my final push to Ki Gompa would transcend such tourist banality and lead me into the true heart of Tibetan spirituality.

Fewer than 200 metres up the mountain – and with these happy delusions still floating in my head – a giant mastiff charged out from behind a rock, bared his teeth and tore off my right trouser leg at the knee. Spooked, I ran all the way back down into Kaza, blood oozing into my socks. Since I didn't know of any other options, I jogged over to the government-housing complex.

'You have come back to celebrate Holi!' Mr Singh exclaimed upon seeing me.

'Actually, a dog bit me and I need some first aid.' I pointed at my bleeding wound.

With the formal air of a person who is doing his best to feign sobriety, Mr Singh shook my hand in sympathy and led me to a small cinderblock hospital just up the road. One tetanus shot and one roll of gauze later, I was back in the housing complex, being introduced to Mr Singh's colleagues – Mr Gupta, who was as bald and chubby as Mr Singh, and Mr Kumar, a thin middle-aged man with hunched shoulders and owlish eye-glasses. Mr Singh merrily explained that they were all road engineers from the Delhi area, and that they hated living in Kaza. 'This is an ugly place', he said, 'and it is filled with country people who have no culture or sophistication.'

Mr Gupta proposed they give me a Holi blessing, so I followed them into Mr Kumar's room, which, with its stovepipe oven, peeling wallpaper and magazine photos of Bollywood starlets, looked like a cross between a college dorm and a miner's cabin. Three bottles of Director's Special whisky sat empty on the top of a dresser. Mr Gupta produced a jar of chalky red pigment and smeared a *tikka* mark on my forehead, while Mr Singh opened a fresh bottle of Director's Special and poured me a glass.

'So why do Hindus celebrate Holi?' I asked.

'It comes from a story in our ancient book, the *Mahabharata*', Mr Singh slurred. 'Exactly one million years ago there was a goddess who tortured her brother to death. So now we celebrate.'

'It is a very enjoyable holiday', Mr Gupta added.

'What do you do when you celebrate Holi?'

'Sometimes we throw buckets of coloured water at our friends or at strangers. But today, since you are our guest, we will watch movies of the colour blue.' Mr Singh shot me a conspiratorial look. 'Of course, you know which movies I mean.'

'I don't think so', I said. 'Are they movies about the *Mahabharata*?'

'No, these movies are much more interesting.' Mr Singh gestured to Mr Kumar, who popped a videotape into the VCR. Throbbing synthesizer music crackled out of the TV speaker, and a fuzzy image shuddered onto the screen. The movie had such poor picture quality that I could barely tell what was going on – though it appeared to be the writhing of two or more naked bodies. Presently, the synthesizer music was offset by slurping, slapping and moaning noises. 'Oh yeah', a voice from the TV said. 'Ride me harder!'

I shot Mr Singh a quizzical look, and he giggled boyishly. 'Mr Kumar wants to know why that man has such a long penis', he said.

'Long and fat', Mr Gupta said.

I looked back at the TV, but still couldn't make out a clear image. Apparently, these men had rewound and fast-forwarded the movie so many times that it had deteriorated into jumbled images of static and fuzz. Only the soundtrack remained.

Assuming it was a fairly standard porno movie, I considered my answer. 'I guess it's part of the job qualification', I said. 'Men in blue movies need to have big penises, just like men who build roads need to have engineering degrees.'

Mr Singh translated this for Mr Kumar; the men nodded seriously.

'What about this', Mr Singh said, gesturing at the screen. 'Is this normal for married men in America?'

I squinted at the TV, but couldn't make out what was going on. 'Is what normal?'

'To have two women licking one man's penis', Mr Gupta said.

'Only one of them is his wife', Mr Singh clarified, 'and the other woman brought them a pizza on her motorcycle.'

'Oh my God!' the TV crackled. 'Don't stop.'

'Listen,' I said, 'these kinds of movies are just fantasies. You can't assume they represent anything about normal American life. I mean, what if everyone thought life in India was exactly like a Bollywood musical?'

'But Bollywood movies are very accurate!' Mr Singh exclaimed. 'They show many good things about India.'

'But they don't represent normal Indian life', I said. 'I mean, do you and Mr Gupta and Mr Kumar break into song and dance every day at work?'

'I like to sing and dance', Mr Gupta offered.

'That's right', the TV interjected. 'Give it to me, you big stud!'

Before the conversation could deteriorate any further, there was a knock on the door and a teenage boy walked in to serve us bowls of dhal. 'This is Vikram', Mr Gupta said. 'He is a student of English.'

'He will look at this movie, and then he will want to run off for hand practice', Mr Singh giggled, making a wanking motion.

Vikram gave me a sympathetic look as he handed me the dhal. 'These guys are hammered', he whispered. 'Just let me know if they start to bother you.'

Ten minutes later, I caught up with Vikram in the housing-compound kitchen. 'Look,' I told him, 'I travelled for three days on some of the worst roads I've seen in my life just to get to Kaza. I have nothing against Holi or Hindus, but I was hoping to meet some Tibetans here. Do you know of any way I can stay at one of the Buddhist monasteries?'

'You've come here at the end of winter', he said, 'and only a handful of trucks and buses have made it through since November. The monasteries are running low on food, and the guesthouses won't want to turn on their generators for just one person. You should stay the night in Mr Kumar's room. It's pretty comfortable.'

'But isn't there any way to meet some Buddhists while I'm in Kaza?'

Vikram shrugged. 'Maybe, but people stay indoors during this time. And they don't know much English. You'd probably get bored if you don't speak any Tibetan. You should come back in June or July. That's the best time for tourists.'

For some reason, the word 'tourists' triggered an instant and vivid fantasy. I imagined myself off in the streets of Dharamsala – eating muesli, flirting with Norwegian back-packer girls, sending emails to friends back in the States and swapping Dalai Lama-sighting stories with star-struck Canadians. Suddenly, this scenario didn't seem so bad at all.

Resigned to my fate, however, I returned to Mr Kumar's room. There, as we fast-forwarded through several more scenes from the movie (which appeared to be about a team of unusually libidinous pizza delivery women), I served as an informal ambassador of American marginalia.

'Yes,' I told them, 'I'm pretty sure Viagra works. No, I haven't tried it. Yes, I'm aware that Bill Clinton and Monica Lewinsky had sexual relations. No, I don't think they still keep in touch. Actually, I don't think they were ever in love to begin with. Yes, there are many famous black Americans named Michael. Yes, I know all about Michael Jackson's career. No, I don't think that would make Michael Jordan want to get plastic surgery.'

Eventually Mr Singh and Mr Gupta staggered off to bed, and I fell asleep on Mr Kumar's floor, next to the woodstove. A little after midnight, I awakened to see the stoop-shouldered Indian sitting on the edge of his bed, intently watching the snowy image of a naked man and woman engaged in a sexual act that was technically outlawed in numerous states and countries.

Seeing that I was awake, Mr Kumar grinned over at me and, with a knowing wobble of his head, said, 'Back-door entry!'

This was the only English I ever heard him speak.

———— — ————

Sometime before sunrise, Vikram came into the room and shook me awake. 'I know of a fuel truck that is leaving in ten minutes. It can take you as far as Pooh, and you can catch a normal bus from there.' He paused for a moment. 'Or, if you want to stay in Kaza longer, the regular bus leaves next week.'

Two minutes later, I was fully packed and sprinting for the fuel truck.

The ensuing three days were not too eventful. Though the muddy Himalayan highway was just as precarious as it had been on my inbound journey, I didn't let it get to me; I merely looked forward to getting back to the well-worn grooves of the tourist trail. As a new series of buses rattled me back down towards Shimla, I stared out at the steep mountain canyons with Zen-like patience.

I had indeed, it seemed, achieved something approaching enlightenment.

A SPECIAL KIND OF FOOL

BILL FINK

Bill Fink is a freelance writer based in San Francisco. He is a regular contributor to the *San Francisco Chronicle* and a variety of regional and international publications. More of his true tales of stupidity can be seen at www.geocities .com/billfink2004. He is currently working on a book about his year of basketball-themed misadventures in the Philippines entitled *Dunked in Manila*.

According to a Japanese saying, there are two kinds of fools: those who have never climbed Mt Fuji, and those who have climbed it more than once.

I didn't want to be either kind of fool, so I decided to climb the mountain once, and to do it right.

As a college exchange student in Japan, I had been studying the language for six months. So I was able to translate – a little – when I saw a Japanese TV segment showing jolly people climbing gentle, well-marked paths up the mountain: '*Something-something-something* Mt Fuji *something-something* walking *something-something* this spring.'

March seemed early in the year to climb a 4000-metre snow-capped mountain, but the televised hikers were wearing T-shirts and shorts, so I assumed it was unseasonably warm. My guide-book said that reaching Fuji's summit at sunrise was the perfect way to conclude the hike, so I decided to start climbing at night, battery-operated torch in hand. Ben, a fellow exchange student, volunteered to join my quest.

I figured we could hitchhike the 480 kilometres from where we lived in Kobe to the base of the mountain by midnight. We'd climb to the top by sunrise, be down by early afternoon, and catch up with our sleep on the car rides home. Ben recommended we start early, and bring sleeping bags, just in case.

Our friends called us foolish – but what did they know, they were foreigners. Our home-stay families didn't have anything to say, because we each told them, American student-style, that we'd be spending the weekend at the other family's house.

Ben scrounged supplies: a bright yellow raincoat for me, a nylon karate jacket and a safari hat for himself. He also borrowed a couple of ragged sleeping bags from his host family, and brought along a box of large plastic bin liners.

'We'll use these to tie around our feet as gaiters, just in case we have to ford a river or walk through some snow on the summit', he explained.

The next morning we took local trains to the edge of Kobe, where we strolled to the nearest highway entrance ramp. Ben had been growing his hair during the exchange programme, with the logic that if everyone's going to stare at you for being a foreigner, you might as well give them their money's worth. With a monstrous afro and a maniacal goatee, he looked like a member of Grand Funk Railroad on a bad hair day. I stood next to him in my bright-yellow raincoat and blue Chicago Cubs hat. We waved at cars like two lost members of a travelling circus.

'Any idea how hitchhiking works here?' I asked Ben.

'Relax. You know that Japanese hippie guy who's always playing guitar outside the library? I asked him about hitching, and he made us a sign.' Ben pulled out a piece of cardboard covered in Japanese writing.

'What does it say, "Fuji or bust"?'

'No, actually he wrote out some folk music lyrics for us:

"Wherever the wind blows, so too will my feelings take me." '

'That's touching', I said. 'Is it going to get us to Fuji?'

'Sure. I think it's some kind of subliminal Japanese message.'

'You must be kidding.'

'I am. Here's the real Fuji sign. But we should still wave this one as a back-up, to show the people our spirit is in the right place. We'll get a ride in no time.'

Only minutes later a car passed us, then reversed to stop in front of us. We grabbed our packs, happy at getting such a quick ride. Instead, the passenger window rolled down, a camera flashed at us, and the car drove away. We decided to ditch the folk lyrics.

A sequence of truck rides eventually took us to Gotemba, the town nearest to Mt Fuji. It was about 10pm, so we were still on schedule for our sunrise hike. We looked for the famous mountain silhouette and saw – nothing.

'Hey, Bill, we're supposed to be eight kilometres away from the biggest mountain in Japan. Shouldn't we be able to see it from here?'

'I'm sure it's just blending into the clouds or something. Maybe we'll see it once we walk past the foothills.'

We put on our jackets for the walk to town, where we stopped in a noodle shop for a late-night meal and a warm-up. We were the only patrons. Once we finished our steaming-hot bowls of thick udon noodles, the manager approached us.

'Hello. Where you come from?'

'America.'

'Thank you for come to visit Gotemba. You make camping?' He motioned at the sleeping bags hanging off our small day-packs.

'We have come to climb Fuji-san!' I announced. (The Japanese respectfully refer to Mt Fuji as 'Mr Fuji'.)

'*Fssssssss...*' The manager made a special Japanese noise that is done by sucking air through clenched teeth. This usually means the speaker has some worrying news for you, but is too polite to tell you directly.

'Fuji-san a little cold, these days.'

'Oh, not so cold', Ben replied. 'I come from Colorado, in America. Many mountains there taller than Fuji-san, and colder. Cold is no problem; we are *tsuyoi*, tough!' Ben pounded his chest, Tarzan-style.

'*Ahhh so*, so...' The manager didn't look convinced. 'When you climb Fuji-san?'

'*Ima*, right now, tonight', I said. 'We're doing the midnight climb, you know, sunrise at the summit? Sunrise: *asa-no-hi*', I added, checking my phrasebook.

He squinted his eyes and turned his head to the side, like a dog that had heard a strange noise. Then he asked, 'How you go Fuji-san?'

Ben pointed to his sneakers, '*Arukimasu yo!* We're walking, man.'

'*Haaaaaaa...*' he said. This is another untranslatable Japanese worry-sound. If you hear both '*Haaaaaaa*' and '*Fsssssss*' in the same conversation, it pretty much means you're screwed.

'Fuji-san...a little far...'

We waved away the manager's worries. We figured he was just a small-town yokel who'd spent his life in a noodle shop, the kind of fool who never once made it up the mountain. We wouldn't be so meek.

Ben and I marched out of the shop in fine spirits. Thirty minutes later, we wandered alone past empty rice fields.

'You're sure this is the right direction?' Ben scanned the gloom for some sign of Mr Fuji.

I squinted at a map in the weak glow of my torch. 'I think I see the dot of Gotemba, and Fuji is this "X" here...'

'Hey, here comes a car. Maybe we can flag it down for directions.' Ben waved at an oncoming sedan.

Surprisingly, given the time and our appearance, the car rolled to a halt. The passenger window lowered to reveal a familiar face.

'Please. Come. I give ride. Okay?' The noodle shop manager, still with a pained expression, beckoned us to hop inside.

The car turned around. At first we thought he was returning us to town. Instead, after twenty minutes of driving, we saw a dark shape looming up ahead. It was easy to tell the mountain from the clouds, because the clouds were the things dumping snow everywhere. The manager remained silent, perhaps torn between his duty to help visitors and his guilt that he was leading them to almost certain doom.

'Yeah, that does look...a little cold.' Ben reached for his safari hat.

After our posturing in the restaurant, we couldn't back down from the challenge. We must be turning a bit Japanese, as we didn't want to lose face with the manager. So once the car stopped at a Fuji trailhead, we gamely hopped out and sank into ankle-deep fresh powder. We grabbed our woefully empty packs and thanked the manager.

'Yes, yes...' He almost bowed his head in apology, and handed us a small paper bag. 'Please...' and then, with a fatalistic nod, '*ganbatte.*' ('Fight to the finish.') The car turned to leave, and its headlights gradually disappeared behind a curtain of falling snow.

It was past midnight. We were thirty-five kilometres from the nearest town. We were wearing jeans and sneakers in a mountain blizzard. But we had...

'Rice balls!' Ben shouted with excitement, as he looked into the paper bag. 'That manager is great. Not only did he find the mountain for us, but he gave us breakfast!' He tossed the gift into his pack. 'Okay, now it's time to put those bin liners to good use.'

Balancing precariously in the snow we double-bagged our feet and scanned for the trail ahead with our weak torches, but saw only untracked snowfields leading into darkness.

'I guess it shouldn't be too hard', I said. 'We just go uphill.'

We headed off, walking between rows of pine trees on what we guessed was a path. The snow deepened. So did our worry.

'Did you hear something, Bill?'

'Sounded like a tree branch snapping.'

'Do they have bears here? They should be hibernating anyway, right?'

'No worries, I read up on this.' My studies were finally coming in handy. I quoted from memory: 'The last bears around Mt Fuji were captured in the Edo period of the early 1800s. They were used in bear-baiting entertainment in Tokyo courts.'

'Thanks. Any chance you read something about hiking paths?'

A few minutes later I sank waist-deep into a snow-covered ditch. I signalled defeat. 'There's no way we're going to get to the top. We can't see three metres in front of us. We could walk right off a cliff.'

Ben agreed, and we staggered towards the trees to find shelter from the wind. There we spotted a dark shape. It was the size of, oh, two bears, side by side. A shot of adrenaline warmed my body.

'You see that? What the hell?' I shouted.

'Awesome!'

'Huh?'

'We have shelter!' Ben led our charge towards a small storage cabin made of plywood and anchored by ropes against the high winds. A broken window revealed its empty interior.

The cabin had no floor, so we set our sleeping bags directly onto the volcanic flank of Fuji. Snow blew steadily through the window to cover us as we shivered through the night. My teeth chattered in time with the wind-blown rope banging against the cabin, while sharp rocks jabbed me in the back.

At daybreak, we stood up, still inside our sleeping bags, and looked out the door. The sun reflected off a bright white snow-field, a plateau of drifts separating us from the steep upper slopes of Mt Fuji. We were maybe one quarter of the way to the top.

We munched on our rice balls and watched the wind whip snow across the peak far above. We looked at our bag-covered shoes, our sleeping bags torn by the volcanic rocks, and our frozen jeans.

Then we looked at each other and came to a decision. *Any* fool can climb Mt Fuji, and *any* fool can ignore it. But it takes a special kind of fool to climb a quarter of the way up, sit in the snow for the night, and then turn around. So that's exactly what we did.

IGNORING THE ADMIRAL

JAN MORRIS

Jan Morris, who is Anglo-Welsh and lives in Wales, wrote some forty books before declaring that *Trieste and the Meaning of Nowhere* (2001) would be her last. Since then *The World* (2003), a retrospective collection of her work, has been published and she is now working on a long addendum to her allegorical novel *Last Letters from Hav* (1985), provisionally entitled *Hav of the Myrmidons*.

D evoted as I am to the ethos of Lonely Planet, I was never a backpacker. 'The British Navy always travels first class', Admiral of the Fleet Lord 'Jacky' Fisher used to say as he checked into yet another fashionable spa, and I was similarly conditioned during my adolescent years as an officer with the 9th Queen's Royal Lancers of the British Army. At the end of World War II, when we were not getting messy in our dirty old tanks, we were making sure that we ate at the best restaurants and stayed at the poshest hotels.

Nowhere did we honour Lord Fisher's axiom more loyally than in Venice, where we happily made the most of our status as members of a victorious occupying army. Many of the best hotels became our officers' clubs, while the most expensive restaurants were pleased to accept our vastly inflated currency (which we had very likely acquired by selling cigarettes on the black market). And in particular, since all the city's motorboats had been requisitioned by the military, we rode up and down the Grand Canal, under the Rialto Bridge, over to the Lido, like so many lucky young princes.

That was half a century ago, and I have been back to Venice at least a hundred times since. I have never forgotten Fisher's dictum (although he died, I must tell you, five years before I was born), and until last year I had never once in my life so far neglected it as to take a *vaporetto*, a public water-bus, from the railway station into the centre of the city. There no longer being commandeered motorboats available, I had invariably summoned one of the comfortably insulated and impeccably varnished water-taxis which, for a notoriously extravagant fee, would whisk me without hassle to the quayside of my hotel.

My partner, Elizabeth, had not been subjected to the same influences of adolescence. She spent her wartime years as a rating in the women's naval service, decoding signals in an underground war room, subsisting on baked beans and vile sweet tea from the canteen. But she had been to Venice with me dozens of times, and I thought that by now I had initiated her into my own Fisherian style of travel. However, last time we were there she proved unexpectedly recidivist. 'Oh, Jan', she said as I hastened her towards the line of waiting taxis, ignoring the throbbing *vaporetto* at its pier. 'Why must you always be so extravagant? What's wrong with the *vaporetto*? Everyone else goes on it. It's a fraction of the price. What's the hurry anyway? What are you proving? We're not made of money, you know. What's the point?'

'The British Navy always –' I began, but she interrupted me with an aphorism of her own. 'Waste not, want not', she primly retorted. Ah well, said I to myself, and to Lord Fisher too, anything for a quiet life. Humping our bags in the gathering dusk, tripping over ourselves, fumbling for the right change, dropping things all over the place, with our tickets between our teeth, we stumbled up the gangplank onto the already jam-packed deck.

There we stood for what felt like three or four days, edging into eternity, while the vessel pounded its way through the darkness up the Grand Canal, stopping at every available jetty with deafening engine-reversals, throwing us about with judderings, clangings and bumps, while we stood cheek-by-jowl with ten thousand others on the cold and windy poop. When at last we debouched on the quayside below San Marco, looking as though we were stepping onto Omaha Beach, Elizabeth turned to me with an air of satisfaction. 'There you are, you see. That wasn't so bad, was it? Think of the money we saved! After all these years, I bet you'll never take one of those exorbitant taxis again. A penny saved is a penny gained.'

But she spoke this meaningless maxim too late. Pride, I nearly told her, comes before a fall. Standing there upon the quayside slung about with bags and surrounded by suitcases, I had already discovered that during our ride on the *vaporetto* somebody had stolen the wallet that contained all our worldly wealth, not to mention all our credit cards. Off we trudged to the police station to report the loss, and as we sat in the dim light among a melancholy little assembly of unfortunates and ne'er-do-wells, how I regretted ignoring the Admiral! I bet Elizabeth did too, although she was too proud to admit it.

I didn't actually say 'Penny wise, pound foolish'. I didn't even murmur under my breath the bit about travelling first class. Never hit a woman when she's down, I told myself. Virtue is its own reward – and as it happened, it was rewarded. We never got that wallet back, but the *carabinieri* were terribly solicitous, and said how sorry they were, and assured us that no Venetian could have done such a thing – it must have been one of those Albanians – and sent us off feeling perfectly comforted and a little bit sorry for *them*, actually, so palpable was their sense of civic shame.

Half an hour later, feeling emotionally and physically drained, we turned up on the doorstep of Harry's Bar, a hostelry I have frequented ever since those glory days of victory, when I was young and easy, as the poet said, and Time let me hail and climb. With Jack Fisher beside us – he would have loved Harry's Bar – we pushed our way through the revolving door and told our sad story to the people inside.

And lo! They gave us a free dinner (scampi and white wine, with a zabaglione afterwards) just to cheer us up. For once our truisms did not conflict. Every cloud, we agreed, as the three of us sat there in the warmth of our first-class corner, really does have a silver lining.

DUTCH TOILET

DOUG LANSKY

Doug Lansky has spent ten years travelling in over one hundred countries. He is the author of *Last Trout in Venice* and *Up the Amazon Without a Paddle*, and penned a nationally syndicated travel-humour column in North America for five years. He currently contributes to *National Geographic Adventure* and *Esquire*, and makes his home in Stockholm, Sweden, where he has not been trapped in any toilet stalls.

The most reliable, though least utilised, traveller's oasis in any city is the library. In a foreign land, you may not be able to read the books or even get a library card, but it usually has three crucial ingredients: free high-speed Internet access, free international newspapers and free toilets. On an April morning in the town of Maastricht, Holland, I went in search of this traveller's trinity.

There was nothing remarkable about the public library I found; no soul-moving architecture or rare-archive collection that would attract the attention of guidebook writers. It was on the small side, with a low ceiling, and like any sanctuary of literature it was warmed with those hallowed hushed whispers that you could easily mistake for prayers.

When you've used up several passports travelling through more than a hundred countries, had a half-naked native in the

Colombian rainforest draw blood from your head with a machete in the middle of the night and been chased by an angry mob with rocks and torches after you've run a roadblock in the back of a pick-up truck in Ecuador, there's a tendency to let your guard down in safe environments such as this. It's a common problem: Robert Young Pelton, who has been called 'the world's most dangerous traveller', told me he has been robbed only once – while his rental car was parked in the Vatican.

There was no armed robber in this library, no scam artist – not even a gastro-questionable morsel of street food. No, I was foiled by a toilet stall. Three stalls, actually.

The doors were locked. I waited patiently for the occupants to leave, then knocked when the situation started to become dire. All were empty. I tried the doors more forcefully, then looked for alternative entries. There was nothing to crawl under or climb over. Each stall was its own tiny room.

I kicked myself when I finally noticed the small slots in the doors where the handles should have been. Europe is the continent of the toll toilet, after all. I measured up the hole with the coins in my pocket and started inserting them. When they got jammed, I simply tried the next door. I even tried a few German coins. Nothing.

Reluctantly, I waddled out to ask the security guard on duty.

There was a simple answer. 'There's no handle', the guard bellowed, as no fewer than fifty heads turned towards me. I wanted to yell out and assure them, 'I'm not just a dopey foreigner who couldn't find his way into the toilet' – but of course that's exactly what I was.

Where does one get a toilet handle in a public library? The guard pointed me towards the circulation desk. I slapped my forehead. 'The circulation desk. Of course!'

I walked over and noticed six or so handles lying on the counter. I reached over to grab one. 'Not so fast', the librarian seemed to be saying in Dutch. She spun her swivel chair in my direction and levelled me with steely pupils the size of sharpened No. 2 pencil points. I stopped cold. Now what? Would I need a library card to check one out?

There was a lecture, first in Dutch, then in English. Urgent or not, permission is required before obtaining a handle and under no circumstances should one ever reach over the circulation desk. In lieu of a card, I gave my word that the handle would be returned.

I headed back to the bathroom with renewed confidence, inserted the handle into one of the doors (one that wasn't jammed with German coins), opened it, and stepped inside. The door swung shut behind me.

The little room was pitch black. And it had just become my jail cell.

I reached over to open the door but it was locked. After feeling with my hands, I realised I needed the handle to open it. And I had left the handle in the door – on the outside.

I located something that felt like a light switch but it didn't do anything except make a clicking sound. I groped around a little more, but I didn't want to get too enthusiastic for fear of bumping into Palaeolithic wads of chewing gum and fossilised boogers.

I could feel the toilet with my shins, and thought it would be best to handle the most imminent threat first. After a few minutes, my eyes began to adjust to the darkness. There was a light on the wall, a minuscule 'black' micro-bulb that gave off less light than a digital watch. I thought it was a motion detector connected to the lights, so I waved my arms around for a while. When that didn't work, I banged on the door.

After fifteen minutes, I heard someone else enter the bathroom. 'Help', I said, in the most friendly and unalarmed voice I could muster. Apparently, it wasn't good enough. The person left. As did the person after that. If there had only been enough light, I could have simply opened my Dutch phrasebook and learned how to say, 'Excuse me, but there's a dumb-ass American locked in this toilet.'

After nearly an hour, I decided it was time to resort to banging and yelling. A few minutes later, I was rescued by a passing urinator.

'Thanks', I muttered, trying very hard to look natural while being rescued from a toilet stall in the men's room.

With the door open, I searched for a light. Nothing. I opened the other two stalls (keeping a firm grasp on the handle) and couldn't find any lights there, either. I even checked the main bathroom switches. *Nada*. Maybe, I thought, I needed to get a light switch from the circulation desk.

I consulted my favourite security guard on the way out. This only certified that I was the stupidest person he'd ever encountered in all his years of security work. He regarded me calmly, then said in a voice so condescending it would have been psychologically damaging to a three-year-old, 'The light is already on.' I assured him that it definitely was not.

Well, it turned out that the tiny black light was the light. It prevents drug users – 'Mostly Germans who come over the border', the guard confided – from shooting up in the stall because they can't find their veins.

'Of course, you can't find the toilet, either', I pointed out.

As I made my way to the exit, I considered pocketing the precious door part – it might come in handy in some future library emergency. But I couldn't break my solemn pact with the librarian, and anyway, I'd be demeaning the valuable traveller's lesson I'd just learned: I now knew how to handle Dutch toilets.

WALK OF FAME

JEFF VIZE

Jeff Vize has trampled over wet cement, flower beds and innocent bystanders in at least forty countries. He currently lives in Los Angeles with his wife, Charlotte, and son, Loïc. He is currently at work on a travel memoir, *Pigs in the Toilet (And Other Discoveries on the Road from Tokyo to Paris)*, from which this story is adapted.

I'm not a movie star, but I've played one abroad. Not that I know anything about acting, dialogue or even comic timing. I just know what it's like to be famous: I was a celebrity for five days in Bangladesh.

If you've ever been to Bangladesh, you know what I'm talking about. In fact, if you've ever been to any developing nation you've no doubt had the same experience, particularly if your skin colour is a few shades darker or lighter than the locally prevailing hue. But ethnicity isn't all that matters – it can be your clothes, your demeanour or your perpetually confused look. You don't have to appear on TV either; you just need to step out of your hotel room.

But the fame conferred upon foreign travellers in Bangladesh is unique for its intensity. This isn't a nation on most round-the-world agendas. Visitors are rare, and a pale white tourist plodding around in Bermuda shorts is a sight to behold for average Bangladeshis. They stare.

Of course, people stare everywhere, whether it's polite Japan or rowdy India. Yet there is something slightly different about the Bangladeshi's stare. It's not the covertly stolen glance of a Tokyo train commuter, or even the leering gaze that a scantily clad Western woman might attract in India. It's a look of absolute shock: a slack-jawed, eye-popping, dry-tongued stare that startles you as much as you've startled them. *There is a foreigner on my street!*

And it doesn't stop with the stare. A visiting foreigner here has the power to shut down an entire city block. Your presence causes traffic jams as rickshaw and truck drivers slam on their brakes to have a look. Shopkeepers shutter their stores and follow you down the street. Children abandon soccer games and huddle around, trying to touch you. At one point, I entered a small shop and turned to find the exit blocked by twenty curious Bangladeshis. Another day, I was ambushed by a group of a dozen children who led me by the hand to – *voilà!* – another foreigner whom their friends had found some two blocks away. He was the only other foreign visitor I saw in five days.

All of this attention was charming at first, but I soon began to think twice about even leaving my hotel. So I developed some coping strategies. First, never – and I mean never – stop in the street to look at your guidebook. This would be like dropping a blob of honey in an ant farm. I found I'd be surrounded by literally hundreds of locals within seconds, and continuing my journey would require handshakes, ten conversations and possibly autographs. One time, I was forced to employ the services of a child bodyguard, who diligently ordered other voyeurs to back off. His only payment was the privilege of being my friend.

The second rule I followed was to walk fast. People would still stare, but I'd pass them like a phantom – leaving them to discuss whether I actually existed or not.

The third rule was to develop friendly yet slightly dismissive ways of acknowledging my fame. I had fun with this one. The easiest was the Princess Diana wave – a half turn of the hand at face level, punctuated by a slightly demure smile. On more energetic days, I resorted to the Richard Nixon victory pose – arms above my head, fingers held up to signify the letter 'V' – as I waded through the masses. The kids loved that one. When I found myself more or less surrounded, I turned local politician – hand extended for multiple handshakes and pats on the head. If that didn't work, I turned the tables by pulling out my camera and snapping a photo of my admirers. Finally, there was the simple head-nod. This wasn't as nice, but it worked when I was in a hurry, which was often.

My techniques worked well for the first few days; then they backfired spectacularly. The problems began with my visit to the Pink Palace, one of Dhaka's biggest tourist attractions. I arrived at the palace to find its gates locked. It was a Friday – mosque day. The positioning of the gate was not exactly advantageous, as I was essentially boxed into a corner. My only exit was via a street packed with Bangladeshis, all of them surely waiting to pounce.

I took a cautious glance over my shoulder. People were already staring, and a few of them were taking cautious steps towards me. No matter, I'd just walk quickly.

I slung my backpack over one shoulder and morphed into Princess Di. A hundred heads swivelled in my direction.

'Hello!' a group of labourers called out in unison.

'Hello!' I returned.

'Hello!' they repeated.

'I'm from America', I said, anticipating the usual 'What is your country?' interrogation.

That didn't satisfy them. Our dialogue continued as I passed them: 'Hello!' 'America!' 'Hello!' 'America!' Even for Bangladeshi standards, this was a bit bizarre. Then I heard footsteps. They were following me. A dozen or so children were converging ahead as well. I picked up my pace and prepared to turn Richard Nixon.

The children reached me before the labourers did, and there were so many of them that I stopped. It wasn't that they blocked my way; in fact, they stopped a metre away from me. But they were shouting and gesticulating so vigorously that something must have been wrong. Their cries came in Bengali as well as English – a cacophony of 'hellos' and 'hey misters' interspersed with instructions I couldn't understand.

Meanwhile, the footsteps were getting closer. I had to keep moving. I tried another hello and walked forward.

'No!' one of them finally shouted. The others were gesturing and pointing like a group of madmen.

'Hello!' I repeated.

The children erupted into uncontrollable laughter; this was evidently the funniest thing they had ever heard. I was just plain confused. Then the footsteps arrived. It was one of the labourers.

'Mister!' he said, pointing at my feet. 'No!'

I looked down, and could hardly believe my eyes. I had spent the last hundred metres walking on wet cement. My footprints were visible all the way back to the gate.

I guess I'm just not cut out for fame.

THE CULINARY CHAOS PRINCIPLE

DON GEORGE

Don George is Lonely Planet's Global Travel Editor and the editor of this anthology. His most recent book is *Travel Writing*. Don has edited four previous anthologies, including *The Kindness of Strangers* and *A House Somewhere: Tales of Life Abroad*. Before becoming a travel writer and editor, he worked as a translator in Paris, where he subsisted happily on *biftek-frites* and house red wine; a teacher in Athens, where he was honoured to eat the sheep's eyeballs at an Easter feast; and a TV talk show host in Tokyo, where he was treated to sashimi so fresh that the fish literally flipped off his plate.

As a traveller, I am a fervent follower of the Culinary Chaos Principle. This principle is based on the theory that the universe is like an all-you-can-eat buffet that is proceeding ever so slowly but ineluctably past the prime rib, the tandoori chicken and the *kung pao* shrimp towards the baked Alaska. Our goal in this smorgasbord is to sample as much as we can before closing time. The best way to achieve this goal is to leave your menu selection in the good hands of chance – a mysterious force you might best imagine as a dapper figure in a tuxedo saying, 'Hi, I'm Chance, and I'll be your waitperson this evening.'

Life on the road affords many excellent opportunities to cultivate the Culinary Chaos Principle. You enter a smoky six-table den at the end of the world. The grizzled proprietor wipes his hands on his Jackson Pollack apron and leads you to a crumb-covered table, then presses a tattered menu into your hand. This is the Special Guest Menu and features a kind of English you've never seen before. But never mind! You decide to start with Shoo Race Soap, proceed to Mixt Intestine Bean Luck, tuck into a Rusted Ship Chup and end with Frooty Coostard Frayed Kek. Yum.

Of course, if you're really lucky, the proprietor will simply wag his grizzled head to indicate that they don't have any English-language menu at all. Ah, then the potentials of the Culinary Chaos Principle positively shine!

I have been graced with the gifts of this principle all around the world, but the meal that lives most memorably in my mind took place in Naples. My wife and I were wandering along the waterfront on a half-day excursion from a cruise ship and had decided to look for a good place to eat. There were some touristy places right near the water, but we eschewed those and ventured further inland, into a warren of dank, dark alleys and vaguely illicit-looking shops. Laundry was festooned along the balconies, and pedestrians and bicycles and motorcycles swarmed by.

We spied a tiny restaurant that was full of people and walked in. The owner greeted us warmly in Italian and bade us sit down. The other diners all looked at us, and a few smiled kindly and then returned to the platefuls of delicious-looking food in front of them.

The owner raised an imaginary glass to his mouth – '*Vino?*' – and returned with two glasses of strong red wine and a menu that was entirely in Italian. I looked around. The owner and his wife and a young assistant, their daughter we later learned, were preparing and cooking the food in full view of the diners. All the ingredients were on display – strings of garlic and shiny tomatoes and clumps of basil, little white balls of mozzarella, golden coils of pasta and a few fish in a pan. The menu seemed to be extremely limited – a salad, a few pastas, a fish dish. That was it.

The owner brought a plate of rough thick bread. I broke off a chunk and it was delicious. We looked at every single dish on the menu but couldn't recognise even one. Still, it would have been too easy – and fundamentally antagonistic to the Culinary Chaos Principle – to simply point at someone else's plate and say, 'I'll have what he's having.' So after some deliberation we bravely pointed to a dish in the pasta section. I imagined this would bring us the wonderfully aromatic dish that our neighbour was savouring – a glorious heap of spaghetti twirled in a thick sauce, with hints of herbs wafting towards us.

As we sipped our wine and watched the other patrons laughing and calling out to each other – it was lunch time and they all seemed to be workers from neighbourhood offices – I could almost taste that mouth-watering pasta. We waited and waited, watching the wife place handfuls of pasta into a large boiling pot and pour them out a few minutes later, perfectly *al dente*, we were sure. Other diners who came in after us got their plates of pasta, but still we waited. Finally, the owner emerged from a closed-off section of the kitchen, proudly looking our way.

We watched expectantly as he manoeuvred two heaping platters through the tables, subtly showing them off to other patrons as he passed, and placed them before us with a theatrical thump.

Oh no! On each of our plates was a tiny pedestal of pasta. And crowning each pedestal, overwhelming the plate so that it slithered off the sides, was a huge octopus, lightly doused in a brown sauce, staring dolefully at the famished, flummoxed foreigners who had proposed to eat it.

These octopi were mountainous, the biggest ever served in the city of Naples, I'm sure. There was no avoiding them, no pushing them to the side of the plate, no covering them with bread. The pasta was merely a warm-up act; these puckering prehistoric protuberances were the stars.

What to do? I can stomach a little octopus, but this was more octopus than I would normally eat in a year.

Now this is where the ineffable glory of the Culinary Chaos Principle kicks in. What to do? Eat it, of course! We couldn't lose face by asking the owner to bring something else. We had ordered it, he had made it – with considerable pride and pleasure, it seemed, from the way he continued to beam at us from a corner, waiting for our first appreciative bites. There was nothing to do but eat.

Why, I thought, hadn't I just pointed at my neighbour's pasta – he who was even now folding his napkin and rising to his feet with a most satisfied smile? Or why hadn't I walked back to the kitchen and told the cook with a gesture and a smile that I coveted the pasta she was devotedly plopping into a pot?

Well, what would I have learned from that?

So I broke off a handful of bread, took a big gulp of wine, and cut into the octopus. It was astonishingly tender, and the brown gravy was unexpectedly delicious. In fact, it was so ethereally exquisite that... Well, no. It was not an edible epiphany – it was still octopus.

By alternating pasta, bread and wine with bites of octopus, I managed to get down about a dozen forkfuls. We nodded and smiled broadly at the owner and at each other, and tried to express our admiration for this singular speciality of the house. But finally I gave up the pretence and pushed and prodded the octopus around on my plate until I had uncovered and devoured all the strands of pasta I could find. That left me with a half-full stomach and a half-eaten octopus.

It was time to raise the white napkin of surrender.

The owner came solicitously over and we indicated that we were full 'up to here'. Then, as he began to gather up our plates, we served the sentences we had concocted. We praised the restaurant's intimate atmosphere and its friendly diners who seemed to know each other so well; we exulted in the open kitchen where we could watch him and his wife and daughter work; we marvelled at how they seemed to use only very fresh ingredients and how their limited menu meant that everything they did, they did very well.

He listened to our English intently, if quizzically, and nodded and smiled until we were done. And when we rose to leave, he rushed from the back of the restaurant to guide us to the door, pumped our hands vigorously, then pressed his hands to his heart and said, I think, that when we returned to his city, we should consider his humble restaurant our Neapolitan home away from home.

We walked into the garlic-bright street that lilted with the cries of vendors and children, flapping laundry and honking horns. We held hands and smiled into each other's eyes. The Culinary Chaos Principle was alive and well; the proof was right inside.

FAECES FOOT

TIM CAHILL

Tim Cahill is the author of nine books, including *Hold the Enlightenment*, *Jaguars Ripped My Flesh* and *Lost in My Own Backyard*. He writes for many national magazines and is the co-writer of three IMAX films, including *Everest*. Tim lives in Montana with his wife, Linnea, two dogs and two cats.

On expeditions to remote and difficult areas, when conditions can become uncomfortable, if not to say actually agonising, it is customary to restructure the pain by irritating and annoying one's companions. In such situations, a person fully expects to be taunted, mocked, ragged and generally made the butt of some profoundly grating ongoing jibe. Those of us who do this sort of thing for a living assume that giving the other girl or guy a daily ration of humiliation raises their tolerance level and helps them endure physical pain. We get our poop in a pile and fling it in the faces of our companions *for their own good*. No one derives any pleasure out of this. (Okay, I lied. It's really fun – unless, of course, you are the person becoming exasperated beyond measure.) Expedition members generally take turns at being the brunt of the joke.

That's why it's very easy to hate my friend Will Gadd. I hate him because he is impossible to annoy. He can do any outdoor athletic activity better than I can – and, in fact, he can do many of them better than anyone else in the world. Will, for instance, placed first at almost every major ice climbing competition in the world in 1998 and '99, and won the 2000 Ice World Cup. He is the current world record holder in distance paragliding (423.5 kilometres/263 miles), and the first to make a one-day ascent of Mount Robson, Canada's highest peak. He is the three-time Canadian National Sport Climbing Champion and has climbed walls rated 5.13d, which, for those not familiar with rock-climbing ratings, probably means that Spiderman hates him, too. And oh yeah, he writes well, and has been published in many of the leading outdoor magazines. He produces outdoor action films, and does stunt work – kayaking, mountaineering, that sort of thing – in various commercials. Even more detestable, Will is almost intolerably modest about his accomplishments. He's a nice guy, and a great travelling companion. You just want to punch him in the head.

So how was I going to get to a guy like that? Call him – what? Wonder Boy? Mr Ice? King of the Ice Holes? We were just starting this little jaunt to what we hoped would be unexplored sections of caves in northern Thailand, and I had no ammunition with which to rankle Will. This was an intolerable situation. Why should he escape daily degradation just because he happened to be a talented and decent human being? If I was going to aggravate Will, for the good of all, I needed something maddening, some nickname designed to generate an ongoing annoyance. But what?

The answer came some hours after our party landed in Chiang Mai. We had taken a cab from the airport to a small hotel and now, somehow, the cab driver had become infuriated and was screaming at my friend Will Gadd.

'I love a car', the driver spluttered. 'You love a car.' The man's voice rose to a shriek. 'You wouldn't do that to your own car.'

It is my experience that, in Thailand, people generally avoid angry confrontations. You have to do something tremendously insulting or appallingly disrespectful to drive your average Thai into such a spittle-spewing rage.

'I'm very sorry', Will said. 'I didn't know.'

But everybody in Thailand knows. I knew. What Will had just done was, by the driver's standards, unforgivable. The cabbie now assumed he was addressing a disrespectful liar. 'Really,' Will said, more than a bit confused, 'really, I apologise.'

He had no idea what he'd done. I watched carefully. It was possible I could get something out of this.

The driver was not mollified, not even a little bit. A big tip didn't help much. This Thai gentleman stood next to his car, on guard, protecting his vehicle from the barbarian, and continued to mutter about Will's questionable ancestry, his dearth of common courtesy, his severely limited intelligence.

We gathered up our bags and made our way in to the little hotel where we were staying for the night.

'What the hell was that all about?' Will asked, when we were safely in the lobby and the cab driver had left in a squeal of burning rubber.

'It's a bottom-of-the-foot thing', I said. 'It's considered disrespectful to show someone the bottom of your feet here.'

'I didn't show him my feet.'

'You did worse', I said. Something good was going to come out of this, I knew; something I could use as annoyance ammunition.

Tomorrow we would rent cars and drive several hundred miles to the west to explore those caves in the hill country. We were carrying cave gear, several different kinds of backpacks, and clothes. Will, who was making a video of the trip, had brought along a lot of delicate camera and sound gear. When the taxi had dropped us at the hotel, we'd off-loaded that gear, putting most of the equipment on the pavement. Will had grabbed the last of his paraphernalia and his arms were full. He'd turned from the empty cab and closed the back door with his foot. This was the action that had thrown the cab driver into a rage.

'It was about closing the door?' Will asked when I told him what he'd done. 'You're kidding.'

'I'm not.'

'He asked if I did that at home. I do it all the time.'

'So do I.'

'So what's this foot thing all about?'

'I don't know', I said. 'But it happens in India, too. I have a theory about it, though.'

'Tell me.'

'Ah, it's sorta disgusting. You don't want to know.'

'Tell me.'

'I could be all wrong.'

'Listen,' Will said in a menacing Clint Eastwood sort of whisper, 'tell me or I can't be responsible for any violence that may occur.'

'Okay.' I paused, trying to formulate a delicate explication. 'You know what a lot of the toilets are like in this part of the world, right?' They are mere holes in concrete or wooden flooring. There are usually two ribbed rectangles on either side of the hole where the feet are placed. Then one squats over the hole and performs the necessities in question. The ribbed flooring is there because not everyone is entirely accurate and the corrugations prevent slips on the disagreeable material which is often spread on the floor itself, and caked in the concrete ribbing where the feet go. It is for this reason that you really don't want to spend a lot of time examining the soles of someone's feet or shoes.

'Anyway,' I said, 'that's what I think. I'm not sure people here would explain it that way. I think it's just something they grow up with. Bottoms of the feet are disgusting to people here.'

'Ah,' Will said, 'so when I touched that guy's car with the bottom of my foot, he thought...'

'That's exactly what he thought', I said, and Will's annoyance name for the entire expedition popped into my head, unbidden. I felt the need to use it immediately. 'I mean, I think you really have to learn to be a little bit more culturally sensitive, Faeces Foot.'

REAL COWBOYS WEAR POLKA DOTS

JUDY TIERNEY

Judy Tierney took a year-long sabbatical from corporate America to travel through Africa, India, Southeast Asia, Australia and New Zealand. Her current work as a freelance consultant allows her the flexibility to continue to explore and write about her adventures. Her work has appeared in *Backpacker* magazine, the *Dallas Morning News*, the *Denver Post*, the *Atlanta Journal Constitution* and on www.travelerstales.com. A Texas native, she now resides in San Francisco.

'I reckon we oughta get a move on', Jeff said, finishing the last few bites of his three-alarm tacos – a mixture of scrambled eggs, potatoes, cheese, jalapenos and chipotle sauce wrapped in flour tortillas. Back at home in San Francisco Jeff started the day with sourdough toast and jam, but he casually wiped his eyes and nose with a napkin as if he were used to eating peppers for breakfast. He emptied his glass of water in one big gulp and then reached across the table for mine.

As we left Austin's Magnolia Café, Jeff waved at our big-haired, blonde waitress.

'Thank ya', darlin'', he called out in the Texas drawl he'd been practising ever since I'd invited him home with me for the holidays.

I thought Jeff, a California-born and -bred Berkeley grad, would love Austin's eclectic mix of herbal medicine shops, antique stores and taco stands along South Congress Avenue. But as we walked past the funky boutiques, Jeff wouldn't stop to browse. He had one mission on his mind. Four blocks down, a six-foot replica of a red Justin boot standing on a wood-shingled roof marked the spot he was seeking.

Jeff pushed open the glass door of Allen's Boots. Inside, the aroma of leather and a pint-sized sales girl named Amber greeted us.

'How y'all doin'?' she welcomed us in a voice that was larger than her four-foot, ten-inch frame. Amber's chestnut pony tail swayed from side to side as she walked towards us. She wore a Western-style button-down plaid shirt and a smile bigger and brighter than her Texas-sized belt buckle emblazoned with two shimmering silver hearts engraved with roses.

Jeff sensed he had found an expert.

'Ya reckon ya could rustle me up some boots here?' he asked her.

'Yep! We've got 'em all – crocodile, elephant, goat, stingray, you name it', she said. 'The ostrich is my favourite.'

'Ostrich?' Jeff replied in disbelief. 'What do those look like?'

Nodding at her feet, Amber showed off black cherry cowboy boots emerging from painted-on Wranglers. Small bumps covered the surface.

Amber swung her foot up on a wooden bench so we could get a closer look. 'See those dots?' she said. 'Those are where they pulled out the feathers!'

We followed Amber past racks of fringed suede jackets, chaps and thick cowhide belts, and Jeff's eyes grew wide as he stared at aisles upon aisles of cowboy boots. Amber escorted us to the area with his particular size, where wooden shelves were stacked high with every style and colour of boots imaginable. He turned directly to Amber.

'Which do you recommend?' he asked.

Even though I grew up in Fort Worth and Dallas, I'd lived in New York and San Francisco for the past fifteen years. I no longer even owned a pair of boots and was no match for the twentyish Amber, who looked like she could ride the range with the best of them.

Amber sized up Jeff in his silk Nordstrom sweater, tidy jeans and loafers, and pulled one of the most expensive pairs off the shelf, a pair of shiny black full-quill ostrich Lucchese boots. 'One of our best boots, all handmade and hand-stitched.'

Jeff studied the hide. It was as exquisite as the leather of the dozen-or-so pairs of fine Italian dress shoes in his closet at home. 'But these look awful fancy', Jeff replied, reluctantly slipping them on.

I thought they were a perfect fit for Jeff's metrosexual lifestyle, but apparently the city-slicker look was not the one he had in mind.

Swaggering down the aisle, thumbs stuck into his front pockets and jeans tucked into the boots, Jeff looked into the mirror. 'I reckon I oughta go round up the wagons', he said in his best John Wayne imitation. He studied his reflection for a moment, and then shook his head.

'The Duke wouldn't be caught dead in boots this pristine', he said to me, and then explained to Amber, 'I'm looking for something a little more rugged.'

Amber pulled down a pair of golden-hued Tony Lama lizards, while I hummed along to Garth Brooks' 'I've Got Friends in Low Places' playing on the store's radio. The song transported me back to high school and college, riding in pick-ups with guys in ten-gallon hats, line-dancing at the bars in the Fort Worth stockyards, and watching George Strait and my other favourite country-and-western singers perform at the annual livestock show and rodeo.

'These are real nice, but you gotta treat the scales every month with reptile conditioner or they'll dry out', she explained to Jeff. 'It's kinda a pain.'

Jeff tried them on, but wasn't sure about the colour. He looked at the tag. 'Buttercup?' he said, turning up his nose. 'Do you think Jessie James would wear buttercup boots?'

'I don't think anyone at your yoga studio is going to know that the colour is called buttercup', I said.

Amber giggled. Jeff looked at me and rolled his eyes.

He turned back to Amber. 'Don't you have anything that looks more like, well, a cowboy boot?'

While Amber plucked boots from the shelf, Jeff seemed to drift off into a daydream. I imagined him musing about the days when cowboys drove cattle herds along the Chisholm Trail, stopping at 'Big Daddy Joe' Justin's shop in Spanish Fort, Texas, to get fitted for custom boots that would protect against snakes, snow, cacti and other hazards of the range.

Amber handed Jeff a pair of camel-coloured ropers. They were simple and casual, and made of calf skin. I'd dated Jeff for eighteen months and I knew immediately that they lacked the flair that the exotic skins exuded and that he preferred.

But Jeff examined them and pretended to take a liking to their practicality.

He turned and sauntered down the aisle, talking in a Texas twang. 'Well, I guess these oughta be jes fine for workin' out on the ranch.'

'I'm sure they would,' I interjected, 'but you're a software engineer, remember?'

'They're too big, anyway', he said, brushing off my sarcasm. 'My heel slips when I walk.'

'You know, boots don't fit like regular shoes', Amber explained. 'They're supposed to slip about an inch. Plus, once you buy a pair, you'll be wearing a thicker sock, not like that fancy one you got on now.'

Jeff tried on the smaller size anyway, and said they were too tight.

'Trust me. They're gonna feel weird at first', Amber explained. 'But once you break 'em in, you'll love 'em. I work all day in mine.

I won't wear anything else.'

Jeff pressed on for the perfect pair.

Amber showed him more styles. 'These are good for two-stepping', she explained, holding up a pair with a low heel and a short shaft.

A scary image of Jeff in a cowboy bar, wearing tight jeans and swigging whisky, popped into my mind.

'Do you have a pair that's good for wine bars and ethnic restaurants?' I asked.

Jeff ignored me and asked Amber to show him more boots.

I was amazed at Amber's patience. She must be used to this, I thought. I wondered how many tourists visited the store thinking that a pair of boots would instantly turn them into a cowboy. Was buying boots in Texas like buying sarongs in Thailand? Did tourists think that by donning a pair of boots they'd immediately fit right in with the locals?

Jeff contemplated some pythons, but when another customer with a pierced eyebrow and a tint of blue hair walked by in a similar pair, Jeff decided he didn't look like an ass-kicker in them. He wanted boots that would make Clint Eastwood proud.

Feeling a bit guilty and noticing Jeff's increasingly short tone, I told him how good he'd looked in the original pair he'd tried on.

'Boots are so mainstream these days that people wear them for just about anything', I told him. 'Those ostrich boots look like a pair JR Ewing might wear to his office in downtown Dallas.'

'I don't want to look like a cowboy wannabe', he told me.

Amber wrinkled her nose. 'All the pairs you've tried on look great', she agreed. 'Why don't ya just pick one?'

'Slow down thar little filly', he said, holding up another pair – chocolate-coloured kangaroo skins this time.

'Are these any good?' he asked.

'I *told* ya. They're *all* good', Amber replied. 'Well, any of 'em except them roach killers.' She gestured to a pair of boots with extremely pointy toes and twisted her foot on the rug as if squashing a humongous bug. 'We call those Yankee boots.'

All Jeff wanted was to look like a real cowboy.

Feeling confident with his boot education, Jeff eyed a pair of bluish grey elephant skins, with a unique dark streak across one of the toes. 'This must be the natural colouring of the hide', he ventured.

Amber rubbed her fingers on the sticky stain. 'No. I think some kid wiped a sucker across it.'

I sat back among the pile of rejected boots strewn along the aisle – shark, python, eel, American buffalo and caiman. In the last hour and a half, Jeff had tried on practically every pair in his size. He'd tried on Dan Post, Tony Lama, Nocona, Justin and Lucchese. He'd tried them in plain black, tan, peanut brittle, almond, cognac, denim and buttercup.

Alan Jackson crooned 'Way Down Yonder on the Chattahoochee' on the radio while Jeff imitated John Wayne in the mirror. Amber whispered to me, asking what else she could do to help him make a decision.

Jeff overheard and tried once again to explain his perspective. 'I don't look like I'm going out to rope cattle in those polka dot ones.'

'They're not polka dots, they're ostrich!' Amber shot back, exasperated. 'And our other sales rep Dale ropes cattle. Those are exactly the ones he wears.'

Jeff didn't know what to say.

'I can throw some mud on them if that'll make you feel better', she said.

'I think I just need a little time to find the perfect pair', he said as he put his loafers back on.

I took Amber aside and told her we'd probably be back the next day. 'He's a little overwhelmed. It's his first time in Texas.'

'Well, thank y'all for coming in.' The worn-out Amber started to walk us to the door, but to our surprise, Jeff wasn't ready to leave.

'Hold on thar lil lady', he spoke in the best Western drawl he could muster. 'Ain't ya' gonna show this cowboy some Stetsons?'

YOU AIN'T SEEN NUTHIN' YET

SEAN CONDON

Sean Condon is the author of three travelogues, *Sean & David's Long Drive*, *Drive Thru America* and *My 'Dam Life*, as well as the novel *Film* and the humour collection *The Secret of Success is a Secret*. He currently lives in Melbourne, Australia.

'You ain't seen nuthin' yet!' I supposed that was true enough – we were just a few miles out of the station in Springfield, Massachusetts, on a highway heading towards Vermont – and we hadn't seen anything you could really call spectacular. 'Don't even bother looking out the window, 'cause you ain't seen *nuthin'* yet!' This was my Uncle Bill, behind the wheel, giving the orders, telling me what I hadn't seen. What I had not seen so far was a large, crystal-blue lake, lots of trees and the occasional majestic hill with an exclusive girls' school on top – the usual stuff you don't see just outside many small cities in northeast America. The thing was, I'd just come from a week in Manhattan, and I *liked* what I wasn't seeing. It seemed an eternity since I'd been surrounded by anything other than snarling traffic, looming skyscrapers and impenetrable clubs with majestic girls inside.

A few minutes after we crossed the state line into Vermont, the Green Mountain State, Uncle Bill asked, 'What do you see out there now?'

'Umm...more trees?' I suggested. 'I don't know what sort, but they're very nice.'

'And what *don't* you see?'

'Oh not this again, please. I've already adjusted to *seeing* things.'

'Come on – what's not there?'

'Dolphins', I said. 'I haven't seen a single dolphin since I got here. No porpoise, either.'

'Billboards!' Bill shouted, beginning his two-day assault of Vermont-based information. 'This is the only state in the US that has banned billboard advertising on highways.'

It was true – I really *hadn't* seen a lot of towering, hideous signage. No golden arches peeking like sneaky corporate eyebrows over tree lines; no red Texaco stars lighting the late-afternoon skies; just all this green. 'It's very beautiful', I said.

Uncle Bill told me that I hadn't seen anything yet.

A while later, once we'd 'exited' the freeway (to put it in American motoring parlance), we drove through the minuscule township of Guilford, which consisted of a general store selling more varieties of home-made root beer than I've ever seen in my life, and a parking lot where they hold town meetings (and possibly Friday-night rumbles). After another few miles along a winding dirt track we came to Bill's house, which he shares with his girlfriend, Carol, an editor. They're very rural, Bill and Carol. They like being in the middle of nowhere, and they've chosen well.

As soon as I climbed out of the car I was greeted by a very large dog of no particular breed. Ordinarily I don't mind a canine welcome, but this particular fella was foaming at the mouth. Quite a lot. 'This dog's foaming at the mouth, Bill', I reported from the roof of the car. 'Quite a lot. Am I allowed to see that?' Bill's almost fifty, but more fit (and rural) than I am, so he wrestled the mutt to the ground and yelled at me to find some pliers. 'You go', I told Carol, unable to leave my position. (It was a terrific view from up there – trees and mountains, men and dogs.) Carol returned from the garage a few moments later and handed a pair of pliers to Bill, shaking her head wearily up at me. 'You mind taking the luggage inside?' I asked her. 'I'll be down in a minute. Once the dog dentistry's done.'

'It's not dentistry', Bill corrected me, his clenched fist halfway down the dog's throat. 'Rocky's got a mouth full of pine needles.'

'Damn trees', I muttered. 'Only good for Christmas.'

'*Porcupine* needles.'

'Oh.' I realised then that there was a great deal I didn't know about life in the country. Then either Rocky or Bill let out a little yelp. Or maybe it was me – I might have seen a spider.

After Carol unpacked my bags, I was coaxed down from the car and the three of us took a small wander around the large property which has been occupied since about 1770. Ethan Allen even passed through this very spot in 1789, I was informed. 'Ethan who?' I made the mistake of asking. Fifteen minutes later I realised that there was also a great deal I didn't know about American Revolutionary War militiamen. 'What about Ben and/or Jerry?' I enquired, not wanting to seem completely ignorant of Vermont's favourite sons. 'Did they ever pass through on a dangerous ice-cream run?'

Adjacent to the house was a wild maze made from small, dense trees. It was cool and dark in the maze, and as we stumbled about pretending to be lost, I tried to imagine other children (or other thirty-four-year-olds) from centuries before treading these same twisting paths. I cast my eyes to the loamy ground, hoping to find an artefact left behind by some long-gone kid – an ivory button, a slingshot maybe, or a sack of priceless marbles. To my surprise I soon found a coin and, too excited over my discovery to bother with reaching the centre of the maze, I turned and tried to retrace my steps back to the house, about six metres away.

Forty-five minutes later I reached the kitchen and immediately plunged the dirt-encrusted coin into a dissolving solution (white vinegar) and waited for its secrets to be revealed. Could it be a rare Civil War-era silver dollar? I wondered. The exclusive and elusive twenty-dollar coin issued between WWI and WWII? Or could it be an American penny from around the time of the Gulf War? Yes, it turned out, it could.

The next day we took a drive. Bill was behind the wheel, while Carol, wearing a pair of dark, square sunglasses that covered most of her face, navigated. I sat in the back, awaiting visual instructions from Bill. It was a perfect day. Bright sunshine shot through the dense forests of balsam, fir and maple. Vermont's incredible lushness, Bill explained, comes from a combination of warmth and water, subtropical summers and winters that regularly reach twenty degrees below.

Our first stop was Newfane, a small and, I thought, altogether too pretty town of fifteen hundred mostly older people. In the middle of Newfane Common, a gently sloping square of green flanked by a Congregational church and the Union Hall, was the Windham County courthouse, a large, spired building made, like just about every other building in rural Vermont, of white clapboard. Hoping to stumble upon a Scopes Monkey Trial-type situation, we took a look inside and met the bailiff, a pleasant-seeming fellow. 'Where you folks from?' he asked. (I assumed that the question was not directed at Bill and Carol because everybody in Vermont knows each other.)

'I'm Australian, but I live in Holland.'

His face lit up. 'Oh really? My daughter was there just last week.' *Yeah*, I thought, rolling my eyes, *I can just imagine. Typical college kid summer vacation – come over to Amsterdam and smoke pot all day for a week. What a loser!* 'Part of a tour she was on. She just won a Nobel Peace Prize', he concluded with a modest, fatherly smile.

'Oh, that's *your* daughter!' Carol said. The bailiff's daughter, Jodie Williams, had recently collected the prize (Nobel) for her work in landmine clearance. Moments later, as I stood next to him for a photograph, I couldn't help wondering whether, if the bailiff was my father, I might have made more of myself than...me.

Behind the courthouse was a restaurant/inn known as the Newfane Four Column Inn (because it's in Newfane and has four wooden columns on the porch). Mick Jagger held his fortieth birthday here, and Tom Cruise and Nicole Kidman liked to come here to 'get away from it all' – 'it' being those things the residents of Newfane probably wish were just a small part of their own lives. The rest of the town consisted of old clapboard houses which all looked the same. In fact, I figured the only way the Newfanians could tell which was their own particular white clapboard home was by painting the window trim different colours, which ranged from light green to dark green.

'Back in the late nineteenth century about one house in three had somebody hang themselves in it', Bill reported loudly.

From Newfane we drove along more small, hilly roads flanked by apple orchards and maple trees sprouting syrup tubes to another tiny town named Dummerston. There's not much to say about Dummerston apart from the fact that it's named Dummerston. And that the buildings are made of white clapboard, which, around here, is pronounced 'clabberd'.

'Have I seen anything yet?' I asked Bill.

'Look at that house', Bill ordered, pointing left. 'Beautiful house and barn there in a lovely setting.' The barn was red. There was a rusted old tractor next to it. 'Gorgeous old stone walls lining this road', he continued. 'Beautiful. Built – *by hand* – in the early eighteenth century.' They were nice, too – the first few miles of them, anyway.

We stopped for lunch at a genuine roadside barbecue pit owned and operated by a friend of Bill and Carol's (and, I assumed, the rest of Vermont) named Jon Julian. There was rich blue smoke and Stevie Ray Vaughan pouring from the smoker shack out back. It smelt (and sounded) good. 'Shouldn't we be in Texas to be eating this kind of food?' I asked.

'If all you've ever had is Texas barbecue, then you ain't tasted nuthin' yet', Bill insisted.

I had a double-pulled pork sandwich with a side of coleslaw and beans, both of which also contained quite a bit of pork, possibly pulled. I don't know exactly what the 'pulled' element in pork is, but I liked it a lot. It ruined me for regular pork. The view from the terrace where we ate was of a lunatic asylum about a mile away in Brattleboro. The smell of barbecued smoked meat drifting across the valley probably drove all those poor bastards crazy with culinary lust.

After the pork festival we were off to Putney, right on the New Hampshire border. On the way we passed more houses (white; clapboard), trees (green) and stone walls (old). With the possible exception of Santa Cruz, California, Putney is the New Age hippie capital of the United States. Carol explained that according to a popular joke, if there's a support group for any kind of dysfunctionality, it's being held somewhere in Putney on Thursday nights. It didn't take long for me to believe it. Sitting on the grass outside a bookstore specialising in mysticality was a group of three women, all wearing loose, comfortable, purple clothing. I overheard one of the *wymyn* telling her friends that she was home-schooling her girls today. 'Their philosophy doesn't really suit being enclosed by four walls every day', she said slowly. While my companions ate non-Ben & Jerry ice cream, I ventured inside the bookstore and didn't buy anything about channelling, crystals, shamanism, dreams or reincarnation. I asked if they carried *Popular Mechanics* and got a dirty look. Back outside, in what passes for the real world, I saw the young, home-schooled philosophers – a four-year-old sitting in a sandpit banging her head against her seven-year-old sister's toy bucket. I remembered that I used to rather enjoy assaulting plastic with my forehead at that age, too. But I went to a state school, so presumably my head-banging had no deeper meaning.

Three or four miles outside Putney we stopped at the semi-famous Putney School, founded in 1935 by radical thinker Carmelita Hinton. Set in five hundred rolling green (naturally) acres of field and forests, the school housed some two hundred students whose parents were paying $26,000 per year to send them there. Parents like Roy Liechtenstein, Jonathan Schell, William Shawn and at least one member of the Grateful Dead. Probably Ben and/or Jerry, too, but Bill refused to confirm or deny this. For their twenty-six large, the children of America's Bo-Ho elite were almost guaranteed entrance to an Ivy League college; however, while attending the Putney School they had to do pretty much everything except teach themselves. They grew their own organic (naturally) vegetables, tended to the pigs and chickens and cows in the huge red (naturally) barn, baked sixty loaves of bread every day and cooked their own meals. (When Bill reported that about ten per cent of the students were vegans, I couldn't help but think that there would probably be a lot of pizza delivery orders placed on nights when the vegans were on kitchen detail, cooking up sand-and-wood casseroles for their colleagues.) The students also ran a blacksmithery and a literary magazine as well as indulging in plain old scholastic activities such as establishing madrigal societies, playing in hot jazz combos and building their own dormitories. 'These kids developed their own missile defence system yet?' I chuckled, to nobody's amusement.

As a bell rang and the students left their classrooms, I expected to meet some miniature genius in a bow tie and straw hat who would bow and call me 'Sir'. Maybe toss off a wry Shavian ice-breaker. And the more I thought about this encounter, the more I looked forward to it. I like being called 'Sir'. (Only later did I learn that students and teachers at Putney were on a first-name basis, an idea which has always given me the creeps, preferring as I did to address my teachers as 'your highness' and to be addressed by them as 'you there'.) Bill led us around like he owned the place or was an alumnus (neither of which was the case). His magisterial sense of entitlement came from the fact that he was friends with the dean of students. 'So who *don't* you know in Vermont?' I asked.

'Ben or Jerry', he replied. 'I know one of them, but I can never remember which one.' When we finally did come upon a group of students, there was not a single bow tie or straw boater amongst the lot. They weren't required to wear any kind of uniform – apart, it seemed, from spectacles and an unflattering haircut. What the group was replete with, however, were dazzling, confident, mature smiles and greetings to us strangers. Back in my high-school days, if my friends and I saw someone coming, we ran away. (Sure it was because we were usually smoking, but still.) These were very self-contained kids who made me feel extremely inadequate, despite their almost Stepford Wife-like demeanour. I was therefore rather pleased to find out later that there were a few expulsions every year, for such infractions as setting fire to things, drug and alcohol abuse and generally being an idiot. Also, the students weren't allowed to watch TV, whether they'd done anything wrong or not. To me this bordered on cruel and unusual punishment, but I figured these youngsters probably didn't miss it at all. One boy I chatted with told me, 'I need to think. I can't just read and spew back information. I need to call upon everything that I know, and maybe a little bit that I don't, and try to put together what I think is the truth.' I thanked him for his time and ran away, smoking and thinking about various episodes of *The Dukes of Hazzard*.

As we left, passing a sports field full of strong, bright, healthy youngsters playing lacrosse, I couldn't help wishing that I'd attended Putney School. Perhaps if I had, I might have made something more of my life than...this.

Ten minutes after I arrived back in New York City the following day, I realised how much I'd enjoyed my brief time in Vermont and decided that I would definitely return the following October. When the leaves turn, everything explodes into beautiful burnt orange (except the houses, which remain white). I called Bill to tell him the news. 'You've never been to Vermont in the fall?' he spluttered. 'Well, you ain't seen *nuthin'* yet!'

NO FOOD, NO REST, NO...

PICO IYER

Pico Iyer is the author of several books of ill-starred travel, from *Video Night in Kathmandu* and *The Lady and the Monk* to *The Global Soul* and his most recent work, *Sun After Dark*. He tries not to travel with his friend Louis, but somehow they have ended up in Cambodia, Haiti, Morocco, Burma, Turkey and far too many other places (not least the Oakland Coliseum) together. On their most recent trip, to Bolivia, they had a car crash at 3500 metres that left one of them gibbering in nonexistent Spanish and the other training furious glances at their errant driver.

I got off the plane in Addis Ababa and there, as in so many airports so often in the past, was my school friend Louis, extending a shaky hand. 'This place is pure magic', he assured me. 'We can go around the whole country with Ethiopian Airlines – the best carrier on the continent – for not much more than a hundred dollars. The plane stops at five major points of interest, and is perfectly suited to people on their first trip here, with limited means.

'The only other option', he continued – he was always shrewd in getting to places one day before I did, and so installing himself as boss, with the unquestioned upper hand – 'is to rent a car. This isn't very advisable because there are more car crashes than cars in Ethiopia. Also, they don't have much in the way of roads. The car costs $240 a day, and takes at least ten days to make the circuit.'

'Excellent', I said.

'It is', he said. 'The car's coming for us in two days.'

Travelling with Louis was always a bittersweet experience. The bitterness came at the time, the sweetness in happy retrospect. We'd studied together as teenagers, in a dusty classroom in southern England where we'd played out the whole game of cards from Pope's *Rape of the Lock* and been treated to luscious evocations of Antony and Cleopatra's Egypt by an ambiguous teacher. 'The *bhaji* she sat upon'– an inspired transcription of Shakespeare's jewelled 'barge she sat upon' monologue, to capture an England now filled with Indian restaurants – was one of Louis' best party tricks.

Nonetheless, the dilapidated hotel in Paris (Louis walking down the corridor in pyjamas, eliciting tea and sympathy from the staff), the rancid place in Marrakesh (across from the nicest hotel in Africa, where we pretended to be staying), the snow-storm in rural Turkey (the kind locals offering us a daily array of kofta, kofta or meatballs) – none of these experiences had prepared me for this. I'd just flown across the Atlantic from New York on Ethiopian Airlines, and was more than ready to sign up for its frequent-flier programme and ensure free trips to the walled city of Harar for life. The beauty of being on holiday is taking to the air.

'The first point of business', Louis continued, 'is to fix up a visa for Eritrea.' This was arguably worse news. I'd come all this way in order to see Ethiopia, which was just concluding a shaky peace with neighbouring Eritrea, a country it had been fighting for years. One fruit of this peace was that visas were now available for Eritrea; an added advantage, as I saw it, was that there would be even fewer other visitors to bother us in Ethiopia. Louis, however, had met a man who promised to smooth our way into the Eritrea of his dreams.

It was the day after Christmas, and the streets of Addis Ababa slumbered in a pure blue calm. The weather was as perfect as advertised, and eleven days from now the rending celebrations that mark Christmas in Ethiopia would represent the highlight of the ceremonial year. Few other travellers were in evidence, but the locals were surely delighted to meet a distinguished investment banker (my friend) who was celebrating the chance to pay $2400 for a trip that could be made in greater comfort and with more ease for $240.

'He said that we should just go to his house for coffee, and he'd fix up a visa.'

At this point our benefactor appeared: a shifty man, in clothes almost as shabby as my own, whose eyes were red, though not with tears. 'My friend', he said, extending his hand towards me. 'Please come.'

His home was appointed with a young woman in very short shorts who was brewing coffee in an atavistic fashion. Our host pointed out her gestures with some delight, and talk passed to Eritrea. As the diplomatic chitchat went on, more young women in very short shorts drifted in and out of the room. Louis looked quite delighted to meet so informal a member of the diplomatic corps.

We were served the ceremonial coffee, and felt many eyes upon us.

'The visa to Eritrea...' Louis prompted.

'For that, you must go to the embassy', our host averred. Women continued to come and go, talking, as Louis shrewdly noted, of something other than Michelangelo.

'Thank you, my friend', said our host, looking at us out of the side of his eyes, and behaving much as I might at home if a credulous millionaire stopped by for tea. His extended hand was looking for something more than the moist feel of my own.

'It's okay', Louis said, undeterred, as we went back to the Hotel Ghion, an improbably dark place that, by curious chance, reproduced the name of the festive geisha quarter in Kyoto – though the addition of an 'h' made all the difference between heaven and hell.

'Mohammed Aidid is staying in the hotel.'

Strangely, this was true. Aidid, the Somali warlord who had mocked and savaged American soldiers only a few weeks before in Mogadishu, was, by most accounts, the most wanted man in the world right now. Unlike most fugitives from justice, however, he had decided not to hie himself to Paraguay. He was resident in room 211 of the Ghion, perhaps musing on the comfortable benefits of Ethiopian Airlines.

We went along to his room, but on the subject of visas to Eritrea, the beauty of the day or even the merits of the local coffee, he and his press spokesman were silent.

——— —— —————— ——

Louis – in his cream suit and with his reddened complexion resembling, as was his habit, James Bond on an off day – looked forward to the drive ahead of us that was guaranteed to make use of all the clenched teeth and stiff upper lip we had been taught in school, even if the driver couldn't get us to Eritrea.

'There are three laws in international business', he said (as I remember it, perhaps fictitiously). 'The first is, "Always rent a car from an Italian. Especially if he is a she, and is ready to be asked out to dinner." The second is, "Come to a country where driving is an adventure, nothing like the eventless exercise it is at home". The third is, "Don't bother with discounts when you're on holiday".'

The fourth – it wasn't spoken – is, 'Don't trust an investment banker on anything other than finance'.

Two days later, the blue having hardly risen into the sky, a trim, stiff-backed man with greying hair – Nelson Mandela during his prison years, perhaps – appeared at our door. Behind him was a

Toyota Land Cruiser. He took time to show us its amenities. It had locks that didn't engage, seatbelts that didn't close. In the back were two cans of kerosene certain to suffocate us if the roads (or their absence) didn't do the job first.

'Can we play this?' Louis asked, extending a prized copy of *Live Dead* to our new friend and guide.

'Of course, sir', said the driver, and within seconds the tape player had swallowed the cassette and was spitting out strangled sounds.

Hours later, we were on the road. Our driver possessed a military bearing that inspired confidence in his ability to fight, if not to drive. The car bore the scars of previous trips to remind us that driving in Ethiopia is about as safe as eating a pig on the streets of Kabul. Both car and driver handled with the jittery fitfulness of an automatic-trained novice attempting a stick shift.

'Have you been on this road before?' I asked our leader.

'Yes, sir', he called back, over the protesting noises of the car. 'Once. Twenty-seven years ago.'

'A long time', I said.

'Yes, sir. I was a boy then. Travelling by bus.'

Very soon the broken huts and dusty lanes of Addis fell away and we were in the emptiness that is the very soul of Ethiopia. Occasional figures proceeded in a distant line across the emptiness towards the mountains. Petitioners dressed in white walked along the road to far-off churches, to celebrate the season. The purity, the dignity of the place moved me to a deeper part of myself.

The people of Ethiopia have a serious look to them – sharp eyes and heavy beards – and it is easy to feel as if one is moving through the landscape of the Apocrypha in the Bible. People wear crosses and ceremonial scarves over their white clothes. Devotion is intense. The rusted tanks and signs of recent fighting along the road were less potent than the tall, thin figures walking, walking, walking, for weeks, or months, on end.

Our driver allowed us to savour these beauties by flinging the rickety car into top gear and accelerating towards the occasional car that appeared before us, preferably around blind turns.

'What the hell are you up to?' cried Louis.

'Sorry, sir', he said, and then passed another car to put us into the path of an approaching truck.

'Bloody hell!' said Louis, the counter-intuitive benefits of travelling by road forgotten. 'Are you trying to get us killed?'

'Of course not', I mentioned to him under my breath. 'If he did, payment would not be forthcoming.'

Our driver saw another madman approaching on the mountain road and went into the wrong lane again, accelerating around the curve.

'I don't believe this!' Louis exclaimed, and then an exchange of words followed that were not diplomatic. We stopped for a little while to catch our breath, and our driver confided, 'Your friend, sir, is very strict. More strict than military.'

'He is', I conceded. We had already come across travellers who had decided to take the Ethiopian Airlines circuit, looking as if they had enjoyed the holiday of their lives.

The days went on, and often we were caked in dust so as to resemble brown snowmen in the back. To keep the windows closed meant certain death from the cans of kerosene. To open them was to admit all the accumulated sand and grit of centuries. Jerry Garcia would have sweetened the trip considerably, but he was now a pinched squeal of swallowed tape in the Land Cruiser's once state-of-the-art sound system.

'Let's just get to the nearest town and bail out', said Louis, who looked very close to accepting that there was a benefit in paying less and enjoying more. For a dangerous moment I felt that English masochism was going to accept defeat in the wilds of Ethiopia.

Fortunately, our driver protected us from this. 'No lunch', he began to wail piteously, when informed of the new hurry-up plan. 'No breakfast, no lunch, no rest.'

'No end', said Louis bitterly, and with that, communications between the two broke down for good. From then on, for day after day on unpaved roads, the Land Cruiser sending us jolting against its uneven roof, the kerosene directing the perfumes of Araby into our nostrils, the new jolts shaking the dust from us, the sand getting inside our eyes and ears, as if we were crossing the Sahara on camel, both my companions chose to speak only through an intermediary.

'Tell him to slow down', said Louis, as we hurtled around a truck, and then swerved back towards a precipice and the comforting depths of the Ethiopian plateau.

'Please, sir', said the driver. 'No lunch, no rest, no dinner.'

I could only imagine he was driving fast to get to the nearest meal. Louis was telling him to go slow and speed up simultaneously, and I happily translated as we lurched over small streams and the car coughed and collapsed by the side of the road.

We started up again and then, at one traumatic moment, another Land Cruiser zipped past us on the unsurfaced road, at a clip that would have qualified it for attention in a NASCAR rally. Minutes later we met it again, in a ditch, its passengers sitting dazed in the front seat.

'No lunch', cried the driver. 'No breakfast, no lunch, no rest.'

'No hope', said Louis, and I translated this into warm pleasantries to our guide.

Occasionally, in the midst of emptiness, our leader would see a man he had served with in the military. The car would stop, and pregnant reminiscences would be exchanged. Louis had taken to closing his eyes, as if to make it all go away, and burying his head in Richard Price's novel of gangland violence, *Clockers*. The driver spoke of his war experiences with a nostalgia growing by the minute.

In time, near-dead, we approached a hotel where Louis and the driver with whom he had long since stopped speaking were able to go their separate ways: the driver back to his much-missed home, Louis to the horror of spending less to enjoy more comfort, with Ethiopian Airlines. I, now permanently brown – a human sand dune with a simultaneous translation machine inside (which could only offer translations from English into English) – was moved to reflect on the beauty of travel.

We travel, I thought – looking fondly at my heroic old friend – for adventure and fun, to get away from the drudgery of our lives at home. We travel to court hardship and face the dangers and excitements that are themselves a kind of vacation and challenge for us. We meet people for whom our presence is nothing but opportunity, to take them out of the sadness and difficulty of their lives. The smiles exchanged on both sides have something of a nervous edge.

I looked again at my friend, the best travelling companion I knew, collapsed in an exhausted heap in one corner of the car, too tired even to argue the 'no breakfast, no lunch' conundrum, and thought how the more horrifying the trip, the more amusing it is in retrospect. But humour, everything, encountered on the road, is just a gateway. It only really moves us if it comes very close indeed to something that looks exactly like its opposite.

AN IDYLL IN IBIZA

KARL TARO GREENFELD

Karl Taro Greenfeld is the author of three books on Asia, most recently *Plague: The Inside Story of the Killer Virus that Nearly Crashed the World*, about the SARS virus. A former staff writer and editor for *Time* and correspondent for the *Nation*, he is currently Editor-at-Large for *Sports Illustrated*. Karl has lived in Los Angeles, Paris, Tokyo and Hong Kong, and now resides in New York City with his wife and two daughters.

Anya had warned me. Yet I had discounted her descriptions of her wealthy German family as exaggerated. Who wasn't a little embarrassed by their parents? But now, as I sat at the breakfast table with the Becker family and watched them spoon huge quantities of yogurt and muesli into their mouths, pile blutwurst, cheese and ham onto thickly buttered black bread and fit entire open-faced sandwiches between their lips, gulp carafes of orange juice and pots of coffee and then light and smoke Fortuna cigarettes before commencing another round of breakfast, I felt I had landed among some race of aliens who had an entirely different notion of what should constitute the first meal of the day. I sipped coffee and had some toast. Including Anya and myself, there were nine of us around the marble-topped table on the veranda overlooking the Mediterranean. The Balearic sun was already blazing; within an hour it would be so hot that you would feel too fatigued to do the folding and refolding required to read a newspaper and would instead place the paper on your face to shield you as you slept.

Anya and I had met six months earlier in Tokyo, where she was a model and I was a magazine editor. She was tall and blonde with grey-green eyes and a huge appetite which she struggled to curb for professional reasons. We were a good match in our similar fecklessness in our respective fields. She landed second-rate jobs – handing out winners' trophies at motorcycle races, doing fittings for obscure designers – while I worked at a magazine where the stories, even after several passes through the editorial process, would still fall short of professional standards. At some point as our careers were careening into prolonged skids, Anya mentioned that her family had a house in Ibiza. I immediately conceived the idea of fleeing there as an ideal escape from Tokyo. By the time we left for the Mediterranean, Anya's contract was about to be dropped by her agency and I had either quit or been fired from the magazine, depending on who you asked.

We arrived late at night, having taken off from Tokyo twenty hours earlier and touching down in London and Madrid along the way. We were greeted at the airport by Anya's mother, Baumy. She was a handsome woman in her early fifties, and her six-foot frame allowed her to carry the additional weight of middle age without appearing fat. She was bronzed and toned from hours of golf and boating, and though she was crow-footed around the eyes, from the nose down she still had Anya's complexion. In fact, as I looked from Anya to Baumy, I realised that I had just seen Anya's future. One could do worse.

Her family loved exotic cars, Anya had told me, and I had imagined fine Italian and English sports roadsters. My own family had been maddeningly prosaic when it came to automobiles, my father returning home every few years with a practical new station wagon manufactured in Sweden or Japan. I don't believe he even knew the names of European sports cars. But the car

Baumy led us to in the airport parking lot was not what I would call exotic – it was idiotic. It resembled the car the Munsters drove: a dark brown jalopy with huge fenders and headlights mounted on struts. The roof pitched forward at a jaunty angle, and there were no windows or doors. Nor was there a trunk.

'The buggy', Anya explained, using the family nickname for the vehicle.

We had to slide our bags through the open side of the buggy onto the back seat, and then I climbed in and tried to wedge myself in among the bags. Anya sat in front next to her mother. The car started with a noisy rattle like an old biplane and then Baumy backed out. Someone honked. She stopped.

I realised the car had no rear-view mirror.

Despite our burden and the car's poor visibility, Baumy passed aggressively, honked if drivers paused for a moment at traffic circles and generally threw the buggy into curves and roared down the straight with surprising confidence in the creaky suspension system. Crouched atop a duffel bag, I flinched as Baumy steered the buggy into passing lanes and then swerved back into line just before the headlights of oncoming traffic. Around hairpin turns, I noticed, like cautionary talismans, there were burned-out carcasses of other cars that had apparently taken these turns too fast. Anya's family, I would discover, seldom heeded warnings.

When we finally arrived at the family's house, I gaped at the view and my own good fortune at having washed up here. We had just passed through a dreary winter and damp spring in oriental Tokyo and had now landed in sunny, occidental Ibiza. I had somehow escaped from a crumbling life in Japan and landed in a place that seemed like paradise. The house was built into the side of a rocky spit of land and comprised a series of decks and balconies and stairwells from which spoked bedroom suites. On three sides of the house there was nothing but clear blue sea.

It would have been truly sublime, however, if Baumy had been restrained from decorating. As it was, she had managed to install the widest array of duck paintings and sculptures I had ever seen. Duck pastels lined one wall. On another were water-colours and oils of various forms of aquatic bird. There were even wooden ducks – they might have been hunting decoys – nailed to the ceiling. The spacious living room was diminished by all this avian decor, so that you had to turn sideways to get past the porcelain mallards.

But once you were clear of them, and out onto the veranda, there was the swimming pool and beyond that, of course, the Mediterranean. I stowed our bags in one of the bedrooms. I was looking forward to sleep and then a lazy day by the pool.

Instead, I found Anya undressing and sliding a black dress over herself.

'What are you doing?' I asked.

'We're going out to dinner', she explained.

'We've been on airplanes for two days', I pleaded. 'We haven't slept.'

She shrugged. 'My mother wants to take us to dinner, the whole family.'

Anyway, she pointed out, in Spain, one eats dinner very late.

I had no choice but to join them. I didn't want to appear ungrateful or, even worse, a weakling. I was beginning to sense, from Baumy and even from how Anya behaved around her mother, that this was a family that seldom second-guessed their impulses.

At dinner, I was introduced to an array of Beckers, all of them healthy and blond with strikingly defined cheekbones. There was the father, Lothar, a tall, skinny man with a face like James Coburn who didn't really seem to speak German, English or, actually, any language at all. He communicated with furrowed brows and stern nods. There were Anya's brothers, Wolfram and Gunther, Teutonic giants who had joined the father's business – an indus-trial concern that had something to do with ceramic pellets – and had similarly low golf handicaps. Much of the conversation among the Becker men revolved around golf, eating and ceramic pellets. There were the girlfriends, both blonde with strikingly perfect skin. I don't believe I ever saw either of them smile. And there was the younger sister, Emi, who wore her hair short and was even taller than Baumy and Anya. Even through my fatigue, I detected an attitude of dismissiveness directed towards me from the various women attached to the Becker clan. The men seemed happy enough to have me along, although I imagined they already knew I would never fit into their lives of golf and ceramic pellets.

That night, when I lay down on the platform bed, for an instant the pounding and sloshing of the nearby sea made me imagine I was adrift. Yet just as I was falling asleep with Anya's head in my arms, I was jolted awake by the scurrying sound of a small mammal, the dry clicking of tiny feet on the tile floor. I slipped away from Anya, lifted the mosquito net and, in the dark, made my way across the room to the light switch. We had kept the door propped open to catch a breeze and now, as I switched on the light, I saw, for a moment, an undulating brown and black pelt dart around a corner and out the door.

I tried to wake Anya to tell her that I believed I had seen a rat. She wouldn't be roused.

By the time we gathered for breakfast the next morning, I had concluded the Beckers were different from any family I had ever known. My parents had been writers. My brother had been autistic. We lived in a Los Angeles suburb and while we had been well off financially, my parents, both Depression-era children, had remained parsimonious and resourceful. My Japanese mother, for example, still hung clothes out to dry in the sun. My Jewish American father would sometimes wear my old suit jackets once I had decided they were passé. The Beckers, on the other hand, as I watched them inhale a round of soft-boiled eggs and guzzle glasses of milk, consumed a disproportionate amount of all kinds of resources. The lights in the living room had stayed on all night. There were pumps going in the swimming pool. Showers left running in bathrooms. Air-conditioners blasting in rooms with open windows. The women wore immense diamond earrings. Baumy had a diamond ring the size of a small walnut. The men all wore Rolexes. I had nothing against their gaudy excess – in fact, in some ways I aspired to it – but up close, it came across as joyless. I had never thought of myself as particularly bohemian, yet compared to these industrialists, that's what I was. Still, these were not the kind of people to question or wonder how we would get along; there were meals to be eaten, rounds to be played and internal combustion engines to be operated.

———————— · ————————

Every morning, Baumy would serve as quartermaster of the family motor pool, assigning cars to the various family members. In addition to the buggy, there were three jeeps – two of which were antique Willys that were as hard to drive as tractors – there was a Citroën 2CV, a BMW Isetta with one door that opened, a Land Rover and a small, practical Ford Fiesta that I quickly identified as the one vehicle I could actually operate. Baumy chose a pair of jeeps as our transportation for the day.

The men were scheduled to participate in a match-play tournament, which left the women and myself free for a day of yachting.

I clambered over the side of a white Willys to a bench seat in the back. Anya took the driver's seat, alongside Emi. In the other vehicle were Baumy and the two girlfriends.

The interior of Ibiza resembled the Pacific Palisades coastline where I had grown up, with similar olive and grey shrubs and rocky bluffs. The hills were scarred black from a recent brushfire, just as the Santa Monica Mountains above my house had often been when I was a child. We wound through a series of small parishes until we came to the marina.

I had expected some sort of monstrosity of a yacht, the nautical equivalent of the cars they drove, but instead was surprised by the 7.5-metre powerboat Anya and her sister were now untying. In fact, this boat, the *Ente*, or duckling, seemed far too small for so many large German women.

I quickly discovered that if you weren't doing anything on this boat, there was nowhere to hide the fact that you were idle. Baumy assumed the role of captain, taking the helm and directing Anya and Emi as they pushed off with a pole and made sure the boat didn't scrape its neighbours as we powered out. The girlfriends had arranged themselves on the forward deck of the boat, the spot where they were least likely to be disturbed. I had no choice but to take a seat behind Baumy, who, despite her bikini and Gucci sunglasses, conveyed a sort of U-boat commander-like solemnity on the whole voyage.

When we were out of the harbour, she turned to me. 'Do you have a privet?'

'A what?' I asked.

She frowned. 'For a boat. A licence. Can you drive a boat?'

'No', I informed her.

'Ach', she said, and turned back to the controls.

I felt useless.

Our destination was a sandy island a few kilometres from the marina, across a sea no rougher than a wooden floor and under a late-morning sun whose heat was heavy and oppressive.

As soon as we were out of the marina, all the women took off their bikini tops, and the small yacht was overwhelmed by breasts. Everywhere I looked, there were mammaries being jiggled by the application of sunscreen. On the prow, the girlfriends were like a pair of Aryan figureheads, warning other craft of this boat's female cargo. Emi and Anya sat beside me, their breasts bobbing with the boat's progress, and at the helm, Baumy stood defiantly, her chest sagging and heavier with age but still on proud display. For me, a mongrel mix of races and religions, to be loose amid this much pedigreed flesh was bewildering. I stayed seated and gazed port, the only direction in which there was no skin.

The only purpose to our voyage that I could divine was more consumption. We threw an anchor and waded ashore at a beach restaurant where an appropriately large amount of calamaris and steaks were ordered. There we were, five blonde women and me – I felt as incongruous as a trapezoid stranded among perfect circles.

Still, I should have been able to enjoy the company of five attractive women, and even found some vindication in my ending up here, on this Spanish isle, with all this pulchritude. If my various Tokyo and New York friends could have seen me then, I would have appeared as some sort of ridiculous winner in life's lottery of breast allocation.

But this was weird. In all my previous meetings with girlfriends' families, there had been questions: What did I do? Where was I from? What were my interests? Even if nobody cared about the answers to these questions, there was at least the pretence of getting to know each other. But ever since I had arrived at the Beckers' summer house, they had not evidenced any curiosity about me at all. These folks didn't know if I had a job, where I lived, if I had gone to college, had siblings, parents, infectious diseases. At first I thought perhaps Anya had informed them, but one night she explained to me that she hadn't really discussed me at all since arriving.

'They just don't worry about things like that', Anya would tell me later.

'What? You mean they don't worry about other people's lives?' I asked.

'Or their own', she shrugged.

Now, as I looked around the table and at Baumy laying down a platinum credit card to pay for the lunch, I was struck by a combination of admiration and resentment. How could they not care? I wondered. But then, as I watched these formidable women with their stern good looks and cruel confidence, I had to admit that this indifference must be what allowed them to cut an unfeeling swath through life. They weren't bogged down with the self-doubt that comes from introspection. And if they weren't busy scrutinising their own emotional interiors, then why should they waste their time trying to figure out mine?

They never slowed down, the Beckers; they lived like an army on the offensive. You woke up, you ate as much as you could, and you advanced. There was no time for reading, for wondering about the state of the world, for questioning why we were here. In the presence of the Beckers' sheer physical perfection and splendid material possessions, such matters suddenly seemed the peculiar concerns of hobbyists. I began to envy their thoughtless charge. It seemed a much more pleasant way to go through life than my path of pointless contemplation and ultimately self-defeating introspection. Beyond her appearance, hadn't that confidence been the trait that had drawn me to Anya?

After lunch, Baumy piloted the vessel through a narrow channel to a beach where we played a few rounds of paddleball. When we climbed back on board, Baumy fired up the motor and slid the throttle forward. We bounced over the waves for a few metres and then there was a thump and silence. She pulled back the throttle, jiggled the starter. Nothing. We were adrift.

Everyone turned and looked at me.

What was I supposed to do?

Then I realised, as the only person on board with a penis, it was my job to somehow address any mechanical problems.

'Karl,' Anya said, 'can you do something?'

This seemed a strange request. Anya knew me. I didn't even know how to operate a video camera. And here I was supposed to repair a boat?

'What? I'm no –'

Anya turned away. Emi, who was sitting facing me, covered her breasts.

'Shouldn't we call for help?' I said. There were numerous boats around us, bobbing just fifty or so metres away in the piss-warm Mediterranean. Wouldn't it be better to see if some salty sea dog could lend a hand?

No one paid any attention to my suggestion.

I stood up. Fine, I could pretend to know what I was doing for a few minutes until we called for help. I took up a position beside Baumy, who held up her hands and stared at the wheel as if it had betrayed her. Of course, in her view, it had. Cars, boats, planes – she also had a pilot's licence – these all served her, and their various shortcomings were matters to be addressed by men. (Later, while flipping through a family scrapbook, I would find a German newspaper clipping in which Baumy stood smiling in a potato field next to a wrecked Piper Cub. She had walked away unscathed from her own plane crash.)

'Did you hit something?' I asked as she flicked the starter toggle up and down.

'Of course not', she said.

A conversation ensued in German between the women, at the end of which Baumy dropped anchor. I was handed a diving mask.

I was to submerge myself under the boat to see what might be amiss. I didn't bother pointing out that I didn't know what to look for. The important thing, it seemed to me, was that someone went in the water. Now.

I splashed off from the rear platform, took a breath and dove under the boat. We weren't very deep, that fact I noticed immediately. I became a little claustrophobic in the 1.5 metres between the sandy bottom and the white-painted hull. I surfaced, took a breath, and then went back down again, exhaling a little as I did so. This time I rotated so that I put my hands on the hull. It was cold and slimy. There were streaks of brownish-green moss and algae growing on the fibreglass.

I twisted and kicked for the surface.

Back under again, I noticed a few silver-reddish fish and a submerged bottle. But I could find nothing wrong with the boat until I swam towards the stern and saw what looked like the top of an oversized coffeepot nestled in the sand. I quickly dove and retrieved it, surprised by its weight. I could barely lift it to the surface. As soon as I swung it onto the platform, I recognised it as a propeller. It was only as I looked down at the stripped shaft where our screw should have been that I realised it was *our* propeller.

Baumy leaned over, saw the propeller, and shouted, 'You broke the boat!'

'Me?' I shook my head, gasping from the exertion of diving. 'It was on the bottom. We must have gone over some rocks.'

Baumy had gone back to the bridge.

I climbed back on board. It was a little cooler now; the sun was lower on the horizon. And most of those boats that had been happily bobbing in the late-afternoon current seemed to have headed back to port.

'Can't you fix it?' Emi asked me.

'How?'

She shrugged. The Becker men, apparently, were called upon to repair things whenever necessary. I had no idea how to reattach a propeller.

'Wouldn't this take welding or soldering or something like that?' I asked.

I received no answer.

'Mama,' Anya said, 'we're sinking.'

She was right. We were noticeably lower in the water.

Now I felt like I was vindicated. We were going to sink. We would have to swim for the deserted beach and then spend the night huddling amid sand fleas and mosquitoes all because Baumy and the girls had been too stubborn to get help when it was there for the asking. Unless I could somehow patch the leak. I adjusted the mask and dove back into the water. The screw had been yanked back, cracking the mounting that held the propeller and leaving two large gaps where the cowling had been connected to the hull. It could be fixed, I thought; maybe even stuffed with shirts and towels so that the boat would stay afloat. All we'd have to do then was get a tow.

When I surfaced, I heard laughter.

'*Ciao, bella! Ah, bellissimo!*' a man was shouting. 'Why don't you come aboard?'

A nine-metre powerboat had pulled starboard. On board were a half-dozen vacationing Italian men who were now crowded so closely against the rail of their rear deck that their boat was listing to port. One of the Italians was manoeuvring their vessel closer while another was waiting to swing a pole onto the side of our boat. It was only at the last minute that the various Becker women reattached their bikini tops and gathered their possessions, preparing to abandon ship.

'What about the boat?' I asked.

No one was listening. A champagne cork popped. The girls giggled.

I grabbed my shirt and sandals and swung aboard the *La Vita é Tropa* – Life's Too Short.

The next day, I declined to go out with Anya or her mother, insisting that I wanted to stay around the house. This struck everyone in the family as curious behaviour. Why would anyone stay home when they could be out spending money, playing golf or risking their life at sea, in the air or on the road?

I took a seat on a stone bench on the patio and flipped through old issues of *Ola!* and *Bunte*. Before me was the dappled Mediterranean, the blue far more lovely when viewed from here than from the bottom of a sinking boat. Then, from behind me, I heard the same scratching and shuffling I had heard on our first night as I tried to get to sleep. I peered into the bougainvillea behind my bench, and froze. There, standing on its hind legs, was a huge black rat. It was a male, with surprisingly large testicles. And it clearly wasn't frightened; in fact, it seemed to be begging. We stood for at least ten seconds, the rat looking from my face to my hands. He almost seemed to shrug as he realised I had nothing to offer him.

Finally, he climbed over the bench, jumped down to the patio and then made his way onto a marble coffee table where he sniffed at an ashtray and empty water glass. He was fat and walked with an awkward waddle that made me think he wasn't used to carrying so much weight. I had never seen a wild rat so comfortable around human beings. I tried to shoo him away by waving my arms at him, but he merely paused and calmly observed my antics before sliding off the coffee table and waddling away, past the swimming pool.

I didn't feel like staying outside on the bench. I went inside and tried to explain to the housekeeper what I had seen, but I couldn't think of the Spanish word for rat.

When the Beckers returned home that afternoon, I mentioned the incident.

'He's called Hugo', Baumy smiled. 'He stays in the garden. He never comes in the house.'

'But he was in the house, I saw him', I said.

'No', Baumy said. 'He never comes in the house.'

The girlfriends nodded. They had been feeding Hugo fresh melon and *cerrado* ham.

'If you feed a rat, he will never go away.' As soon as I said this, I already knew that I had completely missed the point.

The boat had sunk. This was mentioned in passing during another breakfast. No one attached any great importance to the matter, nor was there any mention of the fact that it had been abandoned. The *Ente* had been raised and towed back to the marina and was now dry-docked at a repair yard.

As the rest of the family had planned to go out on the yacht of another industrialist family, Lothar asked me if I would check on the *Ente* and approve the 'reparations'.

For a moment, I considered objecting based on my ignorance of nautical matters. But who would listen?

'Fine', I assured Lothar.

'Make him do a good reparation', Lothar ordered with a smile.

Sure. Whatever. I drove the Ford Fiesta down the hill to the Maritimas Pepe, where I parked and entered a warehouse in which dozens of boats were mounted on trailers or suspended on padded yokes like giant slingshots. As I walked up and down the row of boats, looking for the *Ente*, a man in a polo shirt and jeans approached me and asked if I wanted to buy a yacht. His belt buckle was an eagle clutching what I assumed to be a fake diamond in its beak.

I explained that I was here about the *Ente*.

'Ah, yes', he nodded and retreated to his office. I found the Becker's boat next to a much larger, more impressive vessel which had a chunk taken out of the hull like it had been bitten by a giant shark. The man returned with a clipboard on which was written a long inventory with even longer numbers of pesetas listed next to each item.

He translated for me:

Bilge

Motor

Screw

Pump

Starter

Electrical system

Battery

The whole boat had been swamped, and everything needed to be replaced. The amount in pesetas ran into several millions. I tried to convert the figure to dollars, and wasn't sure how to assess whether or not this was a good deal. I had already assumed that the family overpaid for virtually everything. I didn't want Lothar to think I was an inept negotiator, however, so I told the gentleman to lower the fee by 100,000 pesetas.

'Done', he said.

None of the Beckers ever asked about the cost of the repairs.

That night, Anya and I went out for dinner and then to Pacha, a local nightclub. We didn't return until 4am and when we opened the front door and walked into the entry hall and dining area, where the lights had, of course, been left on, we saw

Hugo, the rat, or at least his ass, hanging out of a fruit bowl on the dining-room table, his black fur shockingly vivid amid the red, yellow and pink of the fresh peaches.

Anya screamed.

Hugo, startled, leaped from the bowl and skittered down the table leg. Panicked, he began running around the room, unsure of how to exit. Anya climbed on top of the nearest chair, shouting at me to do something.

'What?' I asked.

'Kill it.' Anya ordered.

'But they feed it –'

Anya pointed at the vermin now catching its breath in a corner, beneath a sideboard. 'Kill it.'

I looked around for a weapon. There were Hummel duck sculptures and a tray with a duck pattern.

Baumy had been woken by the commotion and now strode into the dining room, wearing a T-shirt which reached to the middle of her thighs. She and Anya exchanged words and Baumy retreated down the hall, re-emerging a few minutes later with a wooden racquet, which she handed to me.

'Kill it.'

I took the racquet, unsure of how to wield it, and advanced towards the rat, who was still cowering beneath the furniture. The poor fellow had overestimated his welcome and would now pay the price. The Beckers had no patience for mammals that didn't respect boundaries, even though the Beckers themselves had sent confusing signals. At my approach, the animal began to run back and forth, from one wall to another, desperate to escape.

I backed him into a corner, away from the shelter of the sideboard, and we both froze. Then he made a break for it, attempting to run past me towards Baumy, who stood with her arms folded over her chest, and Anya, who was still perched on top of a chair. I swung the racquet down and caught Hugo between it and the floor and pressed hard. I couldn't finish the job. I let up for a moment and the rat darted out and charged up my leg, over my stomach and down my other leg. Shaken, I swung the racquet at the floor, missing the rat as it scurried back to the shelter of the sideboard.

We were at a standoff when Lothar came into the room wearing nothing but a pair of purple bikini briefs. He took the racquet from me and strode up to the sideboard, kneeling down to see beneath it. He wiggled back a few feet and then, using the side of the racquet, swung hard, making a sickening, muffled thump as he beat the rat to death.

When he stood up, the wall beneath the sideboard had been splattered with blood and the black corpse was shiny with gore. He handed the racquet to me.

'Now we'll smoke a cigarette', he said.

I had to get back to Tokyo.

SNAKE KARMA

LINDA WATANABE MCFERRIN

Linda Watanabe McFerrin has been travelling since she was two and writing about it since she was six. A poet, travel writer, novelist and contributor to numerous journals, newspapers, magazines, anthologies and online publications, she is the author of two poetry collections and the editor of the fourth edition of *Best Places Northern California*. Her work has also appeared in *Wild Places*, *In Search of Adventure* and *American Fiction*. Other book-length works include the novel *Namako: Sea Cucumber* and short-story collection *The Hand of Buddha*. In spite of everything, she is still a great lover of snakes.

The fer-de-lance is an extremely venomous snake. More deadly than a rattlesnake, this pit viper is also missing its genetic cousin's one redeeming virtue – a warning rattle. It strikes suddenly, and when it bites, it injects a substance that is part neural toxin, part anticoagulant and part digestive enzyme, so that the process of digestion can begin at once. You don't have long once it bites: a minute, maybe two.

My friend Dixie and I weren't looking for snakes. We were looking for quetzals, scarlet macaws and other beautiful birds. We were staying at Lapa Rios, a resort built in the middle of Costa Rica's 'snake territory'. We'd been told the *terciopelo*, as the fer-de-lance is known in these parts (the name is Spanish for velvet), was in abeyance but that they *used* to turn up in the rooms. The resort was just north of Panama, on the Osa Peninsula – often called the armpit of Costa Rica – known for gigantic Corcovado, one of the country's most imposing national parks. Preserving hectares of virgin rainforest, it's the slithering grounds of some of the world's most dangerous *serpientes*. Our eyes were fixed on the thick, epiphyte-laden jungle canopy overhead, but in the back of our minds lurked serpents. Was that an eyelash viper snaking its way up the side of a tree? A *terciopelo* waiting patiently for us in the tall dry grasses of the savannah?

I'd just finished reading a cautionary tale by biologist Donald Perry. In his book, Perry relives his encounter with a local who was bitten by a fer-de-lance. The last time he saw this man, the fellow was in a rowing boat being taken back to the mainland, bleeding from his mouth and all of his pores. I shared this gruesome image with Dixie.

Before I left home, Lawrence, my husband, who is entertained by these things, had shared all of his snake stories. He told tales about rattlesnakes and boa constrictors, and recalled a *National Geographic* special he'd seen about the Amazon. In one exciting sequence, he recounted, an Indian guide went up-river to fish, leaving the main party. The Indian didn't return, and the party began to worry. Later, a six-metre anaconda came floating down the river with a big bulge in its middle. Unable to move, it was easily caught and killed. The party, suspecting the worst, cut open the snake, and there, of course, was their Indian guide – all in one piece, but no longer alive.

'I'm not going to the Amazon', I said dryly.

'There'll be plenty of snakes in Costa Rica', Lawrence had assured me.

I was suitably outfitted against snakes, I thought, as I prepared for our day-long hike through the rainforest. In spite of my warnings, Dixie wore high-top tennis shoes, which she replaced with rubber boots for jungle trekking. But I was prepared. I am the happy owner of the world's most perfect and attractive pair of waterproof Timberland hiking boots. These boots have hiked through Death Valley. They have been immersed in the muddy bottom of the Okefenokee Swamp.

'I'm safe from snakes', I announced to Augusto, our guide, proudly tapping my boot. He smiled and shook his head slowly.

'They bite through animal skins', he laughed. 'Your boots cannot stop them.'

I must have looked as deflated as a week-old balloon.

Then, suspecting the impact his comment had made, and in an effort to hearten us, he whipped out a snakebite kit to give us a demonstration of his medical prowess. This kit consisted of a small plastic glass, a match and a piece of cotton. According to Augusto, all jungle guides must carry them. To demonstrate, he doused the cotton in alcohol, threw it into the bottom of the glass, lit the match, threw it in too, and applied this to the selected body part – in this case, his side. Instantly, all of his flesh was sucked into the glass. The whole operation took only a few (maybe thirty) seconds – fast enough, he assured us, to prevent the poison's spread.

We headed off for our trek through the rainforest, but when we reached the edge of the forest, Augusto grew suddenly very serious. Strangler figs overshadowed land that had been planted and cleared. Banana palms formed long, leafy corridors edged in high, sun-bleached savannah grass. Augusto walked ahead of us, arms stretched out dramatically. He was muttering something in Spanish. I asked him what he was doing. 'I am clearing the path', he said, his eyes sparkling like beads of obsidian.

'Tell me what you are saying', I pleaded. He tried to teach me his chant. It was a strange poem in which Jesus figured. I repeated it in Spanish and promptly forgot it, trusting his odd mix of Indian and Christian lore to see us through. It worked like a charm.

That night Dixie and I prepared for bed in the usual way. We washed and hung out clothes that would never dry because of the damp. Every day they made great progress towards further fermentation. Every night we rinsed them out to reduce the thick, yeasty smell that swelled through our bungalow and threatened to throttle us. Then we filled the room with the muffled tattoo of our palms slapping against the sheets, condemning to perdition the insects that had managed to permeate our protective membrane of mosquito netting. We sat up in our beds with our maps, our reference materials and our Deet, an insecticide strong enough to remove nail polish and melt plastic. The rainforest's nocturnal breeze blew in through the rattan walls. It was quiet. Suddenly, high and tremulous, a scream broke the silence. It was right outside our door.

'Of course a woman's scream breaks the silence', I snapped. 'How predictable. How stereotypically lame.'

'Maybe she saw a cockroach', Dixie offered, bringing to mind a particularly large red specimen that we had encountered on one of our late-night rambles.

'Well,' I observed snottily, 'if she's afraid of bugs, she shouldn't have come to a rainforest.'

Dixie and I decided to ignore the scream and the commotion right outside our door – footsteps, yelling, muffled noises. Sensationalism. We didn't want to be bothered. Besides we had, by now, managed to kill every bug that crawled, wriggled or flew within our protective netting. Our seals were complete. We didn't want to invite further intrusion by breaking the mosquito net barrier.

At breakfast the next morning we heard the whole creepy honeymoon story. Two newlyweds had taken a moonlit walk down the winding resort steps. The bride told us that she had turned her torch on right outside our door. I had to wonder what life-saving instinct had prompted this action. There, inches from her sandaled foot, was a six-foot fer-de-lance. She backed up slowly. Then she let out her scream. Hotel staff arrived and dispatched the snake, but the newlyweds were sorry they'd done this. Toxic snakes are a fundamental part of rainforest ecologies, and they believed it was best to adopt a laissez-faire attitude. I told the new bride that we'd pegged her for some sissy girl, squealing because she'd seen a bug. She told us about the time a poisonous green snake had slid across her belly at a beach in Indonesia.

'Everyone says I have Snake Karma', she added with pride.

I considered this for a moment. Snake Karma. Here was a concept I'd never entertained. I flashed back on my own snake encounters: the cobra I'd come across on a run through a Malaysian cemetery; the highly poisonous European adder I'd encountered one morning when I was running alone on a mountain called Radmunderberget, in Sweden; the green mamba that liked to camp out on the top of my tent in Kenya; the rattlesnake I'd met one fine Easter morning on a hike in the hills near my Bay Area home. Perhaps the fer-de-lance on our doorstep had come calling for me, not her. Perhaps *I* have Snake Karma, my inner being shrilled, and I trembled.

That same morning a group of surfers reported killing a 4.5-metre boa constrictor at a spot a few kilometres up the coast. It had a coati-mundi still in its stomach. The coati-mundi is a pleasant animal that looks like a cross between an anteater and a raccoon. It's bite-sized for a 4.5-metre boa. The coati-mundi's eyes were apparently still open. The surfers said they'd cut up the snake and eaten some of it. It tasted, they said, like very tough chicken.

That night while preparing for bed I could not stop thinking about snakes. Adders, anacondas, asps, cottonmouths, coral snakes, kraits, king cobras and sidewinders – a host of vipers slithered about in my mind. Bugs wriggled and sawed their way through my mosquito netting, climbed clumsily over the coverlet, nibbled away at the exposed parts of my body. I paid them no heed. My Deet sat on the table beside my bed, my maps and my reference materials next to it. When Dixie finally turned out the light, I lay in the silent dark and waited. Do snakes have families? Maybe the *terciopelo*'s mate would come to the door in search of its murdered spouse. Maybe this time the serpent would snake its way into our room. I waited and waited with a strange mixture of fear and excitement. If snakes were my destiny, I was ready to meet them head on. After all, hadn't I managed to survive all my prior ophidian interactions? The sultry tropical breeze whispered through the bungalow walls, ruffled our leafy roof of palms. Insects and frogs filled the air with nocturnal arias. I fantasised about dropping in on the East Bay Vivarium when I got home and buying a cute baby corn snake. The minutes ticked by. I finally fell asleep.

Dawn broke, orchid pink, on another paradisiacal day – Eden, yes, but minus the serpent. It had been an uneventful night. No screams had broken the darkness, no fer-de-lance had paid us a midnight visit. The conclusion was unavoidable. It was the young bride, not me, that the snake had been drawn to, and like a jilted lover, my disappointment was soon replaced by indignation.

Later that morning when Augusto came by and tried to interest me in a hike, I was less than enthused. When he mentioned the incident of the snake and started to prattle on about venom and the victims of vipers, I looked bored. My sudden change in attitude seemed to take the guide by surprise. He turned his attention to Dixie while I leaned back in my chair, sipping at my fruity breakfast cocktail, and squinted off into the sunlight. Maybe later I'd read a good book, sunbathe, go for a dip in the pool. Snake Karma, I thought – who needs it?

SNAKING THROUGH ITALY

WICKHAM BOYLE

Wickham Boyle is the daughter of a foreign correspondent and an anthropologist, a combination that provided the perfect springboard for travel writing. After a peripatetic childhood, her first job was working for the international experimental theatre LaMama. Since then she has kept her bags packed and her mind open. When not on the road, she lives with her family in a funky loft in TriBeCa, a New York neighbourhood she and other artists helped colonise decades ago. She has an MBA from Yale and writes for *National Geographic Traveler*, *Forbes*, the *New York Times* and *Uptown* magazine, among others.

Experimental theatre is an acquired taste. You have to be willing to suspend disbelief and relegate logic to another quadrant of your brain. Such theatre usually involves a nonlinear plot and naked thespians writhing, chanting and emoting. There is commonly a sense of occupying a foreign dreamscape. In short, this can be the worst theatre of all, or it can be transporting. Being a producer of experimental theatre, especially on an international level, requires the ability to carry out tasks that would stop any other executive in their well-paid tracks.

I was the executive director of the LaMama Experimental Theatre company for a decade, nearly all of the eighties. In 1986 we produced a trilogy of Greek plays – *The Trojan Women*, *Medea* and *Elektra* – performed in an environmental setting. They were a sensation. The thirty-two-person cast represented nearly as many countries and all seemed comfortable emoting, singing and running through invented theatres nearly naked, screaming at the top of their lungs. The plays were chanted in a guttural version of ancient Greek with wildly percussive music and lighting provided by rough-hewn torches carried by the actors. The audience had to run after the performers in order to keep up with the action.

After one gut-wrenching, heart-stopping weekend we received a letter from a woman who claimed that the show had driven her crazy and she was now in therapy. Although I doubted the veracity of her claim, I wrote a condolence letter. Such was the power of our theatre.

The actors brandished swords, whips and a gigantic boa constrictor that wound its way around Elektra's neck in a harrowing climax that never failed to produce gasps from the audience. The snake was named Lola and was the responsibility of a cast member who had to share a room with her when the company was on tour.

In the summer of 1987 the LaMama Company and the *Trilogy* were in residence at the famed Spoleto Festival. This festival, held in the medieval jewel-box town of Spoleto in Italy's Umbrian hills, attracted artists and audiences from around the world. I sent the company off to Italy without me, believing I could use a summer with less drama and more fund-raising.

Three days after the company landed in Italy I received a frantic phone call from the stage manager. 'Lola has escaped!' The director and the cast were disconsolate. I told him perfunctorily to hop a train to Rome and buy another snake. End of drama. He called back the next day with a long tale of regulated commerce whereby snakes cannot be purchased as easily as in New York City. There was no time to waste.

My assistant got on the phone and in a jiffy I was riding off on my bike to make a quick tour of Manhattan's available boa constrictors. There wasn't much of an audition. I held the damn things – I actually like snakes, so this was fine; I wanted to see how they crawled, if they were too lively or if they had a sense of laconic movement that would hold the audience's attention. There was one with good colour, which seemed calm but not catatonic, so I took it. I gave the pet shop owner 250 bucks and called my assistant to pick up the newly dubbed Max in a cab. I thought the bike basket and bumpy pavement might be too much for the fledgling star.

Back in the office I had to decide the best way to smuggle Max into Italy. There was no time for import visas or cargo shipping. Luckily this was 1987 so security was pretty lackadaisical, especially entering Italy. But I needed to know what to do with this reptile. Most of the snakes I had travelled with were the human variety and I knew you just had to keep the cocktails coming to keep them quiet. I needed expert advice.

I called the herpetology department of the Bronx Zoo and after a protracted explanation the expert on duty sighed, 'You're really going to do this? I can't talk you out of it?'

'No,' I replied, 'you can only make it better for the snake.' I felt as if I had taken a hostage. The scientist told me that reptiles become very sedate, slow and quiet when they are cold. The trick was to keep Max chilly without freezing him to death. My herpetologist felt this could be achieved by putting Max into my carry-on bag the night before and storing him in the fridge. Once on the plane, if I put him on the floor under the seat, the generally chilly temperatures should promise an uneventful flight.

I felt relatively calm. After all, this wasn't a bag full of illegal drugs, it was a boa constrictor. But when I started to spin out various scenarios, I freaked out. I imagined the prospect of spending twenty years in an Italian prison for smuggling with the intent to produce experimental theatre. It was daunting. I had a glass of wine, fed Max a hapless mouse, carefully rolled him into a blue plastic shoulder bag and put him on the bottom shelf of the troupe's refrigerator with a giant note on the door: 'There is no food in the blue bag.' Theatre people are notoriously hungry, always grazing and eager for free food.

The next afternoon I picked up the blue bag, my purse and no luggage and headed for the airport. I would fly to Rome, catch a train to Spoleto, drop the package and head straight home again. I needed to get back to work and to my toddler. I took my aisle seat and slid Max under the seat in front of me. The plane was full, which worried me a little, but I fantasised about sleeping and waking up in Rome.

I had just drifted off to sleep when the woman to my right nudged me. 'Hey, what's in your bag? It's moving.' There was no time for small talk. I stood up, took my bag and headed to the back of the plane. I noticed that the cabin had become very stuffy and hot. I took a deep breath and looked squarely into the eyes of a stewardess standing next to the drinks refrigerator.

'Okay. Please listen to everything I have to say before you stop me.'

I thought she might think I had a weapon in my bag, or was a lunatic, but she leaned back and I let fly.

I told her about the play, about Lola the escapee snake, the fact that I was the producer and had a new snake, Max, in my bag and was on a mission to get him to Italy for the opening. I imparted what the scientist at the Bronx Zoo had advised, that we'd be fine if the snake stayed cold, but something had happened.

'The cooling system is on the blink', she said, cool as a cucumber.

Suddenly her back was towards me and she was shovelling cans of drink out of the refrigerator the way a dog flings sand at the beach. Cans of Coke and Seven Up were flying around. Tomato juice collided with beers. In an instant there was a snake-sized space in the fridge.

'Give me the bag', she said in Linda Blair's voice from *The Exorcist*. 'This is our secret. I am changing your seat. You will sit back here and watch that no one else goes in that refrigerator.'

Together we wordlessly picked up the cans and reorganised them. I took my new seat and pretended to sleep with one eye on Max.

When we landed, I waited patiently in my seat until all the other passengers had disembarked. The stewardess handed me Max in his bag and said, 'Good luck snaking your way through Italy.' She snickered and walked away.

I assumed a haughty, untouchable demeanour and wandered through Fiumicino Airport and the marvellously lax Italian security where one either walks through the green door for 'Nothing to Declare' or the red if you have something. I had *so* much to declare, but kept right on walking through the green door into Italy's humid summer air, marvelling, as I always do, at the palm trees lining the street. I grabbed a cab to the train station and purchased my ticket to Spoleto. We arrived two hours later and I waited under the gigantic orange Calder sculpture in the lower piazza with my now very lively hand luggage wriggling on my back. Luckily, in Italy a dancing bag elicits no curiosity. It was all *buon giorno* and *ciao* – business as usual in a town full of theatre people and Italians.

The stage manager apologised for being late and loaded us into a Fiat Cinquecento barely big enough for Max, let alone the three of us. He ground the car into first gear and began to wind down the hill to the Villa Redenta, where the actors were staying, and whose extensive grounds were to be the backdrop for the *Trilogy*, which was scheduled to open that evening.

The tension was palpable. Musicians were tuning up, and actors were doing voice exercises that could only be described as simultaneously alluring and unsettling. People were wearing togas, torches were blazing and the director was sulking. I greeted him and in his thick Romanian accent, he asked, 'And you have a snake, yes?' No small talk, no thanks for coming so swiftly.

I took Max out of his bag and the director sneered, 'But he is so small.'

I had jet lag; I was exhausted from finding, buying, transporting and smuggling a snake across international borders.

I looked at him and calmly transferred Max to his arms. 'Many actresses say the same about you and yet you seem to do a serviceable job.' I turned and walked out.

I caught a train to the airport, drank a cappuccino and flew home. The reviews glowed, the *Trilogy* was the toast of the festival and Max was taken to every chic party as an accessory worn on the neck of starlets or leading men. For a moment I considered that perhaps this presaged a successful career as a smuggler, but then I realised that only an emergency could contrive to create a scenario as implausible and wonderful as snaking my way across the sea.

Shakespeare once wrote: 'If this were played upon a stage now, I could condemn it as an improbable fiction'. But not if it was experimental theatre, where anything can happen.

THE AFGHAN TOURIST OFFICE

ALEXANDER LUDWICK

Alexander Ludwick was born in Seattle, Washington, and lived for several years in Guatemala as a child. He supports his travels by working part-time on a fish-processing boat in Alaska, though he would like to go to university someday. He enjoys travelling to remote and isolated destinations, and especially likes visiting Islamic countries and meeting their hospitable people. His next trip is to Haiti. This is his first national publication.

I rode in a yellow taxi towards Kabul International Airport, where I had been told the tourist office was located. It was November 2004, and I needed an extension on my Afghanistan visa. To get it I required a letter of support from the tourist office, which was well out of the centre of Kabul. On the way there the driver had to stop and ask directions at a shop, but finally we pulled to a stop in front of a run-down building that looked like an old schoolhouse. I paid the driver and walked through the gate.

Inside the perimeter was a guard's post full of teenage soldiers who jumped out and started gibbering at me, asking questions in Dari that I did my best to answer. One of them took my hand to shake it and refused to let go, no matter how hard I tried to pull away, all the while smiling and asking unintelligible questions. I kept repeating the word 'tourist', and finally he pointed to a man who was sitting at a desk in the middle of a patch of dirt in front of a building.

I walked over and asked him where the tourist office was. He looked at me, slightly puzzled, then after a minute of thinking pointed around the shabby-looking building, indicating that I should walk behind it.

The shabby building turned out to be the Ministry of Civil Aviation, and behind it there was a second, slightly shabbier building, with a sign in Dari over the door. About twenty metres to the left of the entrance, in an overgrown field littered with abandoned cars, broken-down tractors and the remains of military vehicles, a man was talking into a mobile phone. He was standing next to a hole full of garbage, and when he saw me he gestured emphatically for me to come over. Please don't let this be the tourist office, I thought to myself.

The man was wearing a worn checked blazer and wrinkled black trousers. He had unkempt wavy hair and a subtle, but definitely quite mad, gleam in his eye. He shook my hand violently and continued shouting into his mobile for another couple of minutes, while I waited patiently. He finally finished his conversation with a shout, and slipped the phone into his pocket.

'What you want?' he unceremoniously asked me.

'I need an extension on my visa', I replied.

'Come', he commanded, and walked towards the building. As I followed, he asked without turning to face me, 'How long you want?'

'One week should do it', I said.

He stopped abruptly, turned slowly to face me, looked me in the eye, and said in a low, threatening voice, 'No. You want one month.'

I didn't want to disagree with him, so I just gulped and nodded. He kept the intense eye contact going for a few more seconds, then burst into thunderous laughter. He shook his head at me and walked into the building, still chuckling. I followed, now really perplexed by this man. I was beginning to wonder if he worked here at all, or if I had even come to the right place.

He told me to wait in the hall and walked into another room, where he had a loud, rapid conversation with another man. The hall was decorated with signs in rainbow colours, obviously created using Microsoft Word and featuring titles such as 'President of Afghan Tourist Organisation'. The signs were hung over the hall's wooden doors, which were in dire need of a new coat of paint. The place looked like the inside of a poorly maintained Soviet-era schoolhouse.

While I was looking around the hallway, the man I had met in the field quietly crept up behind me. I was inadvertently blocking the hallway, and he suddenly screamed at me, like a German drill sergeant, '*MOOOVE!*'

I quickly scurried to the edge of the hall and pressed myself against the wall so he could pass. He looked at me as if I was the crazy one, and walked up the hall, shaking his head and laughing to himself. I followed him into what appeared to be his office, filled with worn leather furniture and a desk with a miniature red, green and black Afghan flag on it.

He surprised me again by shouting at me, in his heavily accented English, 'Geev me ten dollars!'

I was beginning to become indignant at this treatment, and I even went so far as to say, 'A please would be nice...' as I reached into my pocket.

'Hmmph,' he huffed, and added, 'you geev me money fast, I make you letter fast!'

I promptly handed over a ten-dollar bill.

He started to fill out the form for me when his mobile rang. He had set the ring tone to one of the latest Hindi pop songs. He looked at me and started humming along with it while bobbing his head, apparently expecting me to know the song and sing along. He then started singing along himself, and as he pulled the phone out of his pocket, he stood up and started dancing, swinging his hips rhythmically to the music and shaking his arms back and forth while singing even louder. At first I was stunned, but as his jig became more and more ridiculous, I had to try hard to restrain a laugh. It seemed he was truly trying to impress me with his dancing and singing skills, which were comically bad, and I was afraid I might hurt his feelings.

After what seemed like several minutes, he finally answered the call. The conversation that ensued sounded serious, and I could hear an authoritative voice speaking quickly in Dari. Then, while the speaker on the other end of the line was in the middle of a sentence, the man in front of me appeared to grow bored, and like an enthusiastic fan at a football game, he howled into the receiver, '*Hooooooooo!*'

I looked at him in utter disbelief, and heard the person speaking in outrage on the phone. He yelped again, this time selecting a higher pitch, and holding the receiver close to his mouth, '*Eeeeeeeeee!*'

He tried two other notes, one higher and one slightly lower than the first, before finally screaming, '*Aaaaahhhhh!*' in a high-pitched falsetto, like a woman falling from a high building. Finally he hung up the phone while the speaker was in the middle of an outraged sentence. He laughed proudly to himself, and went back to writing.

After a minute, he put his fingers to his mouth and let out a high-pitched whistle that caused a sharp pain in my ears. A few seconds later, a teenage boy ran into the room with a rubber stamp and then ran quickly out again. In an exaggerated motion, the man lifted the rubber stamp high above his head and with a murderous look in his eye, he plunged it down on the ink pad. Then lifting it again, he stabbed it onto the letter requesting the visa extension. He tossed the stamp and the ink pad casually into an open drawer, slammed it shut, slid my letter and a receipt for the ten dollars over to me, and told me, 'You go now!' Then he walked out of the room and disappeared through one of the doors in the hallway.

I was still somewhat in shock as I wandered outside. It wasn't until minutes later, when I was in a taxi speeding back towards town, that the incredible strangeness of my encounter dawned on me. I couldn't help but burst out laughing, causing the cab driver to look over at me, wondering about my sanity.

LEFT LUGGAGE

JEFF GREENWALD

Oakland-based Jeff Greenwald is the author of five books, including *Shopping for Buddhas*, *The Size of the World* and *Scratching the Surface: Impressions of Planet Earth from Hollywood to Shiraz*. He is a contributing editor for *Yoga Journal*, *Tricycle* and *Travel+Life* magazines, and serves as Executive Director of Ethical Traveller, a global alliance of travellers dedicated to human rights and environmental protection (www.ethicaltraveller.org). In the course of his career, Jeff has celebrated Passover with Paul Bowles, circled Tibet's Mt Kailash with a demoness and interviewed the Dalai Lama about *Star Trek*. He launched his stage career in 2003 with a one-man show, *Strange Travel Suggestions*. Visit his website at www.jeffgreenwald.com.

Most travellers have learned the truth of semanticist Alfred Korzybski's memorable maxim: 'The map is not the territory'. And many of us, I think, have learned this through direct experience in India.

Everyone has an image in their mind's eye, an expectation of what India must be like. And each visitor, no matter their wealth or circumstance, is given the same lesson: no matter how many maps or guidebooks you study, you haven't a clue what India is like until you physically step off the plane.

It isn't even necessary to get out onto the seething streets, to gawk at the heartbreaking slums lining the railroad tracks or wander through the marble-halled museums filled with Buddhas and daggers. My own education, for example, began at Calcutta's airport.

Granted, this was some time ago. I'm sure that by now Netaji Subhash Chandra Bose International, formerly Dum Dum Airport, has come of age, redesigned around an architectural scheme filled with brightly lit food courts and duty-free boutiques selling Shiseido fragrances and iPod slipcases. At the time of my first visit, however, Dum Dum was a place that looked like it had seen its day, or perhaps five minutes of a day, at some long-forgotten moment between its ribbon-cutting ceremony and the arrival of the first British Overseas Airways Corporation flight. The floor was a collage of red betel juice stains, blue ticket stubs and green *bidi* butts. Above my head, bug-filled fixtures flickered a sickly yellow. Mosquitoes dined on the arriving passengers. As for the toilets – as they say, let's not go there.

All this, I had expected. It was when I found baggage claim that I realised something was terribly wrong. Wrong to the core. Westerners, you see, tend to take luggage carousels for granted. If airports around the world look more or less alike, their baggage carousels are pretty much cookie-cutter replicas: oval- or circle-shaped tracks of neatly overlapping metal fins, moving in a smooth, choreographed motion. The bags emerge from a point slightly above us, from behind a curtained duct. There is a momentary sense of suspense as they bow slightly, slide down a moving rubber ramp and halt with a thud against a hard rubber bumper that moves in synch with the polished fins. It's a beautiful thing.

At the Dum Dum baggage claim, the single carousel was nearly annihilated; it looked like a model, in miniature, of an Indian train derailment. The metal fins were bent, and forced their way ahead with a shrieking, grinding noise, like sheet metal being fed into a paper shredder. The little burlap curtain, where the luggage usually makes its entrance, had been torn off. Even the rubber rail had been removed, no doubt reincarnated as the jury-rigged bumper of a Calcutta taxi.

The conveyor ramp leading from the luggage chute to the carousel was jammed, and stuttered in place like a disembodied frog's leg being shocked, repeatedly, by school students. After an interminable wait the bags began to appear. Each suitcase emerged nakedly at the top, pausing as if terrified by the chaos below. Then, shoved by the bag behind it, the case tumbled end-over-end down the spastic belt towards the sharp silver fins, which shucked it like an oyster. The split bag would then smash against the naked metal rail and burst open, spewing its contents in a wide arc across the spittle-rimed floor. The metal track itself was covered with lingerie and earplugs, batteries and sneakers, aspirin and stuffed elephants. Panicked passengers rampaged through the jetsam, trying to recover their underwear and trousers.

A few months earlier, I had been sitting in a long wooden tourist canoe, following another boat along Nepal's Sunkosi River. Our boatmen were local boys. The rains had been late, and the boys were unskilled. Halfway through our journey, we came towards a patch of whitewater. The canoe ahead entered first. It flipped instantly, tossing its passengers, along with their high-end binoculars and camera gear, into the muddy water. Our boatman was wide-eyed, and the passengers braced for disaster. All, that is, but one. A compact but muscular woman from Maine darted forward, expertly balanced. She seized our Nepali pilot by the hips, and tossed him aside. Grabbing the oars, she navigated the rapids without incident.

The lesson had not been forgotten. I positioned myself directly in front of the chute. The moment my suitcase appeared I leaped onto the carousel and darted up the ramp, ignoring the shouts of the security guards and the cries of the other passengers, whose vests and panties clutched at my ankles like Sirens. The bag tipped forward; I grabbed it by the flanks and, with enormous effort, wrestled it past all obstacles and onto the floor.

——— — —— ———

Many people imagine that, as a travel writer, I know how to pack. This is completely false. I have no idea what to take on a trip. If I'm going to Calcutta for a week, I figure, okay, I'll be going for a walk in the morning and I'll sweat through a shirt. I'm also going to walk during the afternoon and evening. So I'll be needing three, maybe four fresh shirts a day, and figure it's going to be four days before I can find the time to do a wash. By the time I'd finished my preparations, I was bound for Calcutta with a suitcase filled with sixteen shirts, eight pairs of pants, sandals, hiking boots, dress shoes (because you never know), socks, sketchbooks, two cameras, an inflatable mattress, copious toiletries and a vintage Scrabble game in an antique metal container.

My suitcase weighed forty kilograms, and the moment I tried to carry it out of Dum Dum Airport the truth of the matter tapped upon my spine. There was no way I was going to haul this behemoth through the streets of India. The only solution was to extract the absolute essentials, put the thing in storage and reclaim it on my departure from Calcutta.

My first thought was that I'd have to find a tourist hotel, and leave the bag in a storage room or behind a desk. But as I glanced around the baggage claim area, I spied a squarish, hand-lettered sign above an open door: LEFT LUGGAGE. A classic arrow pointed redundantly downward, towards the doorway itself. My suitcase had no wheels, so I pulled and hefted it, in stages, towards this specialised exit. Arriving at the doorway, I glanced through it. There was nothing but a huge, empty field: a lost world which seemed to go on for ever, in all directions, under the blinding Calcutta sun.

It was a million degrees outside. A shimmering haze rippled above the ground. But in the distance – could it be? – stood a house of some kind, a tiny hut at least a kilometre away. There was no road to speak of, just a cracked and overgrown concrete pathway covered with spiky weeds and broken glass. Chipmunks ran to and fro. Emaciated cattle grazed on the horizon, and their dung – fresh, dried, and all stages in between – was piled everywhere. I could barely make out the faraway shack, but it did seem to have some kind of sign on the side, something that might have said 'Left Luggage', but which might just as easily have been an advertisement for car tyres, in Hindi.

India's infamous sun beat down on the field, and on my neck, as I dragged my impossible bag along the concrete track. Perspiration soaked through my clothing, and stung my eyes. The broken pathway scraped the corners of my suitcase, and the little plastic feet shredded like hard cheese. Shards of glass tore my sneakers. There was no avoiding the dung, and each time my feet or my case encountered the droppings of a sacred cow a foul brown track followed me along the path.

For many minutes, the shack seemed to get no larger. Finally, with a parched tongue and peeling shoulders, I staggered onto the front step of the square white building. Inside it was cool and dark. There was a single wooden desk, long and venerable, a remnant from the British Raj. Standing behind it, silent and attentive, was an elderly man dressed in an immaculate white *kameez*. With his white moustache and starched collar, he looked like someone straight out of Gandhi's Congress Party. Behind him, through double doors, was the storeroom, filled with high wooden racks. They were covered with ancient luggage that looked like it had been checked in by Rudyard Kipling.

Mustering my remaining strength, I heaved my suitcase forward. The man pressed his eyebrows together, and he began filling out a small tag with the stub of an oversized pencil. His eyes peered up at me.

'Your good name?' he enquired.

'Sir...' I croaked. I was dehydrated, sweating profusely, and at the point where my anger and frustration were ready to erupt and parboil anyone within earshot. 'Sir. Getting here, to this place, was an absolute nightmare. No journey through hell, no walk over glowing coals, could have been worse. Do you understand me? It took me thirty stinking minutes to get my bag to this stupid place. There are no handcarts, no shuttles, and the pathway is a wreck. It's an outrage. An insult! Tell me, if you can, what is this room doing so far from baggage claim? What's the *point*? Shouldn't you be *in* the baggage claim area? Wouldn't that make *sense*? How the hell are people supposed to...'

As I ranted on, the man reached down with both hands. On the desk before him was a huge journal, bound in rich leather, with a ribbed spine. It looked thick enough to be the Calcutta telephone directory. The spine was blank, but on the cover was a single word, stamped in gold script:

Complaints

The man pushed the book forward, and it slid across the dry wood with a hiss. 'Yes', he sighed. 'Please...please, you make a note of this.'

'Oh, I'm going to make a note of it, all right. A *long* note. This is unacceptable. I'm going to give you airport *wallahs* a piece of my mind.' I declined his pencil, and pulled an indelible pen from my passport case.

I opened the book, and began flipping through the pages. The tome was of some antiquity, with the earliest entry dating back to the late 1950s. I don't know when the Dum Dum Airport opened for business, but it is quite possible that the book was inaugurated during the facility's first year of service. The first entry, in fact, was written in 1958, in ink. The blue script was fading, but the words were clear:

Best of luck viz your new endeavour. Airport clean and modern. This storage facility, however, is inconveniently distant from the terminal. Please address this problem for the convenience of your patrons.
Kind regards,
R Sivarakham, Esquire.

Similar entries followed, firm but polite. I flipped ahead a few pages to 1966. These were the halcyon days of the Magic Bus, which plied the overland circuit through Europe and Central Asia, migrating through India before reaching the hashish-clouded teashops of Kathmandu. In fact, a troupe of hippies had passed through the airport in July of that year. Their spokeswoman offered a comment:

Namasté, but why is the Left Luggage place so far from the airport? It took us forever to get here, man. And the cement is so hot that my thongs melted. No lie! Anyway, if you can fix this, we thank you in advance. Otherwise Mother India is the best. Janis.
(PS: Also, the pathway from the luggage place to here is broken in a few places, those rocks are sharp. Owww!)
(PPS: Much fine weed growing in the field, the cows are very friendly!)

Many pages later, in 1974, an Indian visitor named Agarwal weighed in:

Sirs: If you will not change the location of the Left Luggage depository, at least attend to the pathway from the airport. I sprained my ankle in a pit, and my wife lost the heel of her shoe. Also the livestock should not be allowed to roam free. Their mess is not appropriate at an international air terminal. Requesting your immediate attention to this matter.

The tone of the discourse had hardened somewhat by 1980:

What the hell were you thinking, putting this place a kilometre from the airport? I know the place is called Dum Dum, but it's named after the bullet, not the imbecile. Suggest you send one of your peons to carry a bag both ways, you will find it is a huge pain in ass. Correct this problem at once or I will fly into another city on future trips to India.

In 1987:

What the hell is Left Luggage doing so far from the baggage claim?! For the love of Christ, or Buddha, or Krishna, or whoever! Can't you at least fix the goddamned path?

There were many entries I could not read, in every imaginable language, but even the most superficial command of French, German or Spanish revealed an increasing, and increasingly futile, sense of outrage. By 1989, the pleas had become almost absurd:

PAVE THE ROAD. PAVE THE ROAD. PAVE THE ROAD. PAVE THE ROAD. PAVE THE ROAD. PAVE THE ROAD. PAVE THE ROAD. PAVE THE ROAD. PAVE THE ROAD. PAVE THE ROAD. PAVE THE ROAD. PAVE THE ROAD.
(PS: Please see footnote, below.)

I glanced down:

PAVE THE ROAD!

Page after page, spanning five decades and hundreds of pages, the same complaint – until, a week before my arrival, the most recent pilgrim had simply uncapped a thick laundry marker and scrawled, across two pages:

FUCK YOU

I looked up from the register, and regarded the little clerk with astonishment.

'Have you looked through this book?'

The man wagged his head, an ambiguous gesture that could mean anything. I lost it.

'Well check it out, mister! Every complaint is the same! Thousands of them, exactly the same!' I picked up the book then smacked it on the desktop, raising eddies of dust. 'What's the use of this charade? Nobody even sees this book!' I shouted. 'It's never been opened by anyone with the slightest bit of authority! Are you aware of this? Do you care? Yes? No?' I took a single, very deep breath. 'Sir. Listen carefully to what I'm about to ask you. Is there *any way* to get *any official of this airport* to spend *five minutes* with this book?'

The man nodded pleasantly, and pushed the volume back towards me.

'Of course', he pronounced. 'Please. Make a note of it.'

LET THE BUYER BEWARE

EDWIN TUCKER

Staying true to the flightless kiwi of his native New Zealand, Edwin Tucker rode his bicycle 36,000 kilometres across twenty-two countries. Now living in Canada, he is writing the account of his two-and-a-half-year journey, and is still dreaming of the open road.

The harsh open vastness of the Tibetan steppe is largely devoid of life; even oxygen is scarce. The sun blazes as if I have climbed closer to it than my present four kilometres above sea level. Below me, a grey ribbon of gravel, the unpaved road, lies across the yawning desert plains of southwest Tibet. Even without the effects of altitude, the scenery around me is breathtaking. The richly coloured ochre and graphite outcrops of the Himalayas shore up a navy-blue sky as if a deep sea has been turned into the heavens.

Spring is usually associated with the colour green, but not here. Not where the altitude and cold have squeezed the water out of the air to a humidity level of 10 per cent – twice as dry as the Sahara. There is nothing green here in April: no trees, no bushes. Wispy yellow straws of grass are the only vegetation.

Despite its desolation, I am not alone in riding my bicycle across this seemingly empty landscape. Also bumping along the Freedom Highway – the road from Kathmandu, Nepal, to Lhasa, Tibet – are two companions, Matt and Scott. Matt, from Australia, is cycling home from Scotland; Scott is an American, and like me he is riding his bicycle around the world. We have banded together to form our own tour group, birds of a feather on otherwise different migration routes. Staunchly independent and bloody-minded to the extreme (how many other people would ride a bicycle across the 'Roof of the World' to prove a point?), we will not let authority or the world's highest mountain range stop transcontinental progress under our own steam.

We ride more or less together, but the huge scale of Tibet spaces us out and into our own worlds. Matt stops to try to capture the wonder of it all on film. Further on Scott puts down his bike and attends to the only colourful flora around, flourishing and messy stowaway bacteria, gut flora from the waters of Nepal. I ride on, stopping a few kilometres upwind for my own contemplation of the sublime surrounds.

As luck would have it, I have chosen to take a breather within calling distance of the only local I have seen beyond the few small Tibetan villages we have cycled through in the past week. A shepherd, parting a way through his sparse flock of sheep, saunters over. Dressed in dusty black trousers and an earthy sweater, he could be in his late twenties, though his face is haggard from the effects of his harsh life and environment. As with most rural Tibetan men, his long black hair is held in a braid beneath a traditional red headband. He makes a proud figure, as tough as the resolve needed to survive out here.

I give a small wave and say, '*Tashi delek*' – Tibetan for hello. He addresses me with, 'Hello. Pen.'

Someone somewhere is no doubt basking in self-deification with the thought that they have done the world a great favour by handing out pens to children in countries of need. Though this may have originally seemed like a benevolent gesture, a generation of travellers has suffered from those best intentions. Hands outstretched in welcome are now offered palm up in a pandemic bumming of pens across all of Asia. Even here, at 4000 metres, the interaction between a Tibetan and a New Zealander – the only two people in sight on this vast plain – begins with the local greeting to any Westerner, 'Hello. Pen.'

Ironically, the Tibetan has struck – albeit too late – the mother lode of pens. I had bought a hundred snazzy souvenir pens in Iran as gifts to hand out to the friendly people I would meet on my journey to thank them for their hospitality. As one might be nervous when carrying excess cash in their wallet, I had been anxious crossing the pen-hustling continent with a coveted cargo of writing instruments stashed in my panniers. Yet across so many kilometres of cycling, I had met so many worthy people that I had flitted away my supply and was now down to my very last personalised pen. This single pen was tremendously important to me; it was a connection with the ninety-nine other brethren in possession of my 'Around the World By Bicycle' pens.

Just in case I don't understand English, the Tibetan shepherd resorts to that age-old hurdler of the language barrier: he repeats himself. 'Hello. Pen.'

Now, as keeper of the sole remaining souvenir pen at my disposal, I have become the pen miser. How can I try to educate the world's most populous continent that tourists are not all walking pencil cases? A stand must be taken. I decide to educate anyone who asks – starting now, with this man. I do not have a pen to give away. I have a *valuable* pen. This pen is of such great importance to me that I would not trade it for anything less than a life.

'*Tashi delek*. Sheep', I reply. I don't know the local word for his charges, so I point towards his collection of thin cream-fleeced animals as I attempt to teach him a lesson.

Puzzled, he swivels around to look where I'm pointing. Dismissing my nonsensical reference to his two-dozen ewes, some with spring lambs, he returns to what he knows of dealing with foreigners. 'Hello. Pen', he entreats.

After acting like the stereotype of a New Zealander, pointing enthusiastically towards his sheep, I try a different tack.

I produce *the* pen from my handlebar bag. I baa like a sheep and point to the flock with one hand, then toggle the pen forward with the other, mimicking an exchange. With missionary zeal I am going to extremes to save my fellow travellers from this ubiquitous greeting. Obviously, I think, it would be a cold day in hell before a shepherd would give up a precious spring lamb for a twenty-cent pen. This may be Tibet, but as a nation, China produces twenty-nine billion pens annually – more than twenty for each and every one of its men, women and children.

By now Scott and Matt have come upon the scene of a cycle tourist baaing, pointing to some sheep, and holding a pen, all the while being watched by a perplexed Tibetan. The shepherd turns to them imploringly, already sharing with them an affinity regarding my mental state. Though we foreigners speak the same mother tongue, even they are struggling to make sense of my one-man crusade to translate value. 'I'm trying to teach him that pens don't grow on trees', I call over my shoulder.

After more miming from me, the shepherd finally understands. Astounded by my proposal, he throws his arms in the air and walks off. Either he is genuinely appalled at my gall to liken the value of one of his sheep to my pen or he is trying to negotiate a better price. Regardless, he gets my point: in my mind, my pen is equal to his sheep. His understanding is further illustrated when he returns to try and redress the balance of trade. He says his third word in English: 'Money'.

Feigning shock, I continue the ruse that my pen is every bit as valuable as one of his sheep. Having none of it, he strides away to his flock and stoops. Then he comes back with the nearest lamb, turning it under my nose while explaining its value and merits in Tibetan.

Docile and meek as only a spring lamb can be, this cute little animal in a wool tuxedo murmurs a pitiable bleat as it hangs draped across the shepherd's palm.

My heart softens, as does my resolve, at seeing the innocent lamb. However, the haggling gauntlet has been thrown down. I noisily click the pen a few times, make a show of impressing myself by writing on my palm, and theatrically place the pen in my shirt pocket, ooing and ahhing while presenting it as a real prize.

The shepherd harrumphs and nods as he makes a grab for the pen. Uh-uh! I'm not going to fall for that one. This will be an exchange. Not believing that he'll actually go through with it, I call his bluff and hold out my palm while clasping the pen tightly in the other. The lamb is placed in my empty palm and I let go of the pen and drop it into his fist. Done. He has his pen. I have me a lamb.

I have me a lamb! Is this for real? As disbelieving as my cycling companions, I make to ride off, wondering if this is some kind of Tibetan joke. The shepherd, admiring his shiny new blue plastic pen, has already walked away, apparently happy.

It's not easy to ride a fully loaded touring bicycle on an unpaved road while holding a live lamb in one hand. Wobbling on the bike, I continue on the road to Lhasa, glancing back at my trading partner – who watches me leave with no obvious concern. Riding beside me, Scott and Matt ask me what I have just asked myself, 'What are you going to do with the lamb?'

I may come from New Zealand, where sheep famously out-number people ten to one, but I'm also a vegetarian riding a bicycle around the world. The irony weighs heavy. In trying to teach a Tibetan about value, I have just bought a white elephant in sheep's clothing.

'It could be our mascot', offers Scott. 'Or lunch', he adds.

As the shepherd with his flock starts to diminish in the distance, the lamb starts to baa piteously for its mother.

If I am not going to slaughter and eat this month-old lamb, then I have to return it. The fun is over. I turn the bike around.

The lamb, seeing the flock now getting closer, becomes more and more animated, making me place it on the ground before it causes an accident.

I get off the bike and approach the shepherd. The lamb scrambles back to the flock. 'Hello. Pen', I call to him. I have given back his lamb and I want my pen back.

But he seems to feel that all transactions are final and no refunds or negotiations will be considered. At least that's what I think he means when he pulls out his knife.

'Whoa! Hey, buddy, that's going a bit far, isn't it?' I say as I stop in my tracks. Literally drawing a line in the sand, the Tibetan doesn't threaten me physically with his steel but stabs the dagger into the ground between us.

I see that I have gambled and lost. He called me on *my* bluff. As much as I liked the pen, so does he. He's keeping it.

Well, I think, since he's going to be like that, I'll just collect my lamb and be on my way. I wade into the flock, and the sheep scatter as I grope for a lamb, any lamb. The shepherd starts shouting and shows genuine anger. Leaving his dagger in the dirt, he produces a sling, the same simple device the shepherd David used to fell Goliath. This is getting serious.

He picks up a stone, places it in the crook of the sling, and sets it spinning, his fiery eyes fixed on me, screaming his incredulity that I would dare reject his lamb and go for another. Dread rises, along with the hairs on the back of my neck.

I stand stock-still as the stone is released. It hums through the air at a safe distance from my head. I'm glad I'm still wearing my bicycle helmet. I give up the idea of leaving with a lamb, apologise and ask for my pen back. 'Hello. Pen.'

But the Tibetan doesn't want to give up his pen. Scott and Matt are ready to jump to my defence as the sling is loaded with another stone and set in orbit above the shepherd's head. Now a screaming maniac, he is definitely more than I'd bargained for. I walk back to the bicycle with my hands in the air; I am a man in defeat. Punctuating that point, another supersonic crack splits the air and the stone sings past my ear.

Back at my bicycle, Scott and Matt are already doubled over in laughter and having a hard time holding on to their bikes. I start to laugh too. We soon find that hilarity is an aerobic exercise. There's not enough oxygen to sustain laughter at this intensity, yet gasping to catch our breaths causes us to laugh even more. A lack of air, a ridiculous situation and a dumb lesson have us intoxicated.

This was supposed to be a simple lesson in intercultural exchange. In a position of power, I was the tourist lording privilege over a humble shepherd. Now humiliated, I think: how can I tell this story back home? It should have been a steal for any self-respecting New Zealander, but I couldn't trade a lamb for a pen. My hands are empty, like my head and the air.

AN AWARD-WINNING PERFORMANCE

DEBORAH STEG

Deborah Steg took her first transatlantic trip when she was two months old. Since then she has been smitten with a passion to travel. She lives in New York City.

As I was walking along the Croisette towards the far end of the Bay of Cannes, I noticed a large crowd in the distance resembling a beehive surrounded by worker bees. It was a balmy spring afternoon at the height of the Cannes Film Festival, and the sun was just starting to set. The sky was a deep cerulean blue with ribbons of white clouds streaked across the horizon. This location seemed too far from the centre of town for a photo shoot or celebrity interview, and as I approached I realised that it was just locals and tourists dressed casually and gathered curiously around the aftermath of an accident. Rather than styled and coiffed celebrities, there were several policemen on the scene and a large tow truck that was blocking the lane that led back to the centre of town.

Somehow I knew I would find my mother in the mêlée – and there she was, chatting to a very distressed looking Claudia Schiffer doppelganger. She didn't even notice me come up behind her. From what I could piece together from overhearing the eyewitnesses' accounts to the police, a car had come careening down the Croisette too fast and hit one of the parked cars, a white Mercedes-Benz that was now parked kerbside and looked like its driver's side had been used in a crash test. The other vehicle, a Fiat, had not fared as well. The car had flipped over upon impact and looked like a large sardine can.

A tall, athletic and agitated German was talking to another policeman, or at least making his best attempt to communicate half in German and half in English. The Frenchman tried to comprehend as best he could and asked questions in his best Franglais. There was a lot of hand-gesturing and pointing by both the German and the policeman. As they were finishing up, the tow-truck operator lifted the white Mercedes in one effortless movement and placed it on the flatbed behind him. He then manoeuvred the steel claw to the overturned metal box and placed it behind the Merc. The German hopped up beside the driver and the tow truck drove off. All this transpired within minutes of my arrival.

It was the summer of 1989 and I had come to the Cannes Film Festival hoping to make some valuable contacts in the film industry. I had spent a part of every summer in Cannes for as long as I could remember, and when my mother heard I was coming down for the festival, she couldn't resist tagging along. The oddest occurrences happen on trips with her – and this trip, it appeared, would be no exception. She can strike up a conversation with any stranger and become instant friends with them – and soon come away convinced that person is the greatest thing since the French mashed olives to make tapenade.

So there she was with Ulrike, the German girl whose boyfriend, it turned out, had just left in the tow truck. He'd left her behind when she had stepped away to find a WC on the beach. My mother had been practising her high-school German on the poor girl, and in only a few minutes they'd become dear friends. The crowd dispersed quickly once the flatbed left and the police drove away. The only people left were my mother, the German girl and a tall, thin man dressed in khakis and a polo shirt, carrying a red and blue duffle bag. I wasn't sure what his role in all this was.

Ulrike wanted to make her way to Nice to join her boyfriend, and she needed to find a place to exchange some money so she could get a cab. My mother explained to me that the German couple had driven down to Monaco from Stuttgart for a romantic weekend and to catch the Monaco Grand Prix. They had driven down a day early and since the Grand Prix overlapped with the final weekend of the Cannes Film Festival, they had decided to drive over to Cannes for the day. As they were returning to their parked car, the unfortunate accident had occurred right before their eyes.

The tall, lanky Frenchman standing next to us speculated that the driver – who had been taken away in an ambulance earlier – had had a little too much Bordeaux for lunch.

My mother offered to walk Ulrike to a hotel to exchange her German marks. This meant I was stuck with chatty Pierre, my mother's other new friend, who could match her word for word. He yapped like an impatient Chihuahua, describing how he'd heard a loud crash from his mother's balcony overlooking the accident scene and come down to take a look. Apparently, his mother was a wealthy old woman who summered in Cannes, and he was visiting her at her apartment. The accident happened fortuitously for him, just as he was getting antsy after an afternoon of playing the dutiful son. Listening to him prattle on was about as pleasant as having a mosquito buzzing in my ear.

Ulrike changed her money and the concierge at the hotel called a taxi. As Ulrike's cab glided into the flow of traffic, we were left standing in the driveway of the hotel. This was the first pause in conversation since we'd left the accident scene. I could hear the gentle ebb and flow of the waves from the beach across the palm tree-lined boulevard and smell the briny air in the light evening breeze. Pierre quickly jumped in to fill the silence. He invited us out to dinner and before I could object my mother accepted.

We wanted to stop by our hotel and change before dinner, but Pierre insisted we not dress up since he would be going casual. The sun was setting as we found ourselves back on the Croisette in front of the *belle-époque* hotels. We were walking with Pierre towards the centre of town when he suggested we try a small bistro off the main boulevard. We took a left onto a small street lined with bistros fronted by outdoor tables. Each had a different coloured awning, and Pierre, after walking back and forth between them, suggested the second one from the boulevard with the yellow and white awning.

As we walked into the bistro, Pierre took charge and asked for an outdoor table. At first we were offered the table furthest from the street but Pierre insisted on a better one. It was a nice table for four and I could see the beach from my seat. Pierre immediately ordered a bottle of Veuve Clicquot. My mother objected, saying she didn't drink alcohol, but Pierre insisted on the champagne, saying it was a night to celebrate new friends. She conceded that Pierre could order, but made it clear she would not be drinking.

As Pierre chatted up the waitress taking our order, we learned that she was the chef's wife. Since it was a small establishment, she helped out when she could. Pierre asked if there were any specials and Madame indicated that most were on the menu, except the *magret de canard* with *griotte* (a sweet–sour berry) sauce, since there was only one portion left. Madame recommended this dish and assured Pierre that if he didn't like it he could send it back for the one with sauce *au miel* (honey), which she said was just as exquisite. Pierre decided to start with the melon and *jambon de Parme* and follow with the *magret de canard* with *griotte* sauce. I went for the same appetiser and the *magret de canard* with the honey sauce, while my mother ordered the goat cheese salad to start, followed by the turbot.

When the appetisers arrived, Pierre had a flirty verbal repartee with Madame. He then decided to elaborate about his wealthy widowed mother. He told us she had a chauffeured Rolls-Royce that took her for a ride every afternoon before afternoon tea, a habit she'd picked up while living in London. But instead of the limp tea sandwiches the English serve, the hors d'oeuvres were typically French petits fours and mini sandwiches served on silver trays. While he adored his mother and enjoyed visiting her, teatime was all he could take before she started nagging him about Pierre this and Pierre that.

Madame came to pick up the plates and asked us how our appetisers were. Pierre jumped in and told her his was delicious, but the *jambon de Parme* could have been a little less salty and the melon a little less ripe. Otherwise, he said, it was simply wonderful. When the main course arrived, Pierre once again took to flirting with Madame, complimenting her quite brazenly before fixing his attention on the meal in front of him. He took a few bites of the *magret de canard* before he called over Madame and told her that the breast of duck with *griotte* sauce did not suit his taste; the way he said it in French was more mellifluous and almost endearing, if not a touch arrogant: '*Le magret de canard ne convient pas à mon palate.*' And so Madame solicitously took the plate and quickly replaced it with the breast of duck with honey sauce, which, according to Pierre, was remarkably better. Before Pierre let Madame go, he also ordered a second bottle of Veuve Clicquot, as his mouth was parched from the salty *jambon de Parme* (and he had powered through the first bottle while talking about Maman and her hundreds of petits fours at teatime).

When Madame came by to collect our plates, Pierre turned on the charm again, cajoling Madame into telling him if there were any special desserts not on the menu. There was a birthday dinner in progress at a table behind us, and a cake had just been brought out with a lit candle in the middle, and the group was singing '*Joyeuse Anniversaire*' in the background. Pierre asked Madame to send over a bottle of red wine to the table and to put it on his tab. She thanked him for his generosity, and Pierre said it was nothing, and made a dismissive hand gesture.

Madame returned to the dessert selection, and told Pierre that in addition to the wonderful traditional *crème brûlée* – which was made by her husband, who was not only the chef but the pastry chef as well – there was one portion of lavender-scented *crème brûlée* left; this was a dessert that her husband made only occasionally and it was simply delicious. Pierre, after extensively questioning Madame on her preferences and suggestions, decided to order the *crème brûlée à la lavande*. I ordered the traditional *crème brûlée* and my mother decided to try the *île flottante*, puffed egg whites floating like clouds in yellow vanilla cream sauce.

The chef was doing the rounds of the tables, and he came over and introduced himself. Pierre proceeded to compliment him profusely on his exquisite culinary aptitude and to engage him in conversation. Flattered, the chef told us how he had opened the restaurant after toiling at some of the larger establishments in town. He explained how, as times were tough, he normally manned the kitchen with only one waitress outside the festivals and summer season. Instead of hiring additional staff, his wife would help out when she was not taking care of the children. The chef then went on to mingle with guests at the other tables.

As Pierre was preparing to launch into another discourse about his mother, Madame brought the desserts. Pierre complimented her on her youthful figure and told her if it weren't for her husband telling him, he would never have guessed she'd had any children. Madame did not engage in Pierre's repartee as readily as before. His charm was wearing a little thin.

By the time dessert was finished, Pierre wanted a digestif. I was getting tired and starting to yawn; it was almost eleven thirty and the long day at the beach had worn me out. My mother was getting tired, too, but Pierre kept her engaged in conversation, and she was fighting her fatigue. All of a sudden, a group of chauffeurs vociferously barrelled into the restaurant. They had been shuttling celebrities between Mougins, for Elizabeth Taylor's AIDS benefit at the Moulin de Mougins, and Cap d'Antibes, where most of the bigger celebrities were lodging at the Hotel du Cap. They had come in for a nightcap, and began trading stories about the stars they had driven, their outfits and eccentricities. One of them had driven Liz and commented how remarkably well she looked, considering it was the first time in a while she had chaired the event herself.

The chef had now closed the kitchen for the evening and he sat down with the chauffeurs. The conversation was finally winding down at our table and we were about to ask for the bill when Pierre called over to the chef to enquire about something and the chef motioned for us to move over to his table. We reluctantly joined them and the conversation grew to a crescendo as the chauffeurs tried to outdo each other with their star tales. In the middle of this maelstrom, Pierre got up and said he was going to the toilet. Amidst the commotion, he was barely noticed getting up from the table.

About twenty minutes later, the owner was getting ready to close up the restaurant and he brought the bill. Pierre was nowhere to be seen. The owner asked what had happened to him, and my mother and I looked at each other with mounting concern. He'd said he was going to the toilet, but that was over twenty minutes ago. The owner checked the WC but it was empty. Pierre's duffle bag was still by his chair, but when we opened it to see if there was any ID the only thing inside was a well-read copy of *Le Monde*: no ID, no keys, no personal effects.

My mother took a look at the bill and said she would only pay for our portion, not the extravagant bottles of champagne she hadn't consumed, especially since the owner had shared the last bottle with Pierre. The owner became agitated and insisted he would call the police unless she settled the entire bill. She told him to go right ahead.

Monsieur called the police and they arrived swiftly. The young officer, who looked much like the one from the accident scene, listened to both sides of the story, then decided to settle the dispute by telling us to pay our portion of the meal and half the liquor, since clearly the owner had partaken in the drinking in the latter part of the evening. You could sense he felt there was a good chance that the owner had been in on the con. The owner reluctantly agreed. The policeman left us with a warning, that even though Cannes is a resort town, it is a city like any other with its attendant crime and that we should be more careful. Too many tourists let their guard down when they arrive at a sunny destination, sometimes with disastrous effects. With that, he got a call on his radio about a drug bust and took off.

As we walked back to our hotel, weary from the long evening and stunned by the sequence of events that had transpired, we couldn't quite figure out if the owner had been in on the scam. We wavered back and forth on that one. But for the price of admission, we'd been front and centre at an award-winning performance. Our con artist had missed his true calling as an actor, and could hold his ground with any of the stars peddling their films on the Croisette.

CARPET-ROLLING

BROOKE NEILL

During five years based in London, Brooke Neill moved in and out of Europe, Africa, Asia and the Middle East, loving every second of it. She has recently completed a degree in sociology and journalism in Tasmania and is now busily planning her next trip.

We were pulling ourselves up a small hill in Selcuk, Turkey, in sweaty forty-degree August heat, when my travelling companions Rachel and Anna and I stopped to catch our breath. After spending most of our nights drinking *raki* with other back-packers staying at our hostel and being woken up by a huge loud-speaker perched directly outside our bedroom window at every prayer call, we were seriously lacking the athletic ability to climb a small hill. But we had inadvertently chosen the worst possible place to catch our breath – directly outside a carpet shop.

Anyone who has travelled in Turkey knows that the carpet salesmen are very persuasive. Even if you merely glance at the exterior of a carpet shop, you're likely to receive an invitation to a carpet performance. It begins with the carpet-seller saying, 'Lovely jubbly, you from England?' or 'G'day, mate, are you from Australia?' As soon as you reveal where you're from, the carpet-seller marvels that he has a cousin, uncle or random long-lost relative who lives there.

So we weren't surprised when a voice behind us said, 'G'day ladies, come in for apple tea.' Oh no, we thought, another carpet-seller. We were already preparing our excuses as we turned around, but this carpet-seller was dressed in a navy pin-striped suit and a pale pink shirt unbuttoned at the top. He was tall, dark and, yes, quite handsome.

We went in for apple tea. The shop was dark and cool and all the walls, floor and ceiling were covered in colourful weaves. Our host introduced himself as Josef and ushered us towards a huge pile of carpets. 'Have a seat', he said. We climbed up giggling and let our brown legs dangle off side with our flip-flops balancing off our toes.

As Josef boiled a kettle beside the cash register, he asked us if we had thought about buying a real Turkish carpet while we were in Turkey. We said that we had thought about it but didn't really have the money and didn't want to have to carry a carpet around for the rest of our time in Turkey and then back to Australia.

'No worries, mate', said Josef in his best Australian accent. 'My carpets are the best quality for the best price and for a small amount I can send to Australia and you have no need to carry them anywhere.'

He daintily poured four apple teas and passed them around on a silver tray. We politely repeated that we were not going to be the best customers as we were at the beginning of a four-week trip and had a strict budget.

Josef took off his jacket and rolled up his sleeves. He meant business. He began to bring out all sorts of amazing carpets and waited until he got a reaction from one of us. Before long we were saying things like, 'Now that is beautiful, I really like that one. How much would that one cost?' At this, Josef would get out his calculator and frantically prod the buttons, then extend his arm to show us. The prices were a little too high but we figured there would need to be some haggling *if* we were to make a purchase.

After a while a small man walked in and said hello to us and high-fived Josef. They looked very happy to see each other. We were introduced to Ali and he shook our hands, then he and Josef explained that Ali owned the shop two doors up. Then they high-fived again; they seemed very pleased with themselves. The carpets came out thick and fast now, and soon the pile in front of us was as high as the pile we were sitting on and we had lost sight of the door. In fact, all we could see was carpet.

After my third apple tea I had my credit card out and was being assured by Josef and Ali that what I was doing would bring good luck and that I was very sensible. I was feeling guilty about parting with so much money so early in the trip, but figured one day I would have a house big enough to display all my worldly goods – and anyway, I had spent the last three years travelling and not buying anything of any importance. The purchase had been justified.

After he had written down my current London address in case there were any problems and my permanent Australian address as the destination for the carpet, Josef asked us if we had been to the ancient city of Ephesus. Before we knew it, he was locking up the shop and we were piling into his little white Honda and racing through the streets of Selcuk and out to Ephesus with Turkish pop music blaring out the windows. We wandered around the ruins and chatted to Josef and Ali about life in Turkey. They both had many stories to tell and knew the history of the area.

Then Josef surprised us again. 'What are your plans for tonight, girls?' he asked.

We quickly exchanged do-we-want-to-hang-out-with-these-guys-tonight looks. After a quick analysis, I answered, 'No plans.'

'How about we go to Kusadasi to the discos?' said Josef, with Ali smiling beside him. We had no plans to go to Kusadasi, but after more looking at each other, we all answered, 'Why not?'

Back at the hostel we put on our least smelly clothes and some make-up. On the eighteen-kilometre drive to Kusadasi the Turkish pop was so loud that all we could do was communicate with facial expressions, usually just looking at each other and giggling or slightly rolling our eyes like we couldn't believe what we were doing. The music felt like it was lifting the car from the road with every beat.

Josef and Ali knew exactly where they were heading and we looped through the cobbled lanes of Kusadasi past ancient doorways that were gateways to modern Western culture: discos. We passed a few small restaurants and bars before reaching a tiny doorway guarded by two strong bouncers. Our guides obviously knew them and there were more high-fives among the four of them. We were introduced to the doorman and lowered our heads to pass through to the unknown. The club had a strong, musky underground smell to it and tunes that had followed us around Turkey were being squeezed out of an oversized stereo. Lots of eighties neon lights showed us the way to the bar where we ordered *rakis* all around. We didn't leave the club until the doorman told us they were closing and we had to leave.

'Let's go carpet-rolling back in Selcuk', Ali said to Josef. This was the first time we had heard Ali say anything other than agreeing with Josef, so this made his suggestion even more intriguing.

'What on earth is carpet-rolling? Do you want us to help you roll carpets for delivery?' asked Rachel.

'No, no, no', laughed Josef. 'Let's go back to the shop and we will show you. Don't worry, it is all safe', he reassured us. Anna, Rachel and I were definitely not ready to sneak back into the hostel just yet, so we agreed to the 'carpet-rolling', whatever that might be.

We climbed into Josef's car and laughed our way back to Selcuk. The streets were very quiet and only a few streetlights were lit. Back at the shop Josef switched on all the lights and the colours of the carpets jumped out at us like fireworks. Ali and Josef ran out to the back of the shop and returned with a pink bike helmet and a massive roll of bubble wrap. For some reason this sight didn't make us nervous but just made us laugh even more. 'Ok, who wants to roll in the carpet?' asked Josef.

'How about you guys show us how it is done?' said Anna.

'Okay, we need to set up a carpet block down near the bushes at the end of the hill', Josef said as he began carrying carpets out of the shop and making a blockade at the end of the street. Next Josef wrapped Ali toe to neck in bubble wrap and then in two very long carpet runners. Then Josef helped Ali out the door and lowered him down onto the street, using his body as a support to stop him from rolling all the way down.

'Are you ready?' Josef asked Ali.

'Please be careful, guys. Do you know what you're doing?' I asked.

'Ready!' said Ali, and with this Josef moved his body and Ali was rolling flat out down the hill towards the carpet barrier. Josef was jumping up and down and clapping his hands with excitement. Anna, Rachel and I just watched. Ali hit the carpet barrier after at least forty metres of rolling uncontrollably and we all ran down to see how he was. 'Wooowee, that was great!' he said.

I could not believe it when I was being wrapped in bubble wrap and pretending to be fussy about which carpet I would be rolled in. Both Rachel and Anna thought I was crazy and had their cameras at the ready. For some reason, the fact that I had purchased travel insurance at the airport made me feel better about my decision.

After I was wrapped, I could move only my ankles and feet, so it was very difficult to jump onto the street. I remember being amazed at how quiet the street was – especially as we were making so much noise and I was sure we were causing a disturbance. Anna and Rachel walked down to wait at the bottom of the hill beside the carpet barrier, and I lay face down on the road with Josef's legs wedged up against me, waiting to be released.

What was I doing?

'Are you ready?' Josef asked.

'No but yes', I answered.

Josef moved his feet from under me and jumped out of the way. Suddenly I was rolling down a hill in Selcuk wrapped in a carpet. I couldn't see a thing and I had no idea which direction I was heading in.

The next thing I knew I hit the barrier really hard and threw up on myself and on the carpet. Anna, Rachel and Ali rushed over to help me out of my carpet cocoon, and then I started laughing and laughing. I was embarrassed about the vomit, but Ali assured me it had happened before and that I shouldn't worry about it.

We carried all the carpets up the hill back to the shop and had a relaxing apple tea. I offered to clean the carpet but Josef said that his mother looked after that type of thing and that everything was okay.

Two weeks after I returned to London, a deliveryman with a huge cylindrical package turned up at my door. I signed for the delivery and read the note attached: 'Just in case you want to carpet-roll in London.' On the back of the note was written, 'This is the carpet you vomited on. I have sent the other one to Oz. Love, Josef.'

Now I am back in Australia with two carpets – and no room for either of them at the moment. Since that adventure in Turkey my experience with carpet-sellers has stretched from my local department store to Morocco, but no one has matched Josef in knowing how to sell carpets and a good time. Every time I look at those carpets rolled up against the wall, they make me smile. There must be something in that apple tea.

A MATTER OF TRUST

MICHELLE WITTON

Michelle Witton is an Australian actor/writer, currently based in London. She studied law in Australia and at Cambridge University, where she wrote and acted with the *Footlights* comedy revue. A well-travelled backpacker, Michelle's travel stories and satire have been published in *TNT Magazine*, the *Sydney Morning Herald* and *Backpacker Essentials*. This is the first time her work has appeared in book form. This story is dedicated to the man who assured her, 'It never hurts to kick your toe on the moon' – her father, Bill Witton (1932–2004).

My watchband, already old when I started travelling, had served me well in the three months I'd been on the road, but it finally chose the Italian town of Lucca in which to end its short, though eventful, life. Luckily, I'd planned to stay a while in Lucca, visiting my friend Elizabetta and tending to necessary chores such as mending my dog-eared guidebook and spending quality time with a washing machine. Now I added finding a new watchband to the list.

I'd grown fond of my maroon leather watchband and assumed it wouldn't be too difficult to find one similar in Lucca, as its narrow cobbled streets were lined with leather-goods stores. But after a few days, I'd seen more handbags than I could have ever believed existed – and nothing resembling a watchband. In the heat of my fourth afternoon I stopped for a chocolate gelato and collapsed in the shade cast by a nearby wall. It led to an alley, and craning forward I saw a few shop windows further down. I sauntered towards them for no other reason than sheer bloody-mindedness to look in every shop, if that's what it took.

The window of the first store was so dirty I could barely see in. Yet as I cupped my hand to the glass and peered in through the windowpane, there it was – a tray of leather watchbands! A woman in her sixties with a kindly face and dark grey curly hair stood behind the counter. Her generous bosom extended over her waist and flowery blue apron.

'*Buon giorno, signora*', I beamed when I entered the shop.

'*Buon giorno*', she replied with a friendly smile.

Buon giorno, *spaghetti*, *per favore*, *pronto* and *pesto* marked the edge of the known world for my Italian. If any transaction was going to take place from here on, it was going to have to rely on sign language. '*Per favore, signora*', I said and pointed to the window. The shopkeeper walked to the window and hovered, uncertain about which of the items I wanted to buy. They varied fantastically – the tray of watchbands, children's colouring books, a blender, a teddy bear. The shopkeeper bent over and reached for the blender. '*Non, non, signora.*' She stopped and looked back at me, questioningly. I pointed at my wrist and fished my broken watchband from my jeans pocket. Her eyes lit up and she disappeared again into the window and returned with the tray of watchbands.

She laid the tray on the glass shop counter between us. Almost immediately I spied a maroon band. Perfect! I pointed at it excitedly, '*Grazie, signora!*' The shopkeeper picked up the tray and, her plump fingers having some difficulty, slowly detached the maroon band. I put my watch on the counter. The shopkeeper scooped it up, along with the new watchband, inspected both closely and began to try to fit the watchband to my watch. '*Grazie, grazie, signora*', I said, hoping that she'd put down my watch and let me deal with the fitting later.

'*Non, non*', she replied and determinedly continued fiddling.

This was my first chance to look at the store beyond the contents of its front window and it's fair to say that for its sheer diversity of stock – and sheer disorganisation – I'd seen nothing like it before. It wasn't a second-hand store – most things were still in their plastic wrapping – but the line it drew between convenience shop and junk store was very, very faint. There was a half-deflated paddling pool teetering precariously on the edge of a shelf, cascading over a row of large blond and blank-eyed baby dolls. Men's suit coats hung over a pile of bicycle wheels. Under the front counter, a stack of children's Ninja Turtle cartoon sticker-books were fanned out next to an expensive men's pen.

The shopkeeper stopped fiddling with the watchband and suddenly looked at me. 'American?'

'*Non, signora* – Australian.'

'*Aust-rali-en?*' She looked at me blankly.

'*Si, signora*. Australian', I smiled. It was 2000 and the Olympics had just opened in Sydney. I put my arms in front of me like paws and said, 'Australia. Olympics, *signora*', while jumping up and down like a kangaroo.

'Australia. *Si, si*', she laughed. She then said a sentence in which I caught only the words '*familia*' and 'Melbourne'. Melbourne has a large Italian community and it seemed she was telling me it included her family.

'*Mia chiama* Michelle', I said, pointing to myself.

'Maria', the shopkeeper smiled back. Shortly afterwards, defeated in her attempts to fit the watchband, Maria let out a resigned sign.

'*Quanto costa, signora?*' I asked.

'*Non*', she replied and the determined glint returned to her eye. She'd had an idea. Maria held up one of her hands, five fingers splayed.

'*Cinque minuti*', she said.

'Five minutes?' What on earth, I wondered, was going to happen in five minutes?

Maria came from behind the shop counter, took me by the arm and led me outside to the front step. In the alley, against her shop's whitewashed front wall, leaned a very rusty bike. '*Cinque minuti*', she said again, and pointed at the bike. She walked a few steps towards the bike, pointed to it and to herself, then motioned away down the alley with one arm, while holding up my watch in her other hand.

This pantomime was open to numerous interpretations, but one thing was clear: I had little or no say in what was about to happen. Maria was going to get on her bike and disappear down the alley for five minutes – and take my watch with her.

'*Grazie, signora, non, non*', I said, trying to dissuade Maria from her plan.

'*Non, non*', she laughed and took me back inside. She untied her apron and folded it on the counter. But if Maria was going somewhere for five minutes, what was I going to do in the meantime?

'*Mi scusa, signora?*' I pointed to Maria, pointed at the door and mimed locking the door. I pointed to myself and then to the alley. I assumed that Maria would lock her shop and I'd wait outside until she returned. *If* she returned.

'*Non, non*', she laughed. Well, I certainly didn't want to be locked inside the shop!

Maria beckoned me behind the counter. Perhaps she wanted to show me something? She pointed at the cash register, laid a motherly hand on my shoulder and waddled towards the door. I was so stunned that the realisation that Maria had given me her shop to look after didn't hit me for a minute or two, until well after her bike had disappeared. So here I was, with Italian-language skills largely derived from a Pizza Hut menu, the newly appointed deputy manager of an Italian shop. Santa Maria! Supposing someone actually came in – a real customer – how was I meant to sell anything?

During university I'd worked weekends in a department store. I looked at the cash register. This was at least a bit familiar to me.

But the warm glow of familiarity waned when I realised that Maria's cash register had been manufactured sometime in the nineteenth century and still had a lot in common with the abacus. Still, Maria would have locked the register, surely? She couldn't expect me to sell anything. But no. I looked up and there, on top of the register, were the keys. And nestled on the edge of the shelf beneath it was – Maria's purse.

Okay, I was in charge, though it felt more like I was propelled back twenty-five years to the world of children's dress-ups and playing 'shops'. I smoothed my rumpled top, trying to look as efficiently salesperson-like as I could after living out of a backpack for three months. Casting my eyes over the store from my new vantage point behind the counter, I took a quick mental inventory of my stock. As I'd suspected, it consisted of basically, well, everything – including the kitchen sink. I frantically delved into the shallows of my Italian to rehearse potential 'shopping dialogues'. It was hopeless, I didn't know the words for any of my merchandise. There was a high probability that 'Ninja Turtle' was going to be 'Ninja Turtle' in any language, so at least I could sell the sticker books. I was going to have to really push the sticker books on anyone who walked through the door.

Some minutes passed and, having rehearsed a few sales phrases, I began to quietly hope that I would get some customers. But the alley was empty. A cat lolled in the sun by the door, lazily licking its paws. Then there was the noise of feet on the doorstep and a couple walked in. They were well-dressed, middle-aged – and Italian. My heart was pounding. '*Buon giorno signor, signora*', I smiled, and even found myself adding a little curtsey – which was really overdoing customer service for this neck of Tuscany.

'*Buon giorno*', the gentleman replied, taking a moment to unbutton his suit coat. His partner had seen something at the rear of the store that had caught her eye.

'Giovanni!' his partner beckoned him, and an animated conversation ensued about a dinner service or a crow bar, I couldn't see well enough to tell which. The general gist of the conversation seemed to be that she wanted whatever it was – and he didn't. Great! We were speeding into 'shop-assistant-as-counsellor' territory. I'd worked in interior decorating and seen it all before, one half of a couple wanting to paint the bathroom Honeydew Lemon, the other wanting Midnight Black – and neither giving ground. 'Can you believe it!' the woman would turn to me, waving a colour chart in fury. 'He wants to paint the bathroom this! Can you talk some sense into him, because I've given up!'

The couple's animated conversation resulted in much waving of arms by both parties and a victory, it seemed, for the husband. The couple left my shop with a '*Grazie, signora*', – without purchasing either the dinner service or the crow bar. Maria's *cinque minuti* were seeming more like *dieci minuti*, but just as the couple left, Maria's beaming face popped back through the door and in her outstretched hand was – my watch!

'*Grazie, signora!*' I said with relief, both at seeing my watch and at being able to resign from my duties as deputy store manager.

I strapped my new maroon watchband around my wrist, paid Maria and, with many thanks and fond waves, ran to Elizabetta's apartment.

'Betta,' I called, running in through the door, 'the most amazing thing just happened!'

Over coffee, I told my friend of my adventure. I was disappointed to find she thought it nothing exceptional.

'But Betta, she let me look after her shop! She even left her purse there!'

'Why shouldn't she?'

'But I was a total stranger! I could have taken her purse, the money in the cash register...'

'Yes, but you're not that kind of person.'

'She couldn't have known that. I could have taken off with the lot!'

'But you didn't, did you?'

As far as Betta, or evidently Maria, was concerned, there was absolutely no reason why one wouldn't trust a stranger to mind their shop. Regardless, I felt proud that Maria had trusted me. In London, such unquestioning trust seems to come not just from another culture, but from another time. Rarely do we trust completely even those we call our friends, let alone strangers. Maria's watchband served me well until it too broke. Now I keep it in my box of mementoes to remind me of the time when I went looking for a watchband in Lucca and found something far more remarkable – absolute trust.

NAKED IN OAXACA

LAURA RESAU

Laura Resau has lived and travelled extensively in Oaxaca, Mexico, and is currently working on a collection of stories about her experiences there. She teaches college anthropology and ESL (English as a Second Language) in Colorado, and her fiction and essays have appeared in numerous magazines, including *Brain*, *Child*, *Cicada* and *Cricket*. The *temazcal* adventure recounted in 'Naked in Oaxaca' inspired Laura's Master's thesis in cultural anthropology. Her young adult novel set in Oaxaca, tentatively entitled *What the Moon Saw*, will be published by Delacorte Press in 2006.

An impulsive decision to visit a small town in Oaxaca, Mexico, on market day led to a naked, sweating matriarch beating a naked, sweating me with branches.

After several months of teaching English in the mountainous Mixtec region of Oaxaca, I was ready to venture outside the town I was based in to explore. 'I've never felt safer', I assured relatives back in the US when they asked how I liked living in a remote, impoverished village only a state away from guerrilla fighting. Although I attracted attention as the only young blonde woman in town, my skinny body and chunky baby cheeks inspired people to treat me protectively, as a daughter or sister.

At 4.30am, I was waiting alone in the dark on the deserted roadside a few blocks from my apartment. I was fully clothed at that point, with a bulging wallet in my shoulder bag. The day before, a student had mentioned the market in Tlaxiaco that drew people from surrounding indigenous villages. Envisioning women in traditional red woven tunics and long braids selling dried chillies, I decided to go. My student instructed me to wait before dawn for a third-class bus called a *micro*, and in no time, he said, I'd be immersed in Tlaxiaco's colourful market scene.

As it grew lighter, the taco vendor set up her stand, the tamale guy bicycled past, and the matronly bakery owner washed her windows. When I asked each of them when the *micro* would arrive, they said, '*Ahorita, güera, ahorita.*' Any second now, white girl. Any second.

Two hours later, the *micro* pulled up, a white box balanced on four wheels. Next to the driver's seat perched an altar to the golden Virgin of Oaxaca, and behind her, on the window, a sticker of a well-endowed naked woman throwing her hair back in sexual abandon. I squeezed onto a torn plastic seat, with my knees wedged against the metal in front of me. I'm a small person, so this truly was a *micro* bus. Other passengers trickled in, and after half an hour the driver closed the doors, crossed himself, and kissed his grease-stained hand. The *micro* lurched to a rattling start.

We bounced along, stopping every few minutes to pick up people toting bundles of firewood, live chickens and giant sacks of corn.

A chubby teenaged boy in a shiny basketball outfit struck up conversation. '*Señorita!* Excuse me!' he yelled over the blaring *ranchera* music. 'What are you doing all the way out here?'

'Going to the market. And you?'

He was studying nursing in a nearby town and heading home for the weekend. His name was Luís and he was seventeen, six years younger than me, young enough for him to seem like a child. Yet he treated me with a flirtatious deference, hoping, it seemed, that I wasn't too old for him.

'Mind if I sit next to you, *señorita*? It is miss, right?'

I nodded and he scooted onto the seat next to me. For three hours, as the landscape grew greener and lusher, with pines and fertile fields replacing cacti, he told me stories about nearby Mixtec temple ruins and about his friends who had gone to Florida to pick tomatoes. We began to pass more houses, of wood, adobe and concrete, and soon the *micro* pulled into a dirt parking lot in Tlaxiaco. Luís and I shook hands and he pointed me in the direction of the market, down a hill, where blue awnings filled the street.

The market didn't fit my rustic fantasy. Teenaged boys congregated by speakers booming salsa music from bootlegged tapes. They looked like gang members in their super-baggy jeans, gold chains and headcloths. '*Pssss. Güera*', they called. Further on was the household goods section, packed with bowls and lime squeezers and spoons and colanders – all made of plastic. Where were the carved gourds I'd dreamed of?

Just then a woman knocked into me. Once I regained my balance, I saw that my leather purse, which had rested on top of the sweatshirt in my bag, was gone. I hadn't even caught what the woman looked like.

The purse contained about five hundred pesos – fifty US dollars – which I'd planned to spend on hand-woven shawls, pottery and carved gourds. I tried to calm myself down. Really, the fifty dollars wouldn't hurt me economically; I had enough savings. What bothered me was the idea that someone would steal from me. Up to now, all my interactions with local people had been incredibly honest. In my town, vendors at the market threw in free mangoes and invited me into their homes for lunch. If I left without taking my two pesos change they'd call after me, '*Güera!* White girl! Your change!' Well, the thief *could* have been a really poor person who needed food for her hungry children.

But then the reality hit me. I had no money. No back-up money in my pockets or sock, no money belt, nothing, not even any jewellery I could hock. Not to mention the fact that I felt light-headed with hunger. And I had to find a toilet quite urgently.

That's when I spotted Luís. I ran over to him and blubbered out my story. He sympathetically handed me a banana from his bag, and I devoured it while we went over my options. The only bank in town was closed for the weekend, he said, so even if I made a pathetic phone call to my parents, they couldn't wire any money until Monday. I ate a second banana.

'You're still hungry, aren't you?' he asked.

I nodded.

'Come to my house. Eat lunch with my family.'

As I thanked him, I wondered what he'd expect in return. My faith in humanity had, after all, just been shot.

Luís lived on the outskirts of town, in a neighbourhood that smelt of sweet pine and burning trash. Like most of the other buildings, his house was a half-finished and unpainted concrete structure. Scrawny puppies greeted us, and Luis kicked them away with his foot. We walked through the doorway into a kind of roofless courtyard/living room, with squash plants creeping along the beams overhead, and passed a gold-framed picture of Jesus looking blond and radiant and holding up a finger, as if to say, *Just wait and see what you're in for, güera.*

We ducked through a hobbit-sized doorway into a cave-like kitchen, where a stout woman was stirring something bubbling on the stove with a long wooden spoon. Her black braids were streaked with grey, and an apron was tied over her comfortable rolls of fat. She threw her arms up in surprise and hugged her son. Then she looked at me, and back at Luís, her face amused and full of questions. She shook my hand lightly, barely touching it, as indigenous Mixtec people do, and I explained my situation in flustered broken Spanish.

She shook her head. 'Some people are bad', she said. 'There are some good people and some bad people. *Uh-HUNH.*' She spoke

Spanish with the choppiness of native Mixtec speakers, punctuating her speech with the characteristic '*uh-HUNH*'.

I agreed and then excused myself, located the bathroom, and peed for a full minute. After I dumped a bucket of water into the toilet to flush it, I emerged to find a guy my age, two young girls and an older man waiting to meet me. It was the rest of Luís's family, and I repeated my story to them.

Soon Doña Donaciana called us to the table and served us home-made tortillas and *sopa de panza*, which roughly translates as 'gut soup'. In this case, I think it was cow gut, because it reminded me of deli-sliced roast beef that's been left in the fridge three weeks too long. I discreetly spat some of the more unidentifiable chunks of internal organs into my napkin.

As we ate, they asked me what on earth I was doing working here when everybody and his brother were sneaking across the border to work in the US. When they found out I was single, they wanted to set me up with Eleuterio, Luís's twenty-two-year-old brother (Luís scowled at that). I might not have minded – he was pretty cute, with a dimpled smile and sexy eyes. But then Doña Donaciana informed me that Eleuterio's girlfriend had just had a baby, and I shrugged, 'Oh well. Too bad.'

'*Eso no importa!* That doesn't matter!' Eleuterio insisted, winking. 'She won't care!'

Maybe I could be the godmother of the baby, Doña Donaciana suggested. Then I'd be their *comadre* – co-mother, part of the family. This thought provoked rowdy laughter. I suspected it wasn't just the idea of a *güera* daughter-in-law or *comadre* that was so hilarious, more the idea of a *güera* with rudimentary knowledge of Spanish wandering around small Mixtec towns getting herself into trouble.

By late afternoon, just when I was wondering if I'd be sleeping there for the night, sandwiched between the two girls, Ixtli and Fany, Luís disappeared into a bedroom and came back with a handful of pesos.

'For your bus fare back', he said shyly. 'The last *micro* leaves soon.'

Doña Donaciana said, '*Güera*, come back next Saturday for lunch. You will pay my son back then.'

I gushed thanks, my faith in humanity restored.

———— —— ————

Next Saturday I took the *micro* back to Tlaxiaco, this time as a sea-soned expert. Luís greeted me and led me into the kitchen. Slouched in a kitchen chair sat a young woman, her eyes outlined in eyeliner and mascara, lips coated with pink gloss. This must be Eleuterio's girlfriend. She wasn't particularly friendly to me – maybe she'd caught wind of the family joking about her boyfriend marrying the *güera*. Doña Donaciana stood next to her, holding a very tiny baby in one arm and rolling a whole egg over his body with her hand.

The girlfriend mumbled her name, Teresa. I shook her hand lightly, then greeted Doña Donaciana and asked, 'What are you doing with that egg?'

'Oh, nothing', she said breezily, and asked me how my trip was. She set the egg down and handed me the baby. Ixtli and Fany bounced inside, breathless from playing basketball, and kissed me hello like old friends. Then it was time to eat.

This time Doña Donaciana served us each a thin strip of very salty, very chewy beef. She explained that it had been salted raw and hung on a clothesline to dry for a while, and then fried in oil. *Uh-HUNH.* Beans and rice and tortillas were served on the side, and this time I didn't have to spit anything out. Enough grease and salt work magic.

After lunch, Doña Donaciana announced she was going to give Teresa a steambath, which she called a *baño de temazcal*.

'You want to do it with us, *güera*?' she asked eagerly.

What luck! I'd stumbled across a peaceful little spa oasis. Who would have guessed?

'Yes! Sounds great!'

The girls giggled and looked wide-eyed at each other. A devil-ish grin crept over Teresa's face. Luís and Eleuterio and their father just raised their eyebrows, smiling at some secret, while Doña Donaciana threw back her head and laughed a full belly laugh, wiping her eyes. '*Imagínense*, a *güera* in a *temazcal*!'

I wondered what was so funny. I turned to Luís uncertainly. 'Are you doing it?'

He shook his head without hesitation. 'No.'

'Why not?'

'It's for women.'

'And?' I pushed.

'And it's too hot in there. It's like getting burned alive.' Then he ran outside to play basketball. Eleuterio and their father, car-rying the baby, ran after him.

'Don't be scared, *güera*', Doña Donaciana said. 'It's good for you. My daughters are doing it, right?' She glanced at them, and on cue, they nodded nervously. I wondered if the female-bonding aspect and the chance to see a *güera* being tortured outweighed any pain they'd suffer.

So we women gathered in a small room off the kitchen made of pine planks with a tortilla-making hearth in the corner. The room smelt of burnt wood and ash. In the centre of the room, on the hard-packed dirt floor, sat the *baño de temazcal* – a wooden frame, the size of a low one-person tent, half-covered with wool-len blankets. A pile of leafy branches sat next to it, along with a clay bowl filled with herbs soaking in water. Woven palm mats were spread out beside a stack of folded sheets.

I peeked inside the *temazcal*. At one end was a dish of glowing red-hot rocks. I wondered if it was too late to change my mind.

'Take off your clothes, *güera*', Doña Donaciana ordered. She and Teresa and the girls started undressing. I stripped off my tank top and trousers self-consciously, aware of how their smooth, even brown skin compared to my pale limbs, with their

193

blotches and blue veins. My body seemed flimsy and bony next to their ample rolls of flesh. 'You can keep your panties on', Doña Donaciana said, handing me a sheet, which I quickly wrapped around myself. 'But take off your bra.'

Teresa crawled in first and Doña Donaciana followed with the bowl and a bunch of leafy branches. Once inside, she let down the blankets to seal in the steam.

We heard a loud *hissss* followed by a scream. My stomach clenched. Soon the scream tapered off into moans and squeals. With every subsequent hiss, the moans and squeals escalated into screams again. '*Ay ay ay ay AY AYYY!*' It sounded like either a fabulous orgasm or...severe pain. Soon Teresa's head poked out of the entrance and she gasped for air. Sweat was rolling down her pink face, and her eyes were closed tight in deep concentration. At Doña Donaciana's command, Teresa flipped onto her back, and a few minutes later, on another command, she took a deep breath and disappeared into the *temazcal*. After another minute, she crawled out, glistening, wrapped herself in a sheet and lay down.

Now it was my turn. From under the blankets, Doña Donaciana's face emerged, flushed and sweating and exuberant. 'Come in, *güera*! Come in!'

I dropped my sheet and crawled in, utterly terrified. Doña Donaciana threw a cupful of water on the rocks, and *hissssss*, a suffocating cloud of steam filled the air. It felt like being dropped into a pot of boiling water. I was sure that second- and third-degree burns were springing up all over my body.

'Lie down', Doña Donaciana ordered. I obeyed, and stuck my face outside into the wonderfully cool air, while my body boiled inside.

She began beating me with the leaves, starting on the soles of my feet. If I'd thought it was hot before, now, with the moisture of the leaves sizzling on my skin, it was downright infernal. '*Ah ah ah AH AHHH!*'

'Are you okay, *güera*?'

'Um... I mean...' I struggled to find the part of my brain that could form words in Spanish. 'Um, is it supposed to be this hot?'

'Yes!'

But then I lost the connection with the human language part of my brain and just let out animal sounds of pure agony as she beat the back of my calves, my thighs, my rear, my back and my neck.

'*¿Si aguanta, güera?*' I had no idea what she was asking. I was thinking, in a panic, that I knew nothing about this sadistic woman. I'd just met her son on a bus.

Doña Donaciana instructed me to move my head inside, where she brushed the leaves around in my hair. I couldn't see anything except for the glowing rocks. 'Turn over', she said. 'You can put your head back out.'

As I sucked in the cool outside air, she beat the leaves over the front of my body, and then mercifully asked if I wanted more or was ready to get out.

'Out', I creaked.

A strange thing happened after I crawled out.

I wrapped myself in a sheet and lay next to Teresa against a pile of rolled-up palm mats, watching her face, her eyelids half-closed in a kind of relaxed ecstasy. A deep peace washed over me, and I stayed in that wordless place. It felt delicious now. I dissolved into the smell of wood smoke and just lay there, breathing and existing. Somewhere in my mind passed the thought, Oh good, my skin is still here.

After the girls finished in the *baño*, we lounged around in our sheets like Greek goddesses and sipped warm Coronas together, which were apparently part of the ritual. Later, as we floated up and got dressed, I felt close to these women, as though they were my sisters. The colour of our skin didn't matter because it was essentially the same – flushed and sweaty and burned. Our bodies moaned and screamed and relaxed. I noticed that they no longer addressed me formally; I was close enough to be *tú*.

Before I left to catch the *micro* back home, I asked Doña Donaciana, 'What were you doing to the baby with that egg?'

She smiled. 'It's our custom. It takes away the evil eye. You see, babies can catch it easily. So we rub our babies with an egg to cure them every now and then. *Uh-HUNH.*'

For Doña Donaciana to trust me with this information was significant, I realised. I had passed some kind of test, undergone a female initiation rite.

She bundled me up for the bus ride home. 'Your pores are open', she said. 'No bathing in cold water and no cold drinks for three days.' She wrapped a scarf around my neck and lent me a baseball cap and a cardigan, and I walked into the eighty-degree afternoon, accompanied by Ixtli and Fany. At the *micro* parking lot, they hugged me goodbye and made me promise to come back next Saturday.

I later learned that since pre-Hispanic times, the *temazcal* ritual has symbolised birth and rebirth. For me, this was the birth of an enlightening friendship and a fascination with Oaxacan healing practices. Stripped of money and naked as a newborn, you simply throw open your arms and embrace the strange and fantastic opportunities that life offers.

THE GARDEN KITCHEN

HOLLY ERICKSON

As a young woman, San Francisco native and resident Holly Erickson ate her way across Europe, sampling the likes of reindeer stroganoff and poached whale – and much delicious food as well. She then studied literature at the University of California, Berkeley, and cooking at the California Culinary Academy. The owner of Mrs Dalloway's Catering service, she is also writing *Lights! Camera! Cuisine!*, a cookbook based on cinematic food scenes, and *The Devil Sends Cooks*, a book about private chefs and their clients, from which 'The Garden Kitchen' is excerpted.

Friends of my family had bought a rambling old house in South London. They were an affable young British couple, who thought that their three-storey renovator's delight was too big to waste on two and so had taken in lodgers. After I graduated from college, but before I'd been to culinary school, they hired me to cook. I would be given one of the vacant rooms and in return would cook for the lodgers and the food-loving couple themselves.

As soon as I arrived, however, the couple took off for a sailing trip in the Mediterranean.

'You'll find the kitchen unusual', sang the lady of the house as she headed out the front door, 'and you'll have some keeping up to do, the garden is so splendiferous!'

One of the lodgers was away for the entire summer, but a burly, good-natured American man and a willowy Jamaican woman remained. I unpacked and took a self-guided tour of the house.

As I passed her bedroom, the Jamaican woman whispered, 'She's having an affair. They're off on their sudden holiday to try to work things out.'

'Very interesting!' I exclaimed.

Downstairs, as I was about to open the door, the American told me, 'The kitchen does work. But it's not really a room. He was gung-ho about do-it-yourself renovating and then he lost steam. You'll see.'

I saw. The husband had torn down three of the kitchen walls and most of the ceiling and hadn't put them up again. The phrase 'kitchen garden' took on new meaning here. The cooker, the sink and the fridge all worked perfectly despite tendrils of ivy, encroaching bean vines and huge marrow plants threatening to overtake them. The pots and pans had been arranged on the piano in the library, but I found the electric kettle near some spiky nettles. I plugged it in gingerly, wondering if the damp of the garden could cause electrocution. It didn't. I made my tea and took it into the dining room to drink. There was no place to sit in the kitchen – unless you wanted to throw down a blanket and have a picnic.

In the morning, I tumbled downstairs, boiled my tea, then scurried shivering back into the dining room and brushed the dew off my slippers and dressing gown. The Jamaican girl was hanging up the telephone, and she informed me that she'd found a cheap flight and would be flying home to Kingston for a few weeks.

'It'll be so lonesome around here I may as well take my camping trip to the Lake District now when everyone else is away', the American told me as he downed the last of his tea.

So just like that I was out of a job. I had no way to contact the lady and man of the house to tell them I had no one to cook for, but I felt I shouldn't abandon my post.

That night, as it began to rain, I hurried to make myself some hot cocoa and then firmly latched the kitchen door while the garden plants gesticulated wildly behind the cooker and over the refrigerator. It was the first night I had ever spent alone under a roof anywhere, and I happened to be in a large, South London home on a quiet street ten minutes' walk from the train station on a night full of thunder and pelting rain. I implored the cats not to knock anything over and scare the daylights out of me.

At around ten o'clock the phone rang. I desperately hoped it was the man of the house so I could tell him the lodgers had fled temporarily and I was unoccupied.

Thank goodness, it was a man calling. But his voice was so garbled I couldn't make out what he was saying.

'Call me back. Call me back!' I shouted and hung up.

My boss might be calling from a dodgy foreign phone, I hoped. It seemed forever before he rang again. My heart was pounding.

'I want you. I want you in every way that a man...pip, pip, pip.' The man was calling not from a foreign phone, but from an English pay phone, because every few seconds the pipping sound that means the caller has to insert more coins interrupted the call. I could hear him plunging coins into the slot to evade the annoying pips.

Aha! The boyfriend of the lady of the house, I assumed. Perhaps he too was married, so felt compelled to leave his house to make this phone call.

'You've got the wrong woman. She's gone on holiday. I'm cooking for the lodgers.'

I felt sorry for him since he hadn't been told his inamorata would be abroad for three weeks. But reaching the wrong woman didn't deter him. His language became more graphic before I realised this was my very first obscene caller. And me alone on a stormy night. He rang a few more times, moving straight into the heavy breathing cliché. I hung up each time, but answered each new ring, hoping beyond hope it would be a different caller.

I wanted to ring my Irish friend Mauvourneen to tell her about the obscene call, but it was too late at night to call a live-in member of staff. I wanted to ring up my friend from New Zealand, but he was staying at a hostel and beyond the reach of a phone. I thought about how pathetic this fellow was to venture out on a wretched night with a pocketful of pence to do his business. I couldn't stop smiling and shaking my head. I fell asleep despite the pounding rain and cracking thunder, wondering which vegetables would be ready to pick from the garden.

The next day when the phone rang I felt nervous about answering it. Thankfully, it was the man of the house. I sighed with relief, yet my hand was still shaking as I held the receiver. Finally I was able to tell him, in full detail, about the obscene caller, and oh, that the lodgers had gone. He told me to enjoy myself and to take full advantage of the garden.

Since I had no one to cook for, I decided to have Mauvourneen and my friend from New Zealand over for an all-American Sunday dinner. I bought a plump chicken from an adorable butcher boy with a blue apron tied charmingly around his narrow hips. I bought some sweet corn from the greengrocers. And then I raided the garden, and discovered that the pallid tomatoes twisting up stakes by the tool shed tasted wonderful. I dug up some stubby carrots and a number of potatoes and found some minute lettuces battling for their very existence between two gargantuan marrows. I came across some eggplants and for the first time understood why they are called eggplants, because these were white and egg-sized and -shaped.

For dinner I'd serve Southern fried chicken with mashed potatoes and chicken gravy, buttery corn on the cob, biscuits slathered with honey, green salad with tomatoes and shredded carrots, and chocolate layer cake, known as Victoria Sandwich in England.

It was a lovely summer's day, slightly overcast but not really threatening rain. I had never needed to worry about rain affecting my cooking before, but here I wanted to have everything ready to go, just in case. I cut up and soaked the chicken in milk, peeled the root vegetables, and washed and sliced the lettuce and tomatoes. All the condiments and spices had been moved to the downstairs bathroom, so I needed to run inside and out a dozen times to find everything. I whipped up a salad dressing, prepared the biscuits and mixed up the cake batter. I would bake the cake and biscuits simultaneously – just in case the clouds burst.

I couldn't find a kitchen timer and there wasn't one on the cooker. I had never owned a watch. There was no clock in the music room-turned-pantry, nor one in the dining room. Nor the living room. There was a clock on the chest of drawers in the master bedroom, but it had stopped. I tiptoed into all three of the lodgers' rooms and found nary a timepiece. So I dialled the speaking clock. It was busy. I dialled again and again. Still engaged. So I turned on the TV and thumbed through the *TV Times* so I could correspond what was airing to the time of day. But on a Sunday afternoon nothing was on any of the three stations except endless soccer scores. I supposed every game ever played by every team from Manchester United to the smallest team of toddlers on the Isle of Wight aired that afternoon. I kept dialling the speaking clock every few minutes with no response but a busy signal.

I finally opened the front door to see if I could hail a passer-by. But no one passed by. I peered into neighbours' lounge windows. The inhabitants all seemed to be on Sunday outings.

How could I not find out what time it was in the middle of the afternoon in a city of eight million people?! I felt Rod Serling might step out of the twilight zone at any moment.

The cake! By the time I had searched high and low to time the cake, it had baked – not to cinders, happily, but to perfection.

The biscuits looked perfect, too. Cooling the cake was a breeze, literally. I frosted it and put the biscuits aside to warm up before serving.

My guests arrived, and I prepared the remaining dishes in a stiff wind but without a drop of precipitation. And even fussy Mauvourneen proclaimed everything tasted delicious. It was truly one of the best meals I had ever cooked.

———— ————————

What a funny man was the man of the house. The next three times his sailing boat docked, he rang me up and the first thing I'd hear was exaggerated heavy breathing and in an attempted cockney he'd whisper, 'I want you. I want you in every way a man wants a...pip pip pip!' And then he'd break into giggles. He'd ask after the health and appetite of the cats and if the rain was ruining the kitchen yet. 'No', I'd answer. 'I love cooking in your kitchen. The food tastes fantastic!'

A few days after my wildly successful all-American meal, as I sat reading on the sofa, I heard the keys in the lock and the man of the house entered all alone. He dumped his bags in the hall then walked into the lounge and poured himself a whisky. I thought maybe I should repair to my room, servant-like, but he launched into a monologue I was meant to hear.

'We thought the holiday together would do us good. But what we really need is some time apart. We've been together since college. Ten years is a long time. We're not breaking up, mind you. We love each other. She just wants to spend some time with her boyfriend. Which I truly think she should do.'

'Right.'

'And I thought...'

'Mmm?'

'I thought. I thought...perhaps...you'd like some grapes...from Greece.' He took some out of his bag.

We sat on the sofa, sipping whisky, savouring the grapes.

'With no lodgers for you to cook for and my two weeks of holiday time left, perhaps you'd care to join me on a culinary tour of Britain?' he suggested.

He was a slight man with a jet-black, late-Beatle haircut, angular features and sharp green eyes. I was all for it.

'That your wife has a boyfriend was the best news I've heard in a long time. I'd love to join you. In fact, I want you. I want you in every way...pip pip pip.'

We put out food for the cats, climbed into his van and set off for the West Country, aglow with infatuation.

'Let's have a row!'

'Huh?'

'Let's fight. Nothing makes two people row and bicker and gripe more than a road trip. Except, of course, household repairs. If we do it now before we take off, we'll have a taste of each other's arguing style. I'd like to know if you are the Cold Shoulder type or a Censorable Diatribe kind of girl.'

So as we drove out of London, through the suburbs and finally into pure country, we practised fighting about money, about toilet stop frequency, about drinking and driving, about dinner choices and about which side of the van to sleep on. I never had such a good laugh. And I found I'm neither Cold Shoulder nor Vituperative Rantings, but more the peevish sort. Needless to say, after the rowing rehearsal, we never bickered for the entire trip.

We stopped often to eat or drink. I broadened my tippling beyond Guinness by learning about beer, lager, ale, stout and half-and-halfs. In Devon we ate ploughman's lunches of crusty bread with pungent, crumbly Cheddar cheese and vinegary Branston pickle washed down with hard apple cider. Some of the cider tasted as good as an apple from the Garden of Eden, while others tasted like vinyl. We ate Cornish pasties. I learned that miners' wives had made their pasties with meat stuffed on one side and sugared blackcurrant with mint, as dessert, on the other.

One morning my travelling companion suggested, 'Let's go to Wales for breakfast. They do brekkies better there than here.'

I never got used to how close everything is in Britain. We spontaneously set off for Wales to park for the night and wake up to a splendid breakfast. Eventually, tired and lost, we drove off the highway to a rest stop flooded with light.

'It must be some kind of industrial park. I know it's not scenic, but I'm knackered. Let's go to sleep and in the morning we'll drive somewhere more picturesque', said my disappointed tour guide.

In the morning it was as if we had been transported, van and all, to a better world. We had not passed the night in any industrial park but a sylvan grove. Groggily we sat up to find a group of kids on horses jumping over a fence situated right at the back of the van. Each of them, sixteen in all, got a big grin when their horse landed and they spied the two of us, in disarray, smiling ear to ear. After the riders had galloped off, three little boys in short pants and jumpers scurried around.

'Who can gather the most manure to put on the fire?' asked one.

'I can!'

'No, I can!'

Enchanted as we were by our resting place, we nonetheless felt peckish, so we drove to a truck stop where my tour guide insisted the best ever breakfast awaited us. We had greasy Irish bacon and greyish ham, cold fried bread, mushy tomatoes and rubbery eggs.

'You must have been mighty hungry to think this breakfast was any good', I scolded.

Ignoring the old advice never to swim until an hour after eating, we bathed in the incredibly warm turquoise sea that looked more like somewhere in Hawaii than Swansea. In the evening we settled on a moonlit hillside by a castle. That night a male choir of a thousand voices happened to be singing. We got a Chinese takeaway and a bottle of wine.

The wine tasted like cough syrup watered down with rubbing alcohol. The spring rolls seemed like Cornish pasty dough rolled and deep-fried. Still, it was a memorable meal because the wine and Chinese food were the worst I'd ever had. And we got teary-eyed, not over the horrid meal but at the glorious voices resounding over the hills.

Back in Cornwall we concentrated on finding a cream tea. There's something so delectable about those words: cream tea. I had had many a fancy Ritz tea with strawberry tarts and finger sandwiches, but I had not had many cream teas. I immediately fell in love with the gooey richness of berry jam, the bland cool-ness of Devonshire clotted cream, and the dry flakiness of just-so scones. After licking my fingers and downing the dregs of my tea, we hopped into the van and drove on, stopping here and there to wade in a stream or visit an ocean cove. Then we came to a particularly sweet-looking teashop that boasted – cream teas.

'Oh, don't look so forlorn', said the man of the van. 'Who's to say you can't have two cream teas in one day?'

So we stopped and had our second cream tea, this one even better than the first.

I was in heaven.

'Let's stop in at Cambridge and I'll show you my old haunts.'

As we neared Cambridge an adorable teashop with a lawn full of cows beckoned to us.

'It's a culinary tour. You need to fully experience cream teas', said my guide as he caught me longingly looking at the teashop.

We enjoyed our third cream tea of the day.

By the time we entered Cambridge my belly was aching and I thought I would burst. We found some public facilities, but I was not up to touring and we had to stop far too often all the way back to London.

Back home we discovered that an army of small green caterpillars had set up camp in the kitchen. We crushed them wherever we walked, they sizzled whenever the cooker was lit, and they had woven cocoons in the handle of the refrigerator. With a heavy heart, the man of the house announced he would order a truckload of building supplies. It was time to permanently separate the kitchen from the garden.

COMING TO AMERICA

AMANDA JONES

Amanda Jones is a travel writer and photographer who lives in northern California. Her work has appeared in *Travel & Leisure*, *Town & Country Travel*, the *Los Angeles Times*, the London *Sunday Times*, *Vogue* and *Condé Nast Traveller*, among other publications. Thanks to a predilection for wandering, she has an embarrassing number of on-the-road tales of woe and misadventure. Amanda was born and raised in Auckland, New Zealand.

In 1982, at the age of twenty, I was still living at home with my parents in Auckland, New Zealand. The product of a spectacularly sheltered and conventional existence, I had graduated from university and had no plans for the future. One day, my father summoned me into his den, accused me of being 'rudderless', and presented me with a truly horrible suggestion. He was president of Auckland's Rotary Club at the time, and he clearly felt the position entitled him to practise the worst kind of nepotism. 'Rotary', he announced, 'is offering a scholarship for an MBA programme in America. I've entered your name. I feel quite sure you'll get it. I think you can rely on the fact that you'll be off to graduate school in a matter of months.'

'What?' I responded, wondering what I had ever done to make him think I would be either good at, or interested in, business. I was, however, suddenly buoyed by the notion that I should pick myself up and move to America. 'Where?'

'Georgia. It's in the southern portion of the country.'

'Christ!' I shrieked. 'Georgia! How desperate do you think I am? They don't even *drink* in Georgia!'

I had no idea if this was true, but we'd all heard the stories about America's dry college campuses – a notion incomprehensible to a New Zealander – and I had no desire to go to the Deep South. It certainly gave my father pause. He stood there speechless, likely imagining visiting me at my dry college and being obliged to exchange his gin and tonic in cut crystal for a Tab, straight from the can. He sloped off, and the scholarship was awarded to some other hapless creature.

That conversation did, however, make me realise that I had to take control of my life before my father came up with more insane ideas. I must leave. And anywhere but Georgia sounded good.

I quickly determined that Gina, an American exchange student who'd lived with my family for a year, was my salvation. We were both fifteen when Gina had come to live with us. Back then she'd towered over me. She had enormous breasts, she smoked clove cigarettes, she had one pierced ear and a mane of frizzy, white-blonde hair that gave her an exotic, feral allure. Boys adored her, my parents despised her, and I desperately wanted to be like her. Gina had hated New Zealand. She'd hated the food, hated the rain, and she'd especially hated being made to go to my all-girls high school wearing a tartan kilt uniform.

Now, five years later, Gina had written telling me she had dropped out of college and was living in San Francisco. She had a grand apartment, a rich boyfriend and a fabulous job. I wrote asking if I could come and stay with her, telling my parents I was considering Californian graduate schools.

'Come on over!' Gina had replied, with what appeared to be great enthusiasm. 'I'm psyched! You can live with us in our apartment! It'll be totally cool!!!' I was beside myself. I was off to smoke clove cigarettes in dim San Francisco bars, to stroll down the infamous Haight Ashbury, to pepper my speech with terms like 'psyched' and 'totally cool'. I was going to be just like Gina.

To my absolute astonishment my mother bought me a plane ticket and my father presented me with an American Express credit card that he made quite clear was 'for emergency purposes only'. At the airport I jubilantly bade farewell to my family and my boyfriend and strode off without a backward glance.

Arriving in San Francisco, I hauled my grossly over-packed luggage through airport customs and out into the propitious Californian sunshine. I stood and watched as my fellow passengers swarmed past me to be met by joyful smiles and tight embraces. I watched until they had all drifted off, leaving me alone with my bags and no Gina. I'd been stood up.

With no other option springing to mind, I slumped in a chair to wait. Twenty minutes later the doors finally opened and an agitated Gina flew through them. I ran towards her, throwing my arms around her feral neck, prepared to forgive.

She pulled away, barking, 'Hurry, I'm parked illegally.'

Outside, commanding a stretch of red curb, was a 1962 Cadillac, fins and all. I'd never seen a car so glamorous. On the inside, however, the car appeared to be stuffed floor to ceiling with Gina's worldly possessions.

'Look, things didn't work out with the boyfriend', she said. 'I had to...leave.'

'So where are you living now?' I asked, the car's contents leading me to fear the worst.

'Well, not sure right now. I thought we could get an apartment. Hey, you got any money?'

'But what about your job?'

'Yeah, well, the boyfriend didn't think I needed to work. I gave it up.'

'But...where are we staying tonight?'

She shrugged, lighting a clove cigarette.

'I met this bartender. He's into me. He said we might be able to crash at his pad.'

'Crash at his *pad*?' I was horrified. I wanted to slap her.

I took a closer look at Gina. She'd lost weight and she looked haggard. Her clothes were tawdry, her boots were scuffed and her make-up was too heavy. Even the nimbus of hair seemed lacklustre. As my mother would have said, she looked *well used*.

It dawned on me that I'd left the tidy security of my former life for a hoax. The only real thing about Gina was her clove cigarette.

The bartender looked normal but he seemed to have no obvious interest in Gina, which was worrying. Finally, after last orders, he extended a half-hearted offer for us to come back to his apartment and Gina jumped at it.

Back at the bartender's 'pad' we were introduced to the half-dozen guys who were lounging about the room. They were a few years older than me, and of all shapes and sizes. Despite it being three in the morning, some were playing musical instruments, others were reading and a few were cooking. I shuffled over to the bookshelf to bury my exhaustion, feeling shy and daunted.

I judge people by their books. I can't help it. Books tell you something substantive about their owners. Between them, this motley-looking group of young men had every book I had ever wanted to read. There, like flaming tablets, stood *Zen and the Art of Motorcycle Maintenance*; *Siddhartha*; *The Tin Drum*; *On the Road*; *The Razor's Edge*; *Doors of Perception*; *Gödel, Escher, Bach*; *The Little Prince*; *The Waste Land*; *The Dubliners*.

I was saved.

Gina, it turned out, was a coke addict who had been kicked out of her drug-dealing boyfriend's apartment. She had no job and was high most of the time. Within days she had drifted off to whereabouts unknown – leaving me in a three-bedroom apartment with half a dozen men. They'd all gone to an Ivy League university back east together and had moved to San Francisco for the same reason as me – to find a life.

I asked if I could stay with them until I sorted myself out.

'You're in luck', the small one said. 'Eric, our roommate, is out of town on business. You can have his bed this week.'

I moved into Eric's room. I slept in Eric's bed. I read Eric's copy of *The Electric Kool-Aid Acid Test* and felt like I was living with the Merry Pranksters. Then, on the fourth night at around two in the morning, the door to the bedroom burst open and there was Eric himself. I was deeply asleep and stark naked, having figured that by sleeping that way I could save on laundry.

'Oh, hi', he said. 'How ya doin'?' There seemed to be no surprise in his voice. Perhaps, I thought, finding an unfamiliar, unclad woman in your bed was one of those tedious occurrences one must deal with when one chooses to live in San Francisco.

'Good, thanks', I said. 'But...look...I'll leave, but I can't...not like this.' Eric left the room and returned with a sleeping bag. I slid into it and hopped out of his bedroom. It wasn't a terribly auspicious beginning.

Fast-forward several months. The boys and I had moved to a bigger house and Phillipa, my best friend from New Zealand, had also moved to San Francisco. The men cooked foreign food for us, they played bongo drums for us, they engaged us in intellectual discourse and listened to our opinions, and they took turns showing us San Francisco. We'd found Nirvana.

One day, I came home and was introduced to yet another new roommate. He'd been to college with the others and had just moved to San Francisco. He was tall, he had a loud voice and he was dressed head to toe in clothing with the name of his former college emblazoned on it. I pegged him for an elitist and he treated me as if I were the interloper in the frat house redux. Here we go, I thought, here's the jerk to spoil the perfect thing we've got going here.

Later I heard that Eric, sweet Eric, had told the new roommate there was a blonde model living in the house. What Eric had neglected to tell him was that I was merely *working* at a modelling agency. After my father had coldheartedly cut off the American Express card (which I had quite comfortably lived off), I was forced to find a job without a work permit. The modelling agency was the only place willing to hire me. When I'd shown up, Greg (the new roommate) was actually thinking, 'So – where's the model?'

Over the next few months Greg began to pay more attention to me. I grudgingly noted that he made me laugh. He was smart and quick-witted and actually very handsome. When he'd lean forward to pick up a beer I'd notice how pleasing his forearm was, or how broad his shoulders were, or how his eyes sparkled while he was being so richly sardonic. Then, on my twenty-first birthday, I confessed to being madly in love with him.

Meanwhile, Phillipa, my New Zealand friend, was having a fling with Eric. Everyone was happy. After a year, however, Phillipa and I had exhausted all our visa renewal options and could not legally remain in America. One sunny afternoon I encountered the stirring words of Emma Lazarus printed on a calendar in a dry cleaner's: 'Send these, the homeless, tempest-tost to me, I lift my lamp beside the golden door!' The poem moved me to send a beseeching letter to a local congressman requesting a visa extension. He wrote back saying, in so many words: *Who the hell do you think you are? You are not the huddled masses of some war-torn nation besieged by disease, poverty and corruption. You are not stricken by some heart-rending disability. You are not a defecting citizen of an enemy country. And clearly you are not a genius of incomparable measure. So piss off.*

Phillipa and I vowed we would not leave. We moaned about the bitter unfairness of being born in the First World. We thought about living on the lam. And then one day Phillipa had an idea.

'We'll have to get married.'

Looking up from his *National Lampoon*, Greg said, 'That'll work. I'll marry you.'

Naturally, I thought he was talking to me, his girlfriend of four months.

He wasn't, he was talking to Phillipa.

I glowered. I sulked. 'Good for you two. But who'll marry me?'

'Dunno', said Greg. 'Maybe you should talk to Eric.'

That night, I found valour in tequila and knocked on Eric's door. 'Hey, I've got a quick favour to ask of you. You know how I am really in love with Greg? Yeah, well, I don't want to leave America. So look, will you be a sport and marry me?'

Ever the gent, he asked to sleep on it.

In the morning, Eric emerged having decided to become my husband, but with one caveat. Chip was yet another college friend who, during his senior year, had replied to an advertisement in *Rolling Stone* magazine to become a minister in a perfectly legal mail-order church. For twenty-five dollars he had become a reverend, and for another twenty he had become the Reverend Doctor. His reasons for doing this were hazy, but they involved clergy not being drafted into the military and the promise of discount airfares and special parking dispensations. So that we would not be forced to lie to a minister of the church or a court judge, Eric suggested we ask Chip to marry us.

Chip was contacted and agreed to come out from Ohio and marry us in a double wedding – Phillipa to Greg, me to Eric. (After serious discussion, Greg and I had decided it would be foolish to marry each other for green card purposes only.)

A frenzy of wedding plans ensued, and on April Fools Day, 1984, the glorious event took place. Unaware that it was a federal offence to reconfigure the US flag, I sewed my wedding gown out of Old Glory, a tribute to my dedication to my new country. Phillipa's gown was a fashionable cut of the New Zealand standard. We were married in the woods, Merry Prankster style, and danced down the aisle to Trini Lopez' 'I Want to Live in America'.

After the wedding, the Reverend Doctor Chip went back to Ohio, quit his job and moved out to San Francisco under the pretext that the rest of us needed moral supervision.

In order to become legal resident aliens, our next step was to have our marriages scrutinised by the notorious bureaucrats who ran the immigration department. By all accounts their philosophy was that transnational love was unseemly. We'd heard rumours of the interrogations. We'd been told they separated couples and asked personal things, like, *What type of birth control do you use? What side of the bed does he/she sleep on? How often did you have sex on your honeymoon? Who in his/her family came to the wedding?* We devised codes and hand signals; we posed for honeymoon photos; we memorised family ancestry; we ruminated on our fictional sex life.

The process took months, but eventually we were summoned to the final interview. After keeping us waiting for four hours, an immigration officer heaved herself through the door and bawled out our names. She was a brute of a woman, with a raw, ham-hock face, a brow protruding over darkened pits of eyes, and ankles as thick as a baby's waist. She wore a blue serge skirt and a white shirt buttoned all the way up to her impressive wattle. Her thinning hair was drawn back into a severe bun and bound in a net. She was a Central Casting dream caricature.

She escorted us into her windowless office with a table in the centre. A bright light swung low over the table, undoubtedly used to crack would-be immigrants during tense grillings. *So, tell me again, what brand of underwear did you say your husband wears?* Behind her head was a picture of a hairless cat and a crucifix. Eric and I sat holding hands, as we'd practised.

'Right', she snarled. 'How'd you meet?'

Eric sighed, glanced tenderly at me and said, 'Do you want to tell the story, sweetie, or shall I?'

'You go right ahead, honey', I smiled, clueless as to what story he meant. This was the one question we had not rehearsed.

'Well,' said Eric, 'I returned from a business trip one night and there she was, asleep in my bed, her golden hair spread around her face like a halo.' Casting his eyes heavenward, he continued,

'I sent up a prayer, "Thank you, Lord. Thank you for sending me an angel." It was love at first sight for me.'

The blood left my face. Surely she'd see through his ridiculous display.

'How *sweeeet*', she gushed girlishly. 'Did you live together before you got married?'

'Well, yes, we did, actually', I said before Eric could draw breath.

'Did your parents approve?'

'Mine were fine with it', I told her. 'But we didn't tell Eric's.'

In reality Eric's parents had never heard of me.

There was a pause. 'I understand', she said. 'My parents wouldn't approve if I lived with a man out of wedlock either.'

We were stunned into silence by such personal information coming from one so formidable. My instinct was to lean forward, stroke her arm and quietly recommend that if she ever got the opportunity to live with a man, wedlock or no, she should, you know, *carpe diem*. Eric chimed in, lamenting the conservatism of Midwestern parents. She agreed, telling us she was resigned to spending the rest of her days with the aforementioned hairless cat because she was so afraid of disappointing her parents.

Ten minutes later, after some chatty checking of forms, she beamed brightly and sent us on our way with a meaty handshake. I was officially a legal resident alien in the United States of America.

Several weeks later, Greg and Phillipa had a similarly pleasant experience.

After two years of blissful, non-consummated marriage living in separate apartments, we threw a party to celebrate our respective divorces – legally blamed on 'irreconcilable differences'. Eric and Phillipa had broken up amicably during those two years and Eric had taken up with his college girlfriend again, who, upon hearing he'd married me, had made a hasty reappearance to stake her claim. They were married shortly after our divorce.

Phillipa and the Reverend Doctor Chip drove across country together, fell madly in love and were married soon thereafter.

Greg and I were married at about the same time. We have all been happily married now for seventeen years.

In retrospect, I am eternally indebted to that long-ago drug dealer: three solid marriages and six beautiful children have come into the world because he threw Gina out that day.

And as for the moral of this story: not all misadventures remain misadventures. Travel plans gone awry can take you places, connect you with people and cast you into situations that may just change your life.

JOURNEY TO THE CENTRE
OF THE EARTH

ALANA SEMUELS

Born and raised in Boston, Massachusetts, Alana Semuels can't seem to shake her travel bug. The Harvard University grad has wandered the world from Antigua to Zimbabwe, stopping to teach English in Greece and to work in a clinic in Botswana. Currently a journalist in Pittsburgh, Pennsylvania, Alana looks forward to future travels – and World Series wins by the Red Sox.

So far, yet so near, two persons, one in the Northern Hemisphere, the
other in the Southern Hemisphere, may shake hands, kiss each other
or embrace while they remain within their respective hemisphere.
– inscription at Mitad del Mundo

If you follow the equator around the globe, you fly over Borneo and the Democratic Republic of Congo and an expanse of ocean so long it is hard to imagine its distance.

Go overland and you might see a peeling sign by a road telling you that you are standing on the equator, but most countries have better things to do than devote their dollars or francs or rupias to an invisible line dividing the world.

Ecuador is not most countries. Near its capital, Quito, it has devoted a whole museum to Mitad del Mundo, or the middle of the world. If you're picturing a journey to the centre of the earth's core, you'll be disappointed. Instead, the Mitad del Mundo is a granite building topped by a metallic green globe, with yellow lines painted on the ground approximating what the equator might look like, if indeed it could be seen.

I am staring up at the globe, balancing on the yellow line, not quite ready to hop into the southern hemisphere, although I know I am already there. I am in Ecuador to witness the wedding of my childhood friend Leah, who joined the Peace Corps, fell madly in love with Jorge, an Ecuadorian mechanic, and surprised her parents and pretty much everybody else by announcing that they were getting hitched.

The wedding visitors, who are all Jewish and American, are Leah's parents and brother, a few assorted aunts and uncles, my parents who have known her since she was born, and me, born one year after her and certainly not one to go off and marry someone who doesn't speak English and has never left his village. Or at least this is what I tell my parents when they make me promise for the ninth time since breakfast that I will never, ever pull anything like this. The adults hope that I am their secret weapon – I will stride in and Leah will come to her senses and realise that she needs someone who can at least speak English, preferably a Jewish doctor with Red Sox season tickets.

But Leah's destiny was sealed before she even arrived in Ecuador. The rate of marriages between female Peace Corps volunteers and Ecuadorian men is much higher than it is in other places where the organisation sends unsuspecting and unmarried young women, Leah tells me. One of the other volunteers has already married an Ecuadorian teacher, and another has been living for decades with her barefoot children and farmer husband in a small village without so much as a TV set to link her to the English-speaking world. It must be something in the water, I think, and can understand why my parents keep checking to make sure I haven't found an Ecuadorian man myself.

Signs at the site say that while standing on the equator, you move at a pace of 1.667 kilometres per hour, which is faster than you are moving anywhere else on the globe. I believe it. My head is spinning and it feels like the earth has started to speed its rotation, because Leah is getting married in Ecuador and I can't even communicate with her groom. She has arranged our trip to the middle of the earth perhaps as a subtle reminder that we Americans are not only on a different continent but also in a different hemisphere. I can only focus on the sobering fact that everyone we pass on the street may soon be Leah's relative by marriage.

My first meeting with Jorge is not smooth. My Spanish is rusty, his English vocabulary is limited to a handful of words, and neither of us can think of anything to say in our shared smattering of phrases.

'How are you?' I ask in Spanish.

'Fine', he replies. He launches into a question, which I pretend to understand.

'Yes', I answer. 'It is very hot.'

He is clearly puzzled. Wrong answer, I think. I try again.

'I like to dance', I say, and then, as my grand finale, I finish up with the last phrase I can remember in my jet lag-induced panic. I try to wish him congratulations on his engagement. '*Feliz Navidad.*'

He nods, pleased. Only later do I remember that this means Merry Christmas.

We pile into two white vans and head to Latacunga, where the wedding will take place. The wedding is here because it is easy to reach from Quito and because the groom's family lives here, but not because it is one of Ecuador's top ten tourist destinations. The Best of Ecuador website sums up Latacunga pretty well: 'This is not an invigorating town'. It's muddy and built of concrete, and our hotel/motel is on the highway leading out of the city. Latacunga's highlights are two volcanoes in the far distance that are spewing smoke. I can see Leah's mother estimate their distance, hoping they might explode, scattering the guests like ashes to their far corners of the world.

The next morning, we are determined to tour at least part of the southern hemisphere before the evening wedding, and take off again in our two dirty white vans to explore the villages outside of Latacunga. We drive along a winding road full of potholes while a nasty wind stirs up the pebbles on the ground.

I am not sure who I feel more sorry for – the driver or myself. He is stuck navigating country roads with a van full of Americans who have funny accents and a deep determination to stop and see everything – and I mean everything – we pass.

'Look at the mountains. Have you ever seen mountains like that?' my mother begins. 'Let's stop and take a picture.'

'Signs in Spanish! I wonder what they say', delights the bride's aunt. 'Stop – we need to take a picture.'

'Look at the poor woman with her children and a goat! Are they naked? She only has one eye! How charming', says aunt number two. 'Let's take a picture.'

We stop at every farm and village we see, buying trinkets and wandering around the chilly landscape. We drift into churches and food stores, through empty courtyards, and snap photos of toothless men drinking cola out of glass bottles with straws.

I feel sure that we are on the other side of the equator now. It's nothing tangible, such as seeing the toilets swirl the other way, or recognising a different set of constellations, but is instead a growing feeling that we are more tourists and outsiders than we are wedding guests. We navigate the dirt roads, discussing wedding presents and conferring about Leah's suggestion that we buy the groom's family a medium-sized pig as a goodwill gesture. Instead of selecting china from the registry of Bed, Bath & Beyond, I am in a white van in the Andean mountains cringing as my parents take pictures of women dressed in wool and buy exotic souvenirs that they will take home and hang on the wall. My world has been turned upside down.

We round off the afternoon with a trip to Latacunga's famed market. Every Saturday and Tuesday, people journey from far-off villages to sell cow heads, Nike sweatshirts and old cassette tapes to the Latacungians and those hapless tourists who got on the wrong bus or in a white van and suddenly find themselves in a decidedly not invigorating city in Ecuador.

I join the father and brother of the bride to ostensibly eat but really just stare at *cuy*, an Ecuadorian specialty. *Cuy* is what Americans know as guinea pig; it looks like a rat that has been zapped by a stray electric wire and frozen in time. It is served on its back, four legs raised with paws desperately in need of a mani-cure. I can't help but think of Leah, who at this minute is getting her nails done in preparation for the wedding, and wonder if she too is a guinea pig in some sort of bizarre cultural experiment.

As the sun sets over Latacunga, we dress for the wedding and I wonder what type of wedding Leah dreamt of when she was a little girl, when she still planned to meet a nice strapping Jewish American boy. Probably long pews packed with visitors, roses and bouquets, a classy band playing 'Hava Nagila', a tow-headed gap-toothed flower girl, and a reception where the bride and groom feed each other cake and smear it on each other's cheeks.

Instead we have a reception room in the hotel/motel, above a room that, judging by the booming bass emanating from below, has already begun to party; an entryway of flowers; ten Americans dressed in their finest packable wedding wear feel-ing as nervous as a pack of guinea pigs crossing the Ecuadorian border; and a roomful of Ecuadorians who look like they bite off guinea pigs' heads with their teeth.

After a few brief formalities – limited by the language barri-ers, and the fact that the parents of the bride and groom don't seem to have much to say to one another – Leah walks down the aisle. I say aisle because the guests are divided as if the line from Mitad del Mundo had been invisibly extended to the parquet dance floor. We Americans stand quietly on one side, the Ecuadorians – and there are dozens of them – just as mute on the other. This set-up has all the characteristics of a battlefield – if someone were to yell charge, I am not at all sure what would happen. We are taller, but there are more of them. And their women wear sharp-looking heels.

The ceremony is over quickly and is mostly in Spanish, leaving the American guests to stare dumbly off into the distance while the Ecuadorian women dab tears from their eyes. The part about there being any reason why these two souls should not be joined in matrimony is definitely done in Spanish, which is wise as most of the American guests are looking surprised that this whole wedding thing is actually happening. There is some Hebrew read, a few Jewish traditions upheld, rings exchanged, and before I know it, the deejay shouts '*Viven los novios!*' and cracks open a bottle of champagne, and the salsa music is pumping.

Before the shock settles in that Leah is now married to an Ecuadorian mechanic who speaks no English, the dance floor erupts into a party of fast-moving couples who know the steps and *man*, can they dance. We Americans shuffle off to the side, shell-shocked, shy. Next to the dark-skinned guests on the other side of the room, we look like white twerps who sit around and watch *Seinfeld* on Saturday nights while the Ecuadorians dance the night away.

But my parents are not ready to give up so quickly. My father, a deejay in his college days, reaches into his jacket pocket and shows me a CD of *Billboard's Top Ten Dance Tunes* he bought at the market earlier that day. He sidles over to the music stand and confers with the deejay by nodding and pointing. He comes back, determined.

'Get ready to dance', he says to nobody in particular.

We stand watching twirling couples until the pumping beat of Little Eva's 'Locomotion' arouses a cheer from the American side of the room.

Everybody's doing a brand-new dance now...

And the American contingent floods onto the floor, shaking booties and nodding heads with vigour. Finding comfort in solidarity, they form a conga line. The Ecuadorians, more surprised than anything else, step off to the side, not sure what to do. The conga line does a slow but well-meaning lap or two around the dance floor, my father leading, then breaks up so that its members can shake their hips now. I can't help but join them; I feel so embarrassed by my elders trying to have a good time on their own terms that I want to add to their numbers.

Even the Locomotion has to end, but the deejay is skilled, blending the last notes into a techno Latin beat that arouses cheers from the Other Side.

Exit the Americans, enter the Ecuadorians. They pair off and spin and twirl and dip and shake while my parents and the bride's relatives catch their breath. They haven't danced this hard since the sixties, and are sweating and gasping for air in the high mountain altitude.

'Just wait till he plays "Respect"', my dad says, pumping a fist in the air.

The deejay tries a few more Latin melodies before the next *Billboard* song, which is a relief because the bride's dad looks like he might need a bit of a breather and I don't know if they even have an emergency room in Latacunga. But the Americans are back in full force by the first chorus of 'YMCA', which scares the Ecuadorians off to the side again, and shows off the sweat stains in the Americans' armpits. The Ecuadorians don't seem to sweat at all. They are also unsure what's so much fun about spelling Y-M-C-A with your arms.

When it ends, the Americans sit down and the Ecuadorians take over again and I realise I am witnessing two different

223

weddings in two different hemispheres and it's a competition more than it is a celebration of matrimony.

This might have gone on for ever, but we are saved by 'The Electric Slide'. Now it might seem laughable that such a terrible song, and one that stirs up so many memories of middle school and forced line dancing, would serve as the virtual bridge between the north and south. But it doesn't drive the Ecuadorians off the dance floor. And since it is in English, the Americans are obligated to dance too.

Sure, my parents don't remember all of the steps, and the Ecuadorians have a different version that involves a little more hip-shaking and twirling that doesn't work out so well for the bride's uncle, but the reality is that there we are, now relatives by marriage or friendship, boogieing down to the electric slide in a hotel/motel room in Latacunga, Ecuador, while the volcano smokes miles away.

And even this might have been an anomaly had not the groom's cousin, a teenager named Gustavo who had already drunk the equivalent of a bottle of champagne, grabbed my mother before she could even say '*Ole!*' and started tangoing with her on the dance floor. His relatives follow. When the Americans try to institute their exodus at the onset of Latin music, they are waylaid by relatives of the groom who are determined to teach them how to salsa no matter how many times their toes are stomped.

And although I know we'll be leaving tomorrow to go back to Quito and stay in the Hyatt while the Ecuadorians will go back home and thank us for our pig in the morning, I cannot help but appreciate the pull of the equator and its neutralising effect. For as much as we Americans had opposed the wedding, the Ecuadorians probably loathed marrying Jorge off to a family of such terrible dancers as well. And now Leah and Jorge are at latitude zero, able to go any which way, north, south, east or west, and here we are, having crossed the invisible line that first divided us, spinning at 1.667 kilometres per hour near the centre of the world.

I find myself a nice Ecuadorian man whose name I cannot pronounce who is one of the taller men in the room and thus only a head or so shorter than me. He is patient and teaches me how to salsa, and we even add a few bells and whistles of our own after I get the hang of it. I can see my parents raising their eyebrows when he dips me, but I am having too much fun to be embarrassed. We could have danced off until the sunset, or sunrise in this case, had not Leah remembered that she forgot to throw the bouquet, and stopped the dancing so she could line up all the unmarried females to participate.

I stand jockeying with a cluster of Ecuadorian women behind Leah, really more interested in avoiding the flying flowers than catching them. But when she throws them, they hit the ceiling and somehow bounce into my hands.

My Ecuadorian man applauds the loudest and I turn to wink at my parents. Another Ecuadorian wedding. Now wouldn't that be nice.

THE MOST PERFECT HOTEL IN THE WORLD

SIMON WINCHESTER

Simon Winchester is the author, most recently, of *A Crack in the Edge of the World*, a centennial account of the great San Francisco earthquake. Among his other books are *Krakatoa*, *The Map that Changed the World* and *The Surgeon of Crowthorne* (also published under the title *The Professor and the Madman*). Simon lives in New York City and on a farm in the Berkshire Hills of western Massachusetts.

This is a story not my own, but one that belongs to a literary figure of so towering a reputation among the *belles lettristes* of London that he feels it rather beneath him to relate it. He complains that the tale is, as they were once wont to say in Rome, *infra dig*, since it concerns such mundanities as the location of hotel rooms, the design of baths and the taps with which they are customarily equipped, the latest reported methods of making gin martinis and the rituals of American wedding nights. The fact that this confection, of what are to most readers really rather interesting items of ordinariness, was assembled for the making of the story in what was at the time one of the world's finest hotels, to wit the Connaught, of Carlos Place, London W1, cuts neither ice nor mustard with the figure to whom the tale belongs – an attitude of such unrelieved stubbornness that it has compelled me to conclude, if somewhat irrelevantly, that the aforesaid literary figure is in fact, and in titanic proportions, a crashing snob.

The setting, the Connaught Hotel, was once an inn of the keenest perfection, a place of Edwardian solidity, quiet and discretion, a hotel where one might live for months and feel quite as civilised and content as though one had never left home in the first place. Lately it has been spoiled by fashion, of course; but at the time of the story its chambers, its drawing rooms, its corner bar and its restaurant were all impeccable in their own ways, needing never to be changed in any respect. The Grill in particular, though it plays no part in the story, was evidently an anteroom to Paradise: it was the kind of place where you might fall gently asleep over a perfect Dover sole, whereupon the waiters would be sure to pad past you with the softest of footfalls, would make certain that your tie made no contact with the butter dish, and on your awakening would enquire quietly if coffee or bonbons would be required as a conclusion to your evidently much-enjoyed repast.

But it is not the Grill that is the subject of this story. It is the suite of rooms, second floor front, that are on the very right-hand side of the hotel as you look at the door that opens onto Carlos Place. Most particularly it concerns the capacious and carpeted bathroom of this suite; and to be specific, without, I hope, any hint of vulgarity, it concerns the bath, and the slight eccentricity of its mechanics.

All the baths in this hotel, together, I am told, with all those in the older bathrooms of the Savoy and Claridge's hotels too, enjoy the same and very singular arrangement, a design that was created to ensure peace and quiet for the bath's intended occupant, as also for those who share his chambers: for rather than have the water flow into the bath from taps that are mounted on the vessel's upper lip, as is customary, the unique design of the Connaught's magnificently antique baths has the inflow pipe sited just above the drain, and so little more than an inch above the bath's base. The consequence of the design will be clear: a few moments after the water has been turned on, its surface will have risen above the inflow, and no further sound – no bubbling or splashing or dripping – can be heard again. The bath thus fills in utter silence, a lavatorial discretion that is very much in keeping with the overall understated nature of this most grand of grand hotels.

However, these are modern times, times when few of the Connaught's guests will travel as one generally did in the days the great structure was built, with one's valet. And frankly, if one does not have one's valet on hand to – in this specific case – turn the taps on and, more importantly, off, the silence that is offered by such an intricate design can lead to most costly consequence.

As was discovered, with much embarrassment, not by the aforementioned towering literary figure, but by his equally towering American literary agent, who had come to London and had wisely decided to stay at the Connaught and, most particularly, in the much-favoured second-floor corner suite of rooms. He was accompanied on his excursion not by his valet, but by his wife.

As she recounts, in chiding terms, it was her husband whose fault it all was. He ran the bath. He poured in a liberal quantity of bath salts. He walked away into the sitting room to await results. The reason for his wife's later chiding arose from the existence of a small sign on the ledge of the bath which read: *Patrons are respectfully reminded that because of a unique design the baths in this hotel fill very rapidly and entirely silently, and it would behoove our guests* (well, maybe it didn't say behoove, but the Connaught is the kind of place where such vocabulary would be entirely acceptable) *not to retire to the sitting room, or to use the telephone, while leaving the silently filling bath unattended, as flooding could occur.*

No, she reported later, her husband did not take any note whatsoever of the notice, and as a result he was not behooven to avoid doing what he, as a towering literary agent, seems to have been born to do, and that was to telephone. He did so, at length, speaking to a number of long-unspoken-to friends in London, while all the time the bath, scented with expensive salts, was filling, filling, filling.

It must have been twenty minutes later when there came a soft rapping on the door. Our agent, exasperated by having his telephoning interrupted, opened it. (His wife was immersed in macramé, or some such.) A small man stood before him, clad in the uniform of a bartender. The man's hair appeared to be wet – as, on closer inspection, did his barkeeper's uniform, which clung limply to his form. An expensive aroma of vague familiarity wafted up from him.

'Excuse me for bothering you, sir', said the functionary. 'But I wonder if you might be having some slight trouble with your bathroom. Water seems to be dripping through the ceiling of the bar – in rather sizable quantities, in fact. More like a steady stream. We're having to close down.'

Oh. My. God. *Of course!* Agent, wife and the damply fragrant *cocktailmeister* ran as one to the bathroom – to find water silently washing over the edge of the bath and sheeting down onto a floor that was already six inches deep in warm suds. The room was a ruin. Good shoes floated about, wildly. An American newspaper lay sodden on the bubbled surface. Tufts of carpet drifted like eelgrass on a tropical beach. Oh. My. God.

A hurried turning-off of taps. A torrent of apologies. Offers to pay. Offers to leave. Offers to read all notices next time – it was all just *ghastly*. But the Connaught being the hotel it is, our friends and their luggage were whisked off to another suite, and all were made to feel as though it was the hotel's fault, even though our guests knew full well it was all down to their own carelessness. They crept through the halls of the mansion like furtive spies for the next few days, shamed by the error of their ways.

And never more so than that very evening, when they dared briefly to enter the bar – the ground-floor bar which, in all its oak-panelled magnificence, turned out to be situated in the hotel's right-hand corner, exactly, exactly, below the room they had until lately occupied. The bartender was there, cheerful and newly and drily uniformed, looking for all the world as though nothing untoward had happened.

But happened it most decidedly had. And there was evidence. For in the very corner of the room, directly beneath a slightly sagging ceiling, was a red and tasselled velvet rope suspended from a pair of brass stanchions. An aspidistra in a Chinese pot stood where a banquette once had been, and there was a small handwritten sign regretting that owing to a leak of water, this area of the bar would be closed for a day or two. The humiliation! The pair slunk immediately from the bar and headed to the Grill next door, saying almost as little to each other and to the waiters that evening as those elderly diners who were sleeping so contentedly over their Dover soles.

However, time heals. The following night, perhaps emboldened both by drink and by time, the pair confessed their mistake – and they did so to the towering literary figure who first told me the story. He chortled merrily at their discomfort, and said that he would write something about it.

As indeed he did. Five days later he came to see off our heroes at London's aerodrome, and after the usual obeisances and valedictories had been made, he pressed into his agent's hand an envelope. Read it on the aircraft, he said. You might be amused.

And this is what our agent and über flood-maker read.

A young American man, a Boston Brahmin of impeccable family and taste, had lately married a young and beautiful girl from the American Midwest, a somewhat innocent treasure of a colleen whose father had made a fortune in dry goods, but whose family had travelled little in their lives, and whose daughter had travelled not at all. No matter, said our Lowell or our Cabot or whatever he might have been: I shall take you on our honeymoon to the great and wonderful city of London, England; and there we shall put up at the world's finest hotel, by name the Connaught, and we shall sit in my favourite corner seat in my favourite oak-panelled bar in all the world, and there shall we toast one another with a pair – maybe more – of the finest gin martinis that were ever made by human endeavour. I have been there a hundred times; I know all the attendants and they know me; we shall have a time that will in all senses be memorable, a perfect first excursion into the known mysteries of the outer world.

And so they flew across the ocean, our Mr and newly Mrs Lowell or Cabot or Lodge. They were collected at the aerodrome by the Connaught's magnificent black Daimler, they were shown to an impeccable suite on the fourth floor, they bathed – carefully and obediently adhering to the Rules, for this was a couple fastidious in their habits. They changed into proper evening clothing and in due course came into the oak-panelled bar and they sat in the corner, on a banquette, together in peace and style, the flickering of the fire before them, the rosy glow of London glimpsed behind the velvet curtains.

A bartender approached, smiling with easy familiarity. Two martinis, George, said our Brahmin. Certainly, sir – gin, of course? Of course. Certainly, sir.

And within moments, after nuts and napkins and knives had been arranged by silent men in white linen jackets, and after the sounds of tinkling and shaking and stirring from a very scientific-looking person who stood before an immense array of bottles and behind a brass and cherry-wood bar, so two glasses were brought to the table, and on a silver salver. And what glasses! – perfectly shaped crystal, elegant stems and necks, gleaming and sparkling, and filled almost to the brim with a clear and sparkling liquid, two small olive-green spheres within, an oval film of lemon zest floating on the meniscus above. The glasses were placed, carefully, reverently, before the happy pair. The waiter silently withdrew.

Our man then picked up his glass and motioned to his lady to do the same. He held it up, almost at eye level, gazed into it with awe, the firelight flickering and refracting about its inner mysteries. He spoke. Darling, he began. I have so wanted to bring you here, the world's most perfect girl, to the world's best hotel, to begin our married life with a toast taken with the world's perfect martini. So may I say simply this: I love you, I adore you, and I toast you for a lifetime of happiness and contentment.

He leaned forward, clinked crystal to crystal, brought his glass to his lip and tasted.

And for what was only a second or two, but which his wife later said seemed a lifetime, he hesitated.

Eventually he spoke again. *Almost* perfect, he said. *Almost*. But just – how shall I say it? – just the tiniest bit *too cold*.

And he held his glass before him, at arm's length, gazing with gimlet eye into its glassy depths.

As he did so, suddenly, without warning, a drop of warm and fragrant water fell from the ceiling above him, directly into his glass. He looked up, grinned, put the glass to his lips once more. And smiled.

There, he declared. Now that's just right. He looked up at the ceiling again, then over to the waiter – to whom he flashed a conspiratorial look – and finally to his wife.

See that? he said, delighted. Now didn't I tell you – this *surely* is the world's *most perfect hotel*.

THE PRINCE AND I

KATHIE KERTESZ

At the age of nine, Kathie Kertesz started dreaming about international travel – and saving her money. By the time she was fourteen she was able to pay for her first trip to Europe. Now a happy grandmother of six, in the past year she has had essays published dealing with her major passions: travel and dancing. In her professional life she coaches people in high performance and *joie de vivre*. Visit her website at http://home.earthlink.net/~kkertesz.

It never occurred to me that I would meet a prince looking like this: dressed in blue jeans, slightly damp from spilled sparkling water, and carrying a long Hungarian sausage under my arm. I am half-Hungarian – which means that I was brought up with a strong romantic streak. I learned the Viennese waltz when I was five. When I was a girl my favourite fantasy was of attending a ball and meeting Prince Charming. I would, of course, be dressed in a beautiful long gown. He would be wearing a formal tuxedo and tails, or possibly the dress uniform of his country. It would all be very proper and formal, and I would fall madly in love.

But when I met this particular prince, I was seated in a first-class compartment on a train between Vienna and Geneva, using up the final section of a Eurail pass. I was in my mid-thirties, and was returning from a visit with my father's relatives. As a special parting gift I had been handed a very long Hungarian hard sausage, a delicacy – one of my father's favourites. They had also loaded me down with cheeses, bread and bottled water. As it was nearing lunch time, I had decided to have a snack.

You have to understand that I was feeling a bit shy. I was travelling in first class on a Swiss train, surrounded by a number of slightly forbidding men and women, all of whom were dressed in formal, expensive business attire. I, on the other hand, was wearing jeans and a faded T-shirt, and was loaded down with strange-looking, slightly smelly parcels. As if that weren't bad enough, when I uncorked the sparkling water, it gushed up in an arc, narrowly missing the people beside me and wetting our compartment. I decided to make a quick exit, so loaded up my packages and started down the hall, looking for a less-crowded, less-critical space.

Within minutes I had found one. As I peered into an open door, I was waved in by an affable-looking man who appeared to be in his early thirties. Though dressed formally in a pin-striped suit, he had taken off his shoes and had his feet propped up on the seat across from him.

'Come in', he said. 'There's plenty of room.'

When the two other people occupying the compartment left at the next station, we introduced ourselves.

'Call me Hans', my seat companion said.

I noticed that he was reading a book about science and, telling him that I had grown up surrounded by scientists, I asked if he was a scientist. He gave me a rueful look and told me that he was going through a career crisis. The book was being used to clear his brain.

Soon we were deep in conversation. Still a bit self-conscious about my large Hungarian sausage and slightly dishevelled appearance, I explained that I was travelling back from my father's fiftieth-anniversary high-school reunion in Ordeal, Romania, two miles from the Hungarian border. I also told Hans that I lived in a small town near San Francisco, California. He asked me all sorts of questions about my interests and activities, saying that he had visited the Bay Area and had enjoyed it a great deal. Earlier I had noticed a wedding ring on his finger, but thought, philosophically, At least I am getting the chance to talk in depth with someone who lives in this part of the world.

Our conversation grew more and more animated, and before I knew it, I was showing him aikido moves, teaching him eye exercises and discussing my knowledge of the field of accelerated learning. He said that he was interested in educational reform and asked me a series of intelligent, very specific questions. I found myself enjoying our conversation even more than I could have imagined.

'Tell me about your daily life? What was it like to grow up near here?' I asked Hans.

'My parents brought me up in a very strict and formal manner, so my wife and I vowed that we would raise our children in a more relaxed, informal and loving atmosphere. Our children attend the local public schools. We often do our shopping in the local marketplace, and our cars are Volkswagens, not Mercedes. I am wearing this suit because I had a special business meeting, but I usually like to dress more casually. And I am only travelling first class because of this meeting', he answered.

Hans was so friendly that I pulled out my business card and gave it to him.

'If you and your family ever come to the San Francisco area, do call me up. I would be happy to tell you about special places known only by the locals, and to show you some of them.'

Hans hesitated for a moment, then pulled out his business card and gave it to me. I noticed that it only had his first name with 'von Liechtenstein' on it and then the name of that country below it. I did think the card a bit strange, but thought that maybe they were more formal around here, and didn't have cards with addresses on them.

Looking at it, I said slowly, 'Oh, you are from Liechtenstein?'

'Yes,' he said dryly, 'my family is in agriculture there.'

I smiled at him.

'Actually,' he said, 'I am the Crown Prince of Liechtenstein.'

For a second I thought that I had fallen asleep and this was some sort of dream. Or perhaps he was just joking with me. I considered answering, 'Yes, and my mother is Queen Elizabeth II!'

Hans must have noticed the expression on my face. 'It's really true', he said, 'and we are as informal as I told you.'

'I'm sorry to have seemed so stupid', I replied, feeling like an idiot that I hadn't recognised his name on the card.

'Forget it', he answered. 'I just wish that we could always be like this – like ten-year-old friends, Hans and Kathie, being enthusiastic about our lives.'

'Well, we are right now', I replied. 'I want to hear what it was like when you were growing up.'

Relaxing back into our seats, we munched companionably on my Hungarian sausage and drank the beers he had bought us. I looked outside – we were passing snowcapped Alps with tiny chalets perched upon them.

'Once upon a time...there was a country called Liechtenstein', Hans began. Stillness settled upon me. If this was a dream, I would never forget it.

———————————

A few years passed and once again, I was on my way to Europe. 'Why don't you write to the Prince', a girlfriend of mine teased. 'I bet you don't have the guts to do it.'

The gauntlet had been thrown down. I couldn't pass on the challenge, but I wanted to hedge my bets. I would write to the Prince, but not too far in advance of the trip I was about to make. That way I could tell my friend that I had met the conditions, but wasn't able to make a connection. I wrote a fairly formal note, on letterhead stationery, mentioning the time and place where I had met him, and saying that I was going to be passing near his country and would like the opportunity to talk to him again.

I arrived in Paris, and just as I walked into the apartment I was staying in, the phone rang. 'Ms Kertesz,' a woman's voice said, 'the Prince of Liechtenstein [his father had died] would be happy to see you in his office in ten days.' I felt faint.

It was winter in Liechtenstein. When I asked directions to Hans's office, everyone pointed up to a fairy-tale castle perched high above the town. The taxi driver told me that it had been built in the fourteenth century and was where the Prince's family lived. He deposited me at the end of the drawbridge and I walked slowly inside the castle walls and down a cobbled road that led to a spacious courtyard. As I rounded the corner, I couldn't believe my eyes. There were two Volkswagens parked there, just as Hans had told me. I couldn't keep the silly smile off my face. It was all true.

I had been told to go to a specific door in the courtyard, and I knocked and was directed to enter. My eyes were still dazzled from the snow and the blindingly blue sky, so at first I didn't see Hans. He jumped up and bounded across the room, holding out his hand to greet me. I had vowed to appear more professional this time, so was wearing a dress and had groomed myself carefully. Hans, on the other hand, wore corduroy pants, a shirt with rolled-up sleeves and sandals.

He looked at me and grinned.

'Do you remember those eye exercises you taught me?' he asked. 'Well, I have used them and they work. And all of your information about accelerated learning inspired me so much that I have now put an accelerated learning programme in all of the schools in my country.'

I can still feel the wave of excitement and pleasure that went through me at those words. I have always believed in fairy tales – but I never expected to play a role in one!

WANGARA'S CROSS

JOSHUA CLARK

Joshua Clark, founder of Light of New Orleans Publishing, contributes fiction, travel and photography to various US publications, from the *Los Angeles Times* to the *Miami Herald*. He is also the associate editor for *Scat* magazine. An oyster-eating champion, certified personal trainer and retired bartender, Joshua was raised in Washington, DC, got a somewhat irrelevant economics degree from Yale University, lived in Spain, Australia and Argentina, and now resides in New Orleans.

There is a part of the Simpson Desert in Central Australia where day is split clean into red and blue, earth and sky, with only bone-white trees between the two. And dusk is the same as dawn. The small leafless trees reach like hands, the branches fingers grasping for sky, silhouetted against the red above the horizon. Above the red is a strip of orange and above that canary yellow and pastel blue which gets deeper, then darker overhead, until it's black against clouds of stars you can't see in the Northern Hemisphere. It was below those stars and between those trees that my overturned '74 panel van lay hulking against the red horizon.

I hadn't been near it since noon, when the world was still split clean between red and blue, when the van had stopped being an extension of my body, as cars usually are, and started being a three-tonne hunk of metal that you're trapped inside while it's succumbing to the forces of gravity after you've helicoptered off the road and walloped your third tree.

I hadn't even been going fast. Over the last eight days I'd lost traction and spun out four times on the dirt roads here. But there was nothing to hit, just dirt and sky to slide through until I stopped. And trees. It was the trees that got me. That third one anyway.

When the van started rolling, I thought that was it. But I also thought about how, if I lived, this would make a good story I could tell my girlfriend sometime. Like most people, I'd often wondered what I'd think about right before I died. And that was it. A story.

When the van finished rolling I realised there was blood all over my shoulder and I was probably in shock. I did a limb check. Then a broken bone check. Then I tried to open the door but it wouldn't budge. There was ground where the window used to be. I turned the other way to see sky where the passenger-side window used to be. Both doors, along with the sides of the van, were caved in. After making my way through my belongings heaped on top of me – bottles of water, a gas can, canned beans, CD cases, books, clothes, pillows, a cooler – I kicked open the passenger door, climbed up, leaped from the van and started running like hell because as everyone knows from the movies your car always blows up after you have a bad accident.

It didn't blow up. It just lay there on its side exhaling Cyndi Lauper. It was part of a CD mix my girlfriend had given me for the trip. My finger had been on the way to hitting the 'skip' button when the van lost traction. I'd always wondered if the stereo would keep going after you got into an accident.

Finally, the song ended. For five seconds there was silence in the thin, still July winter sun. I inspected my shoulder, and saw it was only a scrape. Then the synthesizer and drum machine started up again and Cyndi kicked into gear. Something somehow in the tumult must have hit the 'repeat' button.

When I lifted my head from my hands I found myself staring at a pair of emus, each a good six feet tall. They regarded me with curiosity, their fist-sized heads bobbing up and down on spaghetti necks. They were likely not used to seeing college kids covered in red dirt, bleeding and crying about the prospect of having to listen to Cyndi Lauper for infinity. And I was naked. I hadn't seen a person in two days and it felt pretty cool to be driving around naked. Not that it made a difference to the emus. They sniffed through the debris left in the van's wake from the road – my camera in pieces, more CD cases, more canned beans, more books, bottles of water, a compass, underwear, a boot, two pairs of shattered sunglasses, pens, paper, a cowboy hat, coins, cash, until they reached the van itself and got an earful of Cyndi's chorus. At that, the emus ran off to wherever it is they run off to. Me, I had nowhere to go. The next town was about 200 kilometres away. I picked up a pair of underpants that had fallen out of the van and put them on. The cowboy hat and the one (right) boot too. And waited.

Now, while patches of the Milky Way blossomed overhead, and the red of the desert was hugging the bottom of the sky, Cyndi was informing me of exactly how much fun girls just wanna have for the seventy-fourth time. It was getting cold. The matches were still somewhere in the van, next to my mattress, along with all my other worldly belongings. The thing had eaten them all. It had tried to eat me. And I felt like it might get up at any time and have another go at it. But I needed those matches for a fire. Then I saw the smallest blob of light on the horizon, as if the sun was coming back for me at the end of the road. Headlights.

It took a long time before the lights got any bigger, and then impossibly long before I could see the camper van. The red sank below the horizon, then the orange, and finally the canary yellow. The sky was all black and blue and stars by the time the camper van got me in its headlights.

I flailed my arms wildly as though they might not notice some bleeding guy standing in the middle of the road in the middle of nowhere in his underwear, one boot and a cowboy hat. They came within three metres of me and stopped. Blinded in the headlights, I heard the windows roll up. Then the doors lock. Did this look like a carjacking to them? I pointed to my van. The camper van, the size of a small home, crept towards me nervously over the lumpy dirt and rocks that made up the road. It pulled up alongside me. The window came down and from within the dark interior a small voice asked, 'What in God's name is that noise?'

'That's Cyndi Lauper, sir', I said.

'Sounds like Satan', he said.

'You're telling me, sir.'

'What's a Canadian doing out here?'

'American, sir.'

'America?!' said another voice, a woman, from a bit further back in the darkness, probably the passenger seat. 'Graceland?'

'Nope. New Haven, Connecticut, ma'am.'

'Oh.'

'Connecticut?' said the man. 'No kidding? We've been to Detroit before. Went to a dry-cleaning convention there in '84.'

'Really.'

'Do they still have Old Landmark Church of God in Christ there?'

'Not really sure.'

'Have you been to Graceland?' asked the woman. 'We've been to Graceland.'

'Nope', I said. 'Anyway, I'm kinda bleeding and cold and my van's over there on its side and –'

'What are you doing in Australia?' asked the man. I could make out the top of his bald head now, and the woman's silhouette – big glasses and big hair.

'I was spending a semester abroad', I said. 'Studying at the Queensland College of Art. Just got done and wanted to see the country before I have to go back to the States and my van's over there on its – '

'Just travelling ourselves. Bought this camper van after we retired four years ago, started driving and forgot to stop. This is our fifth lap round the bush. We keep it at a slow clip, that way it stays right-side up. I'm Joseph and this is Mary.'

'Josh.'

'Well, Josh, where in God's name are your clothes?'

'In the van.'

Silence. I didn't feel like explaining that I had become scared to death of my own car. Then he said, 'Well, Josh, did you see that sign way back there at the start of the desert that said "Four-wheel drive vehicles only, contact police before you begin and when you get through" or something like that?'

'Yup.'

'Was your van four-wheel drive?'

'Nope.'

'Did you contact the police?'

'Nope.'

'Connecticut, huh?'

'Yup.'

Joseph opened the door, smiling. He was a cherubic old man with a thin horseshoe of white hair around his head. He got an enormous chain out of the back and we fixed it to the trailer behind their camper van. First we turned my van right-side up, put two of their spare tyres on it, then dragged it to the road. I picked up my belongings from the ground, tossed them into the van, and we set off towards what they said was a small town ahead. The beast seemed a lot less menacing now that it was on a leash. It resembled a gargantuan, crinkled egg blasting Cyndi Lauper as we putted along in second gear.

To this day I can't recall much that was said in that camper van. But I remember they were good people. I remember they said they were 'believers'. And that they were explaining their philosophy of 'B's' – beers, bananas and Bibles – when Joseph slammed on the brakes and I, along with several Bibles and bananas (I had yet to see any beers), went flying into the dashboard.

When I looked through the windshield there was a flock of camels walking through the yellow headlights, oblivious to us. It took a good two minutes for them to cross the road. I was in the process of smacking myself to try to wake up when Mary explained that camels were brought here before cars and then left to roam the deserts with nothing to do but procreate and now Australia had more wild camels than anywhere on earth.

When the last camel walked off the road ahead it was replaced by an Aboriginal man in jeans and a T-shirt, waving his arms. His clothes, hair and face were caked in red dirt like mine. Behind him was a small station wagon, and next to that a woman, also covered in desert, holding a backpack. The car, other than being upside down, looked just fine. Joseph and Mary rolled their windows up and locked their doors.

Ten minutes later Freddie and his mother-in-law Awoonga were sitting on either side of me as we jiggled along the road. We left their car where it was. Like Joseph and Mary, they had avoided hitting the camels, and, like me, they had knocked over a tree. They'd been travelling from Awoonga's family's farm to Freddie's farm. Both farms were about 400 kilometres from this road on different sides of it. I asked them what they grew and they looked at me oddly. They said they had met a Canadian like me once down in Perth. I told them I was American. Freddie asked me how the black people were in America. I told him they were fine. He asked if their situation was like his. I told him that the predicament of the Native Americans was more like that of the Aborigines. He asked me the same question again. When I didn't respond he asked me to ask his mother-in-law if she had remembered to bring the tomato sauce in her bag. He explained that tribal law forbade them to speak to each other. I asked him why. That was just the way it was, he said. We should all be so lucky, I said. After I asked her, Awoonga said the tomato sauce was on the back of Freddie's shirt. She said it had exploded all over the car and it had made her very scared because she thought it was her insides. Freddie swore under his breath in some language I couldn't understand, then asked if Mary had any tomato sauce. She said no, sorry, and gave us all bananas. Ten minutes later we pulled up to a small tin-roofed house adjoining an enormous garage, all by itself on the side of the road.

'Told you there was a town here', said Joseph.

At least the lights were on. He pulled alongside the house and said they'd sleep here in the camper van for the night. Freddie, Awoonga and I stepped out, walked up to the front door, and knocked.

A couple of minutes later a woman opened the door, screamed, and slammed it shut. Another minute passed and a small man came to the door.

'Where in the death of Adam are your clothes, mate?' he asked me. His jaw was so slight and his chin so long it turned his face into a triangle.

I explained the situation and he asked what in the death of Adam that had to do with my clothes. Before I could think of an answer he asked if that was Cyndi Lauper. 'I love that song', he said. '*I wanna be the one to walk in the sun. Oh girls just wanna have fu-un!*'

I asked if he might be able to work on my van and get Freddie's and work on that too. He informed me that he was watching the Tri-State Rugby Championship and that his wife was the mechanic but she too was watching the Tri-State Rugby Championship and they'd have to do it in the morning and he'd met a Canadian in Melbourne last year and we were very nice people. I said thank you.

'See any dead roos on the way in?' he asked.

'There were a couple kangaroos', I said. 'I think there was one a few k's south.'

'Puffed up yet, was it?'

'Not really.'

'Bang on. Need to feed the chooks out back. Julia'll grab it in the morning when she gets your mate's ute.'

I thanked him.

Freddie just stood there, staring at the small man.

Finally the man said, 'What is it, blackfella?'

Freddie cleared his throat. 'Do you have any tomato sauce?' he asked.

'G'night.' And the small man closed the door.

On the other side of the road Freddie and I dug a small pit in the hard earth. While we scavenged for firewood he told me about a large rock fish named Alakitja who swam between endless white water lilies in the river known as the Milky Way. The lilies were so bright you could see them from the earth. 'Stars', said Freddie as he picked up another handful of twigs for kindling. 'While hiding from the hard sun, Alakitja was caught by two brothers and they sit up there now eating him by their campfire which is also named the Southern Cross.' He pointed to it.

The entire band of the Milky Way, which isn't as clearly visible in the Northern Hemisphere, arched overhead from horizon to horizon. Although I had never spotted it, I knew from the Australian flag that the Southern Cross was five stars and I did not understand how you could draw two brothers eating at a campfire out of five points, and I had no idea which stars he was pointing to but I told him they were nice. He tossed the kindling in the pit we had dug and began to cry. I told him they were better than nice, beautiful. He said it was not that. Then he walked off to a tree and I heard branches snapping off it. For the first time, my left foot began to hurt pretty bad.

Once we had the fire going, Awoonga joined us. As did a peacock, but I seemed to be the only one surprised by its presence. Its head drooped and it ignored us and looked very tired but happy to be warm. Freddie dug through Awoonga's backpack, pulled out something the size of a subway sandwich and unwrapped the tinfoil around it. I told him it looked gross, like a cow's tongue or something, and he said that was what it was. He cut it in three pieces and gave one to me and one to Awoonga.

'Sweet, eh?' he said, biting off a decent-sized chunk. 'If only we had tomato sauce. If only.'

It was sinewy but broke apart easily once you really got to chewing it. Like you'd imagine your own tongue probably would if you had the guts to really truly chew on it. And he was right, it would have been better with tomato sauce.

He asked where I was going and I explained that I'd spent four weeks driving around the country and was now headed to Sydney to meet my girlfriend. I asked him if he had a girl.

'I have three wives', he said. 'But I only have love for one.' He nodded towards Awoonga. 'Her daughter Wangara.'

Awoonga smiled. 'I have not seen her in one year', she said. 'Freddie is taking me back to his farm in his new car to see her.'

'It is true about loving Wangara', said Freddie. 'I am not just saying it. I love her ever since she come to our place with Awoonga when she was eight years old and me ten. We would sleep on the floor next to our mattress so that we could listen for the Sun Woman. You see, the Sun Woman rises in the morning and lights a fire below the horizon and there she uses red ochre powder to decorate her face. Often it spills into the air and this is the red of dawn. She goes west to her other camp site and carries her torch, our sun, across the sky. The camp site is just below the horizon and there she smothers the torch and takes off the make-up she uses and it rises again into the air and creates the colours of dusk. To return to her morning camp she walks through a tunnel underground and everything is dark.

'It is an old tale. But me and Wangara would lie on the floor and listen for the Sun Woman in her tunnel. We would lie across from each other and look at each other in the starlight through the open window until starlight went away and the Sun Woman put on her make-up and only then could you see the five gold spots like the Southern Cross in Wangara's left eye that trembled each time she shifted her sight from one of my eyes to the other and the sun came into the room through the window on the wall then down onto the floor making our feet warm as it went higher in the sky and then over our bodies until it went into our eyes and we had to close them and not look at each other any more and only then did we sleep. I love her ever since then and many many suns afterward I still love her and the gold spots in her left eye.'

Joseph came up to the fire and handed each of us a paper cup. 'Banana oatmeal chocolate stout.' He pointed to the small trailer behind the camper. 'Our brewery', he said. 'Happy Independence Day!'

'Whose independence is it?' I asked.

'Yours', he said. 'Isn't yours July fourth?'

'Didn't realise it was July', I said.

I used the beer to wash down the last bit of tongue. The drink was thick as tar, but sweet. Joseph said he had better climb back into bed with Mary but he had two extra sleeping bags in the camper van. Awoonga went with him to get them.

Freddie glared at the fire across from me, his eyes like twin embers. His hair shot straight back, wiry and thick, grey and black like smoke. He sipped his beer. 'What are you doing out here, Josh?' he asked.

'Looking for nothing.'

'Nothing?'

'Well, you see, New Haven – it's a city in the States – is the smallest place I ever lived. Finding a place which is empty, where there is nothing, is everything to me. I drove across the American desert last summer only to find the roads paved and the land fenced off. So I thought I'd give your country a go.'

'You should come to work for me on the farm.'

'What do you grow there?'

'Grow? It is a farm.'

I let it drop.

'Car accidents happen quite often here', he said.

'No kidding.'

'I was in another one last month.' He lifted his shirt to reveal a bruised and glistening tangle of flesh below the left side of his ribs. 'The gear-shifter did this. It speared me. But, Wangara, her face smashed, she died. I have not been able to tell Awoonga – or have someone tell Awoonga – this. None of her farm knows. But tomorrow we will be at my farm where everyone knows.'

Awoonga walked back into the glow of the fire. She sat beside Freddie and lay the sleeping bags between them. Freddie looked up from his beer to me. His eyes were welling up, the fire's reflection building in the bottoms, the tops white with starlight, and in between his pupils filled with bottomless supplication. Cyndi Lauper, mid-chorus, came to an abrupt halt. There was only the fire. There was none of the insect noises I had heard in other parts of Australia.

I said goodnight, but Freddie was silent, unblinking, afraid to knock those twin reflections down his cheeks. The peacock stuck its head up as I passed it and entered the cold starlight. I crossed the road and opened the back of the panel van and crept onto my mattress. Everything I had was in pieces around me, bathed in dirt the colour of dawn. I put my ear to the floor and heard the Sun Woman's footsteps move further and further away, and waited for sleep until she lit her torch. It looked like dusk. Just on the other side of the road.